MW00675793

Maccabean Martyr Traditions
in Paul's Theology of Atonement

Maccabean Martyr Traditions in Paul's Theology of Atonement

Did Martyr Theology Shape Paul's Conception of Jesus's Death?

JARVIS J. WILLIAMS

WIPF & STOCK · Eugene, Oregon

MACCABEAN MARTYR TRADITIONS IN PAUL'S THEOLOGY OF
ATONEMENT
Did Martyr Theology Shape Paul's Conception of Jesus's Death?

Copyright © 2010 Jarvis J. Williams. All rights reserved. Except for brief quotations
in critical publications or reviews, no part of this book may be reproduced in any
manner without prior written permission from the publisher. Write: Permissions,
Wipf and Stock Publishers, 199 W. 8th Ave., Suite 3, Eugene, OR 97401.

Wipf & Stock
A Division of Wipf and Stock Publishers
199 W. 8th Ave., Suite 3
Eugene, OR 97401
www.wipfandstock.com

ISBN 13: 978-1-60608-408-3

Manufactured in the U.S.A.

For Ana,

With much love and appreciation

Contents

List of Abbreviations

AB	Anchor Bible
AJBI	Annual of the Japanese Biblical Institute
BDAG	*Bauer, W., F. W. Danker, W. F. Arndt, and F. W. Gingrich.* Greek-English *Lexicon of the New Testament and Other Early Christian Literature.* 3rd ed.
BECNT	Baker Exegetical Commentary of the New Testament
Bib	*Biblica*
BibSac	*Bibliotheca Sacra*
BJRL	*Biblical Journal of Religious Literature*
BJS	Brown Judaic Studies
BN	*Biblischen Notizen*
BSC	Bible Study Commentary
BThSt	Biblisch-theologische Studien
BTS	Bible Themes Series
BZ	*Biblische Zeitschrift*
CBQ	*Catholic Biblical Quarterly*
CBQMS	Catholic Biblical Quarterly Monograph Series
CJAS	Christianity and Judaism in Antiquity Series
CQR	*Catholic Quarterly Review*
DSS	Dead Sea Scrolls
EKKNT	Evangelisch-Katholischer Kommentar zum Neuen Testament
EvQ	*Evangelical Quarterly*
EvRTh	*Evangelical Review of Theology*
EvT	*Evangelical Theology*
FRLANT	Forschungen zur Religion und Literatur des Alten und Neuen Testaments
HDR	Harvard Dissertations in Religion
HNTCS	Harper's New Testament Commentary Series
HUCA	*Hebrew Union College Annual*

ICC	International Critical Commentary
JBL	*Journal of Biblical Literature*
JBLMS	Journal of Biblical Literature Monograph Series
JETS	*Journal of the Evangelical Theological Society*
JJS	*Journal of Jewish Studies*
JPSTC	Jewish Publication Society Torah Commentary
JQR	*Jewish Quarterly Review*
JSJ	*Journal for the Study of Judaism in the Persian, Hellenistic and Roman Period*
JSNT	*Journal for the Study of the New Testament*
JSNTSup	Journal for the Study of the New Testament: Supplement Series
JSOT	Journal for the Study of the Old Testament
JSPSup	Journal for the Study of the Pseudepigrapha: Supplement Series
JTS	*Journal of Theological Studies*
KEKNT	Kritisch-exegetischer Kommentar ber das Neue Testament
LXX	Septuagint
MBT	Münsterische Beiträge zur Theologie
MNTC	Moffat New Testament Commentary
MT	Masoretic Text
NAC	New American Commentary
NCBC	New Century Bible Commentary
NEB	Die Neue Echter Bible
Neot	*Neotestamentica*
NIBC	New International Biblical Commentary
NICNT	New International Commentary on the New Testament
NICOT	New International Commentary on the Old Testament
NIDNTT	*New International Dictionary of New Testament Theology*
NIGTC	New International Greek Testament Commentary
NIV	New International Version
NKZ	Neue kirchliche Zeitschrift
NovT	*Novum Testamentum*
NovTSup	Novum Testamentum Supplement Series
NRSV	New Revised Standard Version
NSBT	New Studies in Biblical Theology
NTC	New Testament Commentaries

NTM	New Testament Monograph
NTS	*New Testament Studies*
NT	New Testament
OBO	Orbis biblicus et orientalis
OT	Old Testament
OTL	Old Testament Library
OTP	*Old Testament Pseudepigrapha*
PNTC	Pillar New Testament Commentary
PTR	*Presbyterian Theological Review*
QR	*Quarterly Review*
RevExp	*Review and Expositor*
RSPT	*Revue des Sciences Philosophiques et Thèologiques*
SBET	*Scottish Bulletin of Evangelical Theology*
SBL	Society of Biblical Literature
SBLDS	Society of Biblical Literature Dissertation Series
SBLMS	Society of Biblical Literature Monograph Series
SBLSP	*Society of Biblical Literature Seminar Papers*
SBT	Studies in Biblical Theology
SCJ	Studies in Christianity and Judaism
SCR	*Studies in Comparative Religion*
SCS	Septuagint Commentary Series
SJSJ	Supplemental Journal for the Study of Judaism
SJT	*Scottish Journal of Theology*
SNTSMS	Society for New Testament Studies Monograph Series
SP	Sacra Pagina
SBFLA	*Studii Biblici Franciscani Liber Annus*
ST	*Studia theologica*
TBei	*Theologische Beiträge*
TDNT	*Theological Dictionary of the New Testament*
THNT	Theologischer Handkommentar zum Neuen Testament
TNTC	The New Testament Commentary
TRu	*Theologische Rundschau*
TS	*Theological Studies*
TTZ	*Trierer theologische Zeitschrift*
TQ	*Theologische Quartalschrift*
UBSGNT	United Bible Societies Greek New Testament, 4th ed.
VC	*Vigiliâe Christiannae*
VD	*Verbum domini*

VT	*Vetus Testamentum*
WBC	Word Biblical Commentary
WMANT	Wissenschaftliche Monographien zum Alten und Neuen Testament
WTJ	*Westminster Theological Journal*
WUNT	Wissenschaftliche Untersuchungen zum Neuen Testament
WW	*Word & World*
ZAW	*Zeitschrift für die alttestamentliche Wissenschaft*
ZNW	*Zeitschrift für die neutestamentliche Wissenschaft und die Kunde der Älteren Kirche*
ZTK	*Zeitschrift für Theologie und Kirche*
ZW	*Zeitschrift Wissenschaft*

Preface

THIS BOOK IS A modification of my doctoral thesis (Maccabean Martyr Traditions in Paul's Theology of Atonement), which I successfully completed and defended under the supervision of Dr. Thomas R. Schreiner at the Southern Baptist Theological Seminary in Louisville, Kentucky in December 2007. Although the thesis argued in this work is the same as the one argued in the original doctoral thesis, this monograph offers a revised analysis of the key texts since I have had the opportunity after the completion of my doctoral program to present scholarly papers related to my thesis, to do more exegesis and research of the relevant texts and literature, and since I have had the opportunity to think about my thesis and method of argumentation more carefully after my doctoral thesis than when I was in the thralls of trying to finish my Ph.D. program. As with the original doctoral thesis, I owe many thanks to several scholars and people who have made this work (I think) better than the original doctoral thesis and who have helped me tremendously with getting my doctoral thesis off of the shelves that are reserved for unpublished Ph.D. theses in the back of Southern Seminary's library and into published print for the broader academic community. But I am solely responsible for any deficiency that the reader might find in this work.

I owe thanks to my dear friend Micah Carter. Micah encouraged me to pursue publication with Wipf and Stock. I owe thanks to the team at Wipf and Stock for accepting my doctoral thesis for publication. I am especially grateful to K.C. Hanson (editor-in-chief) and Christian Amondson (assistant managing editor). K.C. promptly responded to my inquiries about pursuing publication with Wipf and Stock. Christian promptly responded to all of my tireless e-mails and guided me through the publication process with much professionalism and pastoral care for my work.

I owe many thanks to Dr. Thomas R. Schreiner, my beloved *doctor-vater*, mentor, pastor, and friend. Dr. Schreiner challenged and sharpened my thesis at several points. He also continued to read my work on Martyr

Theology very critically after I completed my doctoral thesis. Words cannot express my indebtedness to and love and appreciation for him.

I am grateful to Drs. John B. Polhill and Brian J. Vickers who served as the other two examiners of my doctoral thesis and who both challenged my arguments and pointed out deficiencies during my oral defense. Dr. Charles Quarles served as my external reader. Dr. Quarles offered several helpful suggestions that have strengthened this work. I owe thanks to Professor J.W. van Henten for reading an article related to the thesis argued in this work and for his helpful comments through e-mail during my early stages of writing the original doctoral thesis. I owe thanks to Dr. Daniel P. Bailey for his willingness to e-mail me a copy of his masterful Cambridge doctoral thesis, which many scholars eagerly await to be published. Although Dr. Bailey would disagree with my thesis, I trust that we have both profited much from our series of dialogues through e-mail regarding Martyr Theology and the background influences behind Paul's conception of Jesus's death.

I owe thanks to Mrs. Ella Prater for reading the original doctoral thesis before I submitted it for publication. In addition to the various scholars who aided the publication of this work, I also owe thanks to Campbellsville University (CU) where I serve as assistant professor of New Testament and Greek. In the spring of 2009, CU provided me with 2 opportunities to present papers related to this monograph at our faculty colloquium and at our biblical studies lecture series. The opportunity to interact with scholars from other disciplines at faculty colloquium and with students during the biblical studies lecture series forced me to think more carefully about the clarity of my thesis. I especially thank Daniel Motley (my research assistant at CU) for checking the footnotes and bibliography for mistakes.

Finally, I owe many thanks to Ana Williams, my sweet and beautiful wife of 8 years, for her relentless love for me and for her tireless support of my work. Without her sacrifices, encouragement, prayers, and love throughout my writing of the original doctoral thesis, I would have given up without finishing the work when finishing became physically, financially, spiritually, and emotionally difficult. In addition to her faithfulness as a wife, she has been just as faithful as a mother to our beautiful son, Jaden Alexander Williams. Her commitment to me and to motherhood challenges and inspires me! It is with great joy that I dedicate this book to Ana with much love and appreciation!

Jarvis J. Williams
Louisville, Kentucky
May 2009

1

Introduction and History of Research

INTRODUCTION

MANY SCHOLARS HAVE INVESTIGATED the nature and significance of Jesus's death in the Pauline corpus. This is evident by the numerous monographs,[1] Pauline theologies,[2] essays,[3] dissertations,[4] and articles[5] that have analyzed Jesus's death in the Pauline corpus. Several of the previous investigations considered the background influences behind, the nature of, and the significance of Jesus's death in Paul,[6] and many of the previous investigations of Jesus's death in the Pauline corpus were significant contributions to Pauline Studies. Since recent scholarship questions whether Paul conceived of Jesus's death as an atoning sacrifice or as a saving event,[7] a fresh analysis of Paul's conception of Jesus's death and of the background influences behind his conception of Jesus's death is needed.

---

1. Dodd, *Bible and the Greeks*; Morris, *Apostolic Preaching*; idem, *The Cross*; Lyonnet and Sabourin, *Sin*; Sanders, *Paul*, 463–74; Friedrich, *Verkündigung*; Breytenbach, *Versöhnung*; Cousar, *Theology*; Hooker, *Not Ashamed*, 20–46; Janowski, *Sühne*; Knöppler, *Sühne*.

2. Ridderbos, *Paul*, 182–97; Beker, *Paul*, 182–212; Dunn, *Theology*, 207–33; Schreiner, *Paul*, 219–36; Schnelle, *Apostle Paul*, 442–54.

3. Käsemann, "The Saving Significance," 32–59; Dunn, "Paul's Understanding," 76–89; Carson, "Atonement," 127–36.

4. Scullion, "A Tradition-Historical Study;" Hedderic, "Akedah Hypothesis;" Frazier, "Comparison;" Bailey, "Mercy Seat."

5. Deissmann, "ἱλαστήριος," 193–212; Dodd, "Hilastērion," 352–60; Manson, "ἱλαστήριον," 1–10; Morris, "Meaning," 3–43; Nicole, "C. H. Dodd," 117–57; Marshall, "The Death of Jesus," 12–21; Buchanan, "The Day of Atonement," 236–49; Breytenbach, "Versöhnung, Stellvertretung und Sühne," 59–79; Bell, "Sacrifice," 1–27.

6. See history of research below.

7. In a series of publications in the 1990s, McLean argued that sacrificial theology was

THESIS

My thesis is that Paul presents Jesus's death both as an atoning sacrifice and as a saving event for Jews and Gentiles, because Martyr Theology shaped his conception of Jesus's death. I do not argue that Martyr Theology was the only influence behind Paul's conception of Jesus's death, but that Martyr Theology best explains why Paul would and could conceive of Jesus's death both as an atoning sacrifice and as a saving event for Jews and Gentiles. I primarily argue my thesis by means of an exegetical investigation and comparison of key texts in 2 and 4 Maccabees and in Paul's letters. I also consider other Second Temple Jewish texts that appear to contain a Martyr Theology. The exegesis serves to highlight soteriological, lexical, or conceptual parallels between Martyr Theology and Paul's conception of Jesus's death.

I develop 4 arguments throughout the book to defend the proposed thesis: (1) the deaths of the Jewish martyrs functioned as atoning sacrifices for Israel's sin. (2) Their deaths were a saving event for the nation. (3) Paul ascribes to Jesus's death language that closely parallels the martyrs' deaths in 2 and 4 Maccabees. (4) The parallels with and similarities between the martyrs' deaths in 2 and 4 Maccabees and Paul's presentation of Jesus's death suggest that Paul borrowed from the ideas and concepts in Martyr Theology regarding the death of the righteous for others to present Jesus's death both as an atoning sacrifice and as a saving event for Jews and Gentiles.

This chapter introduces the thesis, the concept of Maccabean martyrdom, and it presents a history of research of much of the relevant literature pertaining to the thesis. Chapter 2 investigates selected texts from Greco-Roman literature, Leviticus 16, Isaiah 53, and the key texts in 2 and 4 Maccabees to support that 2 and 4 Maccabees speak of the deaths of the martyrs with similar language found in Greco-Roman literature, the OT cult, and Isaiah 53. Chapter 3 investigates Genesis 22, Exodus 32, Numbers 25, and Isaiah 53 to see if these texts could have exclusively shaped the authors' conception of the martyrs' deaths in 2 and 4 Maccabees or Paul's conception of Jesus's death. Since each of the OT texts that I investigate in chapter 3 mentions human sacrifice and since

---

altogether absent from Paul's soteriology. See McLean, "Christ as Pharmakos," 187–207; idem, "The Absence of an Atoning Sacrifice," 531–53; idem, *The Cursed Christ*. Most recently, see Brondos, *Paul on the Cross*; Lampe, "Human Sacrifice," 191–209, esp. 194–95.

three of the four mention human sacrifice for the benefit of others, I limit my investigation to these specific OT texts. I argue that with the possible exception of Isaiah 53, the above OT texts do not exclusively provide the background behind the authors' conception of the martyrs' deaths in 2 and 4 Maccabees or Paul's conception of Jesus's death.

Chapter 4 investigates the key texts in Paul that demonstrate a soteriological, lexical, or conceptual connection with Martyr Theology. By means of both an exegesis of the key Pauline texts and by an analysis of the parallels between the key texts in 2 and 4 Maccabees and in Paul, I offer arguments in chapter 4 to defend that Martyr Theology shaped Paul's conception of Jesus's death as an atoning sacrifice and as a saving event for Jews and Gentiles. Chapter 5 offers conclusions and some implications of chapters 2–4. In the former, I endeavor to coalecse the arguments of chapters 2–4. I especially conclude chapter 5 by suggesting that Martyr Theology's influence on Paul's conception of Jesus's death best explains how he could conceive of Jesus's death both as an atoning sacrifice and as a saving event for Jews and Gentiles. My conclusions also express why Martyr Theology's influence on Paul's conception of Jesus's death does not truncate the saving significance of Jesus's death for the nations in his soteriology.[8]

AN INTRODUCTION TO MACCABEAN MARTYRDOM

What is a Maccabean Martyr?

In contrast to the contemporary understanding of martyrdom, I use the terms "martyrdom," "martyr texts," "martyr traditions," and "Martyr Theology" in this book to refer to Maccabean martyrdom: viz., the martyrdom that occurred in the Second Temple period (STP) during the reign of Antiochus Epiphanes IV. During this period, righteous Jews refused to forsake the laws of their God and refused to yield to the edicts of pagan authorities.[9] Instead, they voluntarily and gladly chose death since they believed to do otherwise would have displeased their God.[10]

---

8. Schreiner (*Paul*, 236) asserts a similar statement regarding Martyr Theology and Paul's theology of substitutionary atonement.

9. So van Henten and Avemarie, *Martyrdom and Noble Death*, 3–4.

10. Van Henten (*Martyrdom and Noble Death*, 3–4) defines martyrdom in 2 and 4 Maccabees in the following way: "A martyr is a person who in an extremely hostile situ-

To make the distinction between the concept of martyrdom during the STP and the concept of martyrdom in contemporary society is necessary, because martyrdom has become a popular expression within recent years.[11] The term has strong religious overtones, and both Christians and Muslims have used the term to describe those who would die a heroic death for a religious cause.[12] Based on the noun μάρτυς ("witness") and the verb μαρτυρέω ("to bear witness"), some ancient Christian sources have historically attached meanings to martyrdom that emphasize the confessional aspect as the most integral element of a martyr's actions.[13] For example, the Martyrdom of Polycarp was one of the earliest Christian documents where μάρτυς occurred as a reference to those who remained faithful to their God by refusing to submit to the edicts of pagan authorities (e.g., Mart. *Poly*. 1:1; 2:1; 14:2).[14] Yet, the concept of martyrdom is much older than the Christian vocabulary traditionally used to describe it.[15]

---

ation prefers violent death to compliance with a demand of the (usually pagan) authorities. This definition implies that the death of such a person is a structural element in the writing about this martyr. The execution should at least be mentioned." According to van Henten, 5 important literary components occur in martyr texts: "(1) an edict issued by the (pagan) authorities is the point of departure for the narrative. Transgression of this edict results in the death penalty. (2) The enforcement of the edict brings Jews into a loyalty conflict, since they cannot stay faithful to their God, the edict, and their Jewish way of life. (3) When Jews are forced—after their arrest—to decide between complying with the government's edict or remaining faithful to their religion and practices, they choose to die rather than to obey the authorities. (4) This decision comes to the fore in the dialogue with the ruler or other officials, which is sometimes accompanied by tortures. (5) The execution is described or at least indicated." Cf. van Henten, *Maccabean Martyrs*, 7–13, esp. 8. For a different definition of Maccabean martyrdom, see Pobee, *Persecution and Martyrdom*, 19–30. In addition, some have suggested that suicide was a type of martyrdom for ancient Jews. For example, see Passameneck, "The Jewish Mandate," 215–41. However, Passameneck offers the following qualification: "Suicide is contrary to both the letter and the spirit of Jewish law if it is the consequence of a rational process. . . Both the Talmud and post-talmudic halakhic literature reflect the fact that the concept of death before dishonor is well enshrined in both the legal (and moral) system of Jewish tradition" (216, 239). See also, Doran, "The Martyr," 189–221; Dorge and Tabor, *A Noble Death*; Shepkaru, "The Evolution of Jewish Martyrdom."

11. So van Henten, *Martyrdom and Noble Death*, 3–4.

12. Ibid.

13. Ibid.

14. Ibid.

15. Ibid.

Jewish Martyrdom and Antiochus Epiphanes IV

The Jewish persecutions, enforced by Antiochus Epiphanes IV (ca. 175–164 BC),[16] during the STP was the immediate background behind Jewish martyrdom in 2 and 4 Maccabees.[17] Antiochus succeeded his father as ruler over the Seleucid Empire (1 Macc 1:1–10). He was a wicked root (1 Macc 1:10; cf. 4 Macc 8:1) and an arrogant and terrible man (4 Macc 4:15). Two years after he defeated Ptolemy, king of Egypt (1 Macc 1:16–28), he deceived many Jews in Jerusalem by making them think that he would be peaceful toward them (1 Macc 1:29–32). Instead, he conquered Jerusalem and converted the city of David into his own fortress. He placed evil men behind its walls (1 Macc 1:33–35). He corrupted the nation (1 Macc 1:36–40; 4 Macc 4–6), destroyed the Torah (1 Macc 1:56), and made an oath to kill any Jew who obeyed God's law (1 Macc 1:60–63). Obedience to Antiochus resulted in honor and reward (4 Macc 8:4–7; cf. 1 Macc 1:11), but disobedience resulted in extreme torture and death (4 Macc 5:4; 6:12, 30; 7:12, 25; 8:8–12).[18]

Jewish Martyrdom and God's Judgment

In addition to Antiochus' role in Maccabean martyrdom, certain martyr texts also suggest that Antiochus' extermination of the Jews who did not obey his reforms was God's judgment against Israel on account of its sin (2 Macc 6:12–17; 7:32–38). Many Jews apostatized from the Torah and obeyed Antiochus' Hellenistic reforms (1 Macc 1:11–15). Consequently, God punished the nation through Antiochus so that it would not undergo a more severe, eschatological judgment for its religious apostasy (2 Macc 6:16–17; 7:35; 12:40–42; Ep. *Jer.* 2; Song of the Three Young Men 1–8, 13; As. *Mos.* 9:1–5). With the preceding background in mind, the reader should be able to understand better the history of research of the major works that have discussed Martyr Theology's influence on Paul's conception of Jesus's death.

---

16. Henceforth "Antiochus" throughout the book.

17. The historical timeline of Antiochus' invasions and his campaigns against Egypt are debated in scholarship. For work on dating, see Tcherikover, *Hellenistic Civilization*.

18. For more thorough presentations of the Maccabeans and Second Temple Judaism, see Moore, *Judaism*; Hengel, *Judaism and Hellenism*; Sacchi, *History*; Feldman, *Judaism and Hellenism*.

HISTORY OF RESEARCH

Not a Background

Ethelbert Stauffer was the first scholar to systematize the various components of Martyr Theology in the relevant literature. He asserts that Jesus was a martyr and that the early church imitated his obedience. Stauffer's work discusses martyrdom from Jesus to Polycarp. He cites a few Maccabean texts, scripture, and post-NT texts that speak of martyrdom. However, his investigation does not clearly discuss the soteriological similarities between Martyr Theology and Paul or whether the former shaped Paul's conception of Jesus's death.[19]

Leon Morris analyzes the various views of ἱλαστήριον. He concludes that it was impossible to give a clear answer as to the meaning of ἱλαστήριον. Nevertheless, he maintains that ἱλαστήριον refers to the removal of God's wrath instead of a reference to the mercy seat or the Yom Kippur ritual. At best, Rom 3:25 simply is a parallel to 4 Macc 17:21–22. However, a parallel does not necessitate the belief that Paul depended on Martyr Theology in his presentation of Jesus's death. Rather, "it is simply that the ideas being expressed in the two passages are similar."[20]

Theofried Baumeister attempts to create a Jewish theology of martyrdom. He surveys the relevant literature from Daniel to Polycarp. The breadth of his study prevents him from answering important questions that pertain to the provenance of and antecedent traditions to Martyr Theology. Moreover, Baumeister does not discuss Martyr Theology with the relevant categories that can be traced throughout the literature. Most importantly, Baumeister neither applies his work strictly to Paul's soteriology.[21]

Ralph P. Martin discusses the similarities between Martyr Theology and reconciliation in Rom 5:9–11 and in 2 Cor 5:18–21. According to Martin, at first glance there appears to be a clear connection between

---

19. He wrote his German work in 1941, but I refer to the later English translation in this work. Stauffer, *Theology*, 185–334.

20. Morris, "The Meaning," 3–43. One of Morris' concerns in his work on the atonement was to refute Dodd's claims that the bible does not teach propitiation. See Morris, *Apostolic Preaching*. Later scholars joined Morris' efforts. For example, see Thornton, "Propitiation or Expiation?" 53–55; Garnet, "Atonement Constructions," 131–63.

21. Baumeister, *Die Anfänge*.

Martyr Theology and Paul's conception of Jesus's death. This connection can be seen by his use of καταλλάσσω ("to reconcile"), God's wrath, judgment, and vicarious suffering for sin (cf. 2 Macc 7:32–38). Still, says Martin, there are clear antitheses between Martyr Theology and Paul's assertion that Jesus's death accomplished reconciliation. First, the martyrs urged God to be reconciled to them, not that they would be reconciled to God. Second, the martyrs presented their lives to God as acts of vicarious piety and merit. Third, Paul and the entire apostolic preaching of the cross accentuate that God was the initiator and originator of reconciliation: "He is always the subject and never the direct object of the verb" to be reconciled.[22]

Stanley E. Porter investigates Paul's concept of reconciliation in Rom 5:1–11. He examines καταλλάσσω ("to reconcile"), καταλλαγή ("reconciliation"), and related concepts in the relevant Greek, Hellenistic, and Jewish literature. He suggests that the correct meaning of καταλλάσσω "has been clouded by great complexity which has grown up surrounding the theological concept [of] reconciliation" (brackets mine). Therefore, the meaning of the term needs clarification.

Porter offers his exegetical and theological investigation of καταλλάσσω and καταλλαγή as a means of arguing the following thesis: while Paul certainly borrowed both Greek and Hebrew metaphors to formulate his reconciliatory language in Rom 5:1–11, his presentation of reconciliation is simultaneously unique to him. First, "God is the initiator of reconciling action, from initial justification to final salvation with God's love forming the basis for his action through Christ." Second, "καταλλάσσω is an intensely personal metaphor for the relationship between man and God which spans the initial act of justification and the final act of salvation." Third, Paul speaks of reconciliation with passive verbs "to refer to God removing the cause of his own anger against man, an idea barely glimpsed by the Hebrews and unknown to the Greeks." Fourth, Paul presents reconciliation as a process and condition in which sinners rest through Jesus's death. Fifth, similar to the Hebrew tradition, "Paul intensifies the emotional sense [of the term] to depict reconciliation as a personal and intimate relationship between parties" (brackets mine).

22. Martin, *Reconciliation*, 105–6.

Porter concludes that the background behind this Pauline metaphor was not Martyr Theology.[23]

Nico S.L. Fryer discusses the different proposals for the meaning of ἱλαστήριον. He also discusses the problems that arise from each proposal. He argues that Paul uses ἱλαστήριον in Rom 3:25 to refer to the mercy seat. Fryer disagrees that there is a reference to Martyr Theology in Paul's use of ἱλαστήριον in Rom 3:25. A martyrological background, argued Fryer, must be rejected for the following reasons: First, 4 Macc 17:21–22 explicitly refers to the substitutionary death of the seven brothers and the other martyrs, but substitution in Rom 3:25–26 is ambiguous. Second, God is the only one who initiates and effects atonement in Paul. Thus, Rom 3:25 must be read in light of the Yom Kippur ritual. Third, ἱλαστήριον appears as an adjective in 4 Macc 17:22, but Paul employs it as a substantive in Rom 3:25.[24]

Cilliers Breytenbach argues that I. Howard Marshall's proposal, that the Martyr Theology of 2 Maccabees was a viable background for Paul, is incorrect.[25] Paul's theology of reconciliation came from Hellenistic literature in which reconciliation terminology neither refers to the relationship between God and humans nor occurs in any religious contexts. Reconciliation terminology only appears in political or military contexts in Hellenistic literature. Moreover, in the literature antecedent to Paul, reconciliation made no reference to the OT cult. The reconciliation language in Paul is different from its use in 2 Maccabees, Philo, and Josephus. Paul does not present Jesus's death as an atoning sacrifice.[26]

G. K. Beale argues that the background behind Paul's conception of Jesus's death was the OT, specifically Isaiah 40–66. Beale's work in this area has primarily focused on Paul's understanding of reconciliation. Beale readily admits that reconciliation terminology occurs nowhere in Isaiah, but the theme of new creation does. Since Paul speaks of reconciliation in the same context of new creation and his apostolic ministry in 2 Cor 5:16–21, Isaiah was his most probable background.[27]

23. Porter, "Reconciliation," iii–iv, 175–78, 188–89; idem, Καταλλάσσω.

24. Fryer, "Hilastērion," 99–116, esp. 103–4.

25. I discuss Marshall's view below.

26. Breytenbach, *Versöhnung*, 40–83; idem, "Versöhnung, Stellvertretung," 59–73; idem, "Christus starb für uns," 447–75; idem, "Salvation of the Reconciled," 271–86. Cf. Porter, Καταλλάσσω, 39–77.

27. Beale, "Reconciliation in 2 Corinthians 5–7," 550–81.

Bradley H. McLean offers what he calls "a new approach for interpreting the concept of atonement found in Gal 3:13." In Gal 3:13, Jesus provides atonement by becoming accursed for sinners. Since Paul did not organize his letters biographically but theologically, Paul does not embellish an historical reminiscence about Jesus's death that the church handed down to him. Instead, Paul offers a unique theological statement in need of interpretation.

McLean acknowledges that many scholars have traditionally understood Paul's conception of Jesus's death in light of Levitical sacrifices, the Servant-Songs, Martyr Theology, or the Akedah Hypothesis. McLean contends that nothing in Paul's letters seemingly supports that any one of these traditions was his background. McLean rejects all Jewish and some aspects of Greco-Roman traditions as the background behind Paul's conception of Jesus's death. Regarding Jewish traditions, McLean boldly states that he does not personally have knowledge of any text in the Jewish tradition that contains the teaching that a righteous man could atone for the sin of others by becoming accursed. On the other hand, McLean asserts that clear allusions occur in Paul's presentation of Jesus's death to Greco-Roman *Pharmakos* rituals, rituals by which spiritual pollution manifested itself through physical calamities (i.e., famines, diseases, etc.). The *Pharmakos* sacrifice was accursed by the gods and consequently expelled from the community. In McLean's view, Jesus was the *Pharmakos* sacrifice who bore the curse of God and experienced divine rejection.[28]

Wolfgang Kraus examines relevant martyr texts, relevant DSS, and relevant OT texts as a means of discerning the background behind Rom 3:25–26. He argues that Rom 3:25–26 was dependent on a pre-Pauline traditional formula that was influenced by both Hellenism and Judaism. Neither the deaths of the martyrs nor Jesus's death was vicarious or an atoning sacrifice, but the deaths of both should be understood as divine inauguration. Kraus predicates his thesis on a rabbinic belief that the blood ritual of the sacrificial system cleansed and inaugurated the temple and that atonement for sin did not occur until the priest placed his hands on the animals. In Rom 3:25, Paul refers to the sanctifying presence of the ritual.[29] He does not demonstrate a dependence on Martyr Theology by doing this.

28. McLean, "Christ as a Pharmakos," 187–207; idem, "The Absence of an Atoning Sacrifice," 531–53; idem, *The Cursed Christ.*

29. Kraus, *Der Tod Jesu.*

Douglas A. Campbell presents an extensive exegesis of Rom 3:21–26 in order to discern its meaning. Campbell briefly summarizes the ἱλαστήριον-debate that Adolf Deissmann, C. H. Dodd, and Leon Morris previously undertook before him. Campbell agrees with Deissmann that ἱλαστήριον in Rom 3:25 does not refer to the mercy seat, but to a propitiatory. Campbell argues that ἱλαστήριον refers to the atoning ritual of Yom Kippur in Rom 3:25 during which propitiatory atonement took place without referring to the actual mercy seat. Campbell's work does not discuss whether Martyr Theology shaped Paul's conception of Jesus's death in Rom 3:25 as he discusses Paul's atonement terminology. Instead, he relegates this discussion to appendix II where he argues for a late dating of 4 Maccabees (ca. AD 135). Consequently, Campbell rejects the view that Martyr Theology (particularly 4 Macc 17:22) shaped Paul's conception of Jesus's death in Rom 3:25.[30]

Margaret E. Thrall discusses the background behind Paul's use of καταλλάσσω in 2 Cor 5:18–21. She states that the term occurs in secular Greek as a non-religious term and that it occurs in Greek-speaking Judaism as a religious term. Thrall contends, however, that καταλλάσσω is unique to the Pauline corpus in the NT, because his "own use of the verb in the active [voice] with the sense reconcile (someone) to oneself has no exact parallel" (brackets mine).[31] The martyrs simply expressed a hope that God would hear their prayers and become reconciled to them and to his people again (2 Macc 1:5; 7:33; 8:29).[32]

Peter Stuhlmacher suggests that Paul uses a creedal text in Rom 3:25 to elucidate God's offering up of Jesus as atonement. This creedal text incorporated the Yom Kippur ritual. Christ's death, seen by all, replaced the Yom Kippur ritual, only seen by the high priest and God. The primitive church's critique of the Yom Kippur ritual may have had its provenance with Stephen and his followers (Acts 6). After Stephen's martyrdom and after the expulsion of his followers from Jerusalem, the tradition probably entered Antioch. Paul and fellow missionaries, who took the gospel to Rome, became acquainted with the tradition in Antioch.

In Rom 3:25, Paul consciously refers to "statements of the faith that unite him with the Roman Christians." The translation "sacrifice of atone-

---

30. Campbell, *Rhetoric*, 102–30, esp. 107–13, 130–37, 219–28.

31. Thrall, *Second Corinthians*, 429–39, esp. 429–30.

32. Ibid.

ment" for ἱλαστήριον has no support in the Greek sources, but can only be derived from a hypothetical reference to the Jewish martyrs in 4 Macc 17:21–22. However, Martyr Theology's influence on Paul's use of ἱλαστήριον does not fit philologically with the content of Rom 3:25 since the NT presents Jesus as more than a Jewish (prophetic) martyr. The term ἱλαστήριον in Rom 3:25, then, refers to the mercy seat.[33]

Stephen H. Travis suggests that Martyr Theology assisted the primitive church's teaching about Jesus. Yet, he deems it a mistake in method "to look to [martyr] texts for an explanation of what Paul's use of ἱλ–αστήριον means" (brackets mine). Travis affirms that Jesus "was judged in our place," but he states that Paul's writings do not present Jesus's death as bearing the wrath of God for sinners who would otherwise experience his retributive justice for themselves. The absence of explicit retributive ideas in Romans 3 makes it unlikely that Martyr Theology shaped Paul's conception of Jesus's death in 3:25. Furthermore, says Travis, Paul teaches nowhere in his writings that Christians suffered vicariously for the sins of others. The absence of this suggests that he wrote from different assumptions from those present in Martyr Theology. His assumptions were informed by the OT cult.[34]

Douglas J. Moo acknowledges the possibility that ἱλαστήριον refers to the mercy seat of Leviticus 16 in Rom 3:25, but he suggests that this interpretation is unlikely. He prefers the simple translation "sacrifice of atonement." Moo does not devote much time to whether Martyr Theology served as a viable background behind Paul's use of ἱλαστήριον in Rom 3:25, but rather he quickly dismisses the idea in a footnote in his lengthy commentary on Romans. In light of the occurrence of ἱλαστήριον in the OT, Moo asserts that "it is unlikely that Maccabean Martyr Theology has had any important influence on Paul's use of ἱλαστήριον."[35]

Kenneth Grayston discusses the relationship between martyrdom and atonement. He argues that in the ancient world, martyrdom and atonement did not necessarily correlate with one another. He mentions the similarities between Martyr Theology and Paul's conception of Jesus's death. His investigation of the Pauline corpus mainly focuses on ἱλ–αστήριον in Rom 3:25 and on Paul's reconciliation motif. He affirms that

---

33. Stuhlmacher, *Romans*, 58–61; idem, "Zur neueren Exegese," 117–35.

34. Travis, "Divine Judgment," 21–38, esp. 27–30.

35. Moo, *Romans*, 230–40, esp. 234, n. 74.

some similarities exist between Paul's presentation of Jesus's death and the deaths of the martyrs in Martyr Theology. Still, he argues that the differences between the two are greater than their similarities. First, the martyrs offered themselves to God as atoning sacrifices in order to appease his wrath, but Jesus's death was offered instead of the ungodly. Second, the martyrs died to reconcile God to Israel, but Jesus died to reconcile the ungodly to God. Third, the martyrs hoped that their deaths would reconcile God to his people, but Paul pleads that Jesus's death should compel the ungodly to be reconciled to God. Fourth, the martyrs thought that their deaths would propitiate God's wrath and dispense his mercy and reconciliation to the nation, but Paul presents Jesus as dying for the ungodly, and his death would result in both the present reconciliation and the future salvation of the ungodly. Fifth, the martyrs suffered for the salvation of the nation, but Paul asserts that only the sufferings of Jesus were efficacious for salvation.[36]

In his Cambridge dissertation, Daniel P. Bailey carefully argues that Paul's use of ἱλαστήριον in Rom 3:25 and the author's use in 4 Macc 17:22 are distinct.[37] Paul uses the term consistent with its occurrence in the biblical world (i.e., mercy seat), and the author of 4 Macc 17:22 uses the term consistent with its occurrence in the Hellenistic world (i.e., propitiatory).[38] According to Bailey, to argue that ἱλαστήριον refers to sacrificial atonement in 4 Macc 17:22 is a mistake. After reviewing the evidence in the relevant Hellenistic literature that supports reading the term as "propitiatory," Bailey argues that various inscriptions affirm that ἱλαστήρια were offered either to propitiate the wrath of offended deities or to ensure favors from them.[39] He also argues that-τήριον words do not regularly refer to actions in Hellenistic literature, but to places (e.g., θυσιαστήριον "altar," ἱλαστήριον "mercy seat," φυγαδευτήριον "refuge," and ἁγιαστήριον "altar").[40] Bailey concludes that the meaning

---

36. Grayston, "Atonement and Martyrdom," 250–63.

37. I am grateful to Daniel P. Bailey for kindly e-mailing me a copy of his dissertation.

38. Bailey, "Mercy Seat," 5–12, esp. 11–12.

39. For the above analysis and summary of Bailey's view, see also DeSilva, *4 Maccabees* (2006), 250–51, who cites Bailey ("Mercy Seat," 31–75).

40. See also Finlan, *Atonement Metaphors*, 200–03, who cites Bailey, "Greek Heroes," 6–7; idem, "Mercy Seat," 1, 4, 12, 237–38. However, Morris ("The Meaning," 3) points out that-τήριον words can also refer to a means (e.g., σωτήριον).

of ἱλαστήριον in 4 Macc 17:22 as it relates to the martyrs' deaths "should be sought against a non-sacrificial background."[41] According to Bailey, 4 Maccabees nowhere states that the martyrs died as atoning sacrifices for Israel's sin, and Paul's background behind his use of ἱλαστήριον is the OT's mercy seat and not Martyr Theology.[42]

After investigating the relevant atonement terminology in the OT and the LXX, Thomas Knöppler argues against understanding Rom 3:25 in light of Martyr Theology. Instead, the martyrs' deaths in 4 Macc 17:21– 22 should be ruled out as Paul's interpretative framework on the basis of historical and theological considerations. Paul's framework was Leviticus and the Yom Kippur ritual.[43]

Charles H. Talbert discusses the various interpretations of ἱλαστή ριον in Rom 3:25 and the interpretation of related terms. He questions whether the Martyr Theology of 4 Macc 17:22 shaped Paul's conception of Jesus's death in Rom 3:25 since Paul did not present Jesus's death as a sacrifice of atonement in his other letters. The absence of sacrificial lan-

---

41. The above quote comes from DeSilva (*4 Maccabees*, 251), who summarizes Bailey's view.

42. DeSilva (*4 Maccabees* [2006], 251) agrees with Bailey in part, but DeSilva asserts that "the effect of the propitiatory gift is, however, fundamentally the same as the sacrifice of atonement: on the basis of the martyrs' loyalty to God unto death, God's anger turns away from Israel, and God turns again to Israel with a favorable disposition so as to deliver her from her enemies (2 Macc 7:37–38; 8:5)." Contrary to Bailey, DeSilva argues that the author of 2 Maccabees used the cultic language from the Yom Kippur ritual to describe the effect of the martyrs' deaths (250–51). In addition to Bailey, other interpreters have understood ἱλαστήριον in Rom 3:25 to refer to the mercy seat as early as Origen (AD 185–254). For example, see Origen, *Romans*, 216–25. The majority of post-Origen NT exegetes have affirmed the mercy seat view. Cf. Calvin, *Romans*, 75; Barth, *Romans*, 104–05; Manson, "ἱλαστήριον," 1–10; Nygren, *Romans*, 156–62; Lyonnet, "expiationis," 336–52; idem, *Sin*, 157–66; Bruce, *Romans*, 104–07; Swain, "For Our Sins," 131–39; Wilckens, *Römer*, 191–92; Käsemann, *Romans*, 97; Janowski, *Sühne*, 350–54; Meyer, "The Pre-Pauline Formula," 198–208; Hultgren, *Paul's Gospel and Mission*, 59–60; Newton, *The Concept of Purity at Qumran*, 76–77; von Dobbeler, *Glaube*, 78–87; Fryer, "The Meaning," 99–116; Barrett, *Romans*, 73–75; Stuhlmacher, *Romans*, 58–61; Hooker, *Not Ashamed*, 43–44; Schlatter, *Romans*, 99; Byrne, *Romans*, 132–33; Williams, *Paul's Metaphors*, 247, 253 n. 19; Bell, "Sacrifice," 1–27, esp. 16–19. Contra Morris, *Romans*, 179–82. He rejects the imagery of mercy seat for ἱλαστήριον in Rom 3:25 and opts for "means of propitiation." Similarly Ridderbos, *Paul*, 187; Murray, *Romans*, 116–17; Mounce, *Romans*, 116–18. While affirming that ἱλαστήριον in Rom 3:25 has the Yom Kippur ritual as its background, Fee ("Metaphors for Salvation," 43–67, esp. 55–60) maintains that ἱλαστήριον does not refer to the mercy seat.

43. Knöppler, *Sühne*, 112–17.

guage argues in favor of taking ἱλαστήριον in Rom 3:25 as a reference to the lid of the ark. Talbert concludes: "if so, then Paul has used two images for the saving work of God in Christ: redemption (forgiveness) and new mercy seat (locus of the divine presence)."[44]

Daniel Stökl Ben Ezra argues that Paul's use of ἱλαστήριον in Rom 3:25 reflects the Yom Kippur ritual in Leviticus 16. The term ἱλαστήριον is the translation of כַּפֹּרֶת in the Masoretic Text (MT). This term clearly refers to an object inside of the tabernacle, which (the object) is connected to atonement in the MT. In virtually all of the literature, lexical evidence affirms that ἱλαστήριον refers to the כַּפֹּרֶת. Martyr Theology (i.e., 4 Macc 17:21–22) cannot be the background behind Paul's conception of Jesus's death in Rom 3:25–26, because 4 Maccabees post dates Paul's writings. Besides, says Ben Ezra, it is hard to believe that early Christian-Jews who were familiar with the LXX "did not immediately make an association with the most frequent usage in the [LXX], especially considering the mention of blood and sins in the context [of Rom 3:25]" (brackets mine).[45]

Tom Holland presents a fresh survey of the influences behind Paul's biblical writings. He challenges the arguments of many scholars who have argued that Greek culture influenced the NT writings more than a Jewish heritage. Holland argues that Martyr Theology's influence on Paul does not convincingly explain other soteriological motifs in Rom 3:21–26. Justification, righteousness, and redemption most closely reflect the New Exodus model of salvation, to which Paul alludes in 1 Cor 5:7 (cf. Rom 3:21–26). Paul explicitly appeals to the OT in Rom 3:21–26 with the words law and the prophets (Rom 3:21; cf. 1:3).

Additionally, to affirm that Martyr Theology was the background behind Paul's conception of Jesus's death is to reduce his death in his thought to nothing more important than the death of any innocent sufferer. This reduction would surrender "the great evangelical doctrine of the unique substitutionary sufferings of Christ." In Holland's view, Paul does not make one clear allusion to Martyr Theology.[46]

---

44. Talbert, *Romans*, 110–15.

45. Ben Ezra, *Yom Kippur*, 198–202. Similarly Deissmann, "ἱλαστήριος," 193–211; Davies, *Rabbinic Judaism*, 227–84, esp. 230–42; Campbell, *Rhetoric*, 107–13, 130–33. However, Deissmann, Davies, and Campbell reject the view that Paul calls Jesus the mercy seat in Rom 3:25.

46. Holland, *Contours*, 157–82, esp. 179–82.

Possible Background

W. Sanday and A.C. Headlam argue that the Yom Kippur ritual was not the background behind Rom 3:25. Their commentary does not explicitly argue that Martyr Theology was his background. Rather, along with other texts, Sanday and Headlam cite 4 Macc 17:21–22 to argue their view of ἱλαστήριον in Rom 3:25. They suggest that Jesus's death was an atoning sacrifice and that although NT authors often use OT cultic language to explain his death, the OT was not the background to Rom 3:25.[47]

Hastings Rashdall acknowledges that Martyr Theology was possibly the background behind Paul's conception of Jesus's death in Rom 3:25. Rashdall maintains that the OT was the immediate background behind a sacrificial understanding of Jesus's death, that 4 Macc 17:22 affirms that the martyrs died as sacrifices of atonement for sin, and that God saved Israel through their sacrificial deaths. Rashdall concludes that it is "highly probable" that Martyr Theology was Paul's source of thought for his sacrificial understanding of Jesus's death.[48]

Jacques Dupont presents a thorough analysis of Paul's reconciliation motif (the most thorough prior to the work of later scholars). He discusses the concept of reconciliation and related terms. According to Dupont, it is incorrect to deny that Paul's reconciliation motif reflects 2 Maccabees, because Paul conformed his reconciliation motif the same as 2 Maccabees.[49]

C. E. B. Cranfield rejects the popular belief that ἱλαστήριον refers to the mercy seat. He suggests that Martyr Theology's impact on Paul in Rom 3:25 is clear (esp. 2 Macc 7:30–38; 4 Macc 6:27–29, and 4 Macc 17:21–22). Cranfield downplays the wrath of God in Rom 3:25, but he observes that the deaths of the Jewish martyrs served as sacrificial atonement. He states that this idea was both popular for many Jews and was well known to Paul. Martyr Theology was an important background behind Paul's conception of Jesus's death, but scholars should also take seriously the influence of both the *Akedah Hypothesis* and Isa 53:10.[50]

I. Howard Marshall suggests that Paul's motif of reconciliation appears most frequently in 2 Corinthians and that 2 Maccabees prob-

---

47. Sanday and Headlam, *Romans*, 87–88, 91–94.

48. Rashdall, *Atonement*, 130–32.

49. Dupont, *La reconciliation*. Cf. Käsemann, "Reconciliation," 49–64.

50. Cranfield, *Romans*, 1:214–18, esp. 1:217–18.

ably has provided the catalyst to the development of Paul's use of the category of reconciliation. Martyr Theology presents the deaths of the martyrs as sacrificial offerings (2 Macc 7:32–38). Their offerings were the means by which God ended his wrath against the nation. Paul likewise presents Jesus's death as the means by which God ends his wrath against the nations (2 Cor 5:18–21). The influence of Martyr Theology on Paul's conception of Jesus's death cannot be categorically proven, but it can be argued and affirmed with a high degree of probability that Paul borrowed from the Martyr Theology of 2 and 4 Maccabees to present Jesus's death as an atoning sacrifice.[51]

Robert J. Daly argues for a connection between Martyr Theology and the suffering of Christians in Paul. Although he argues for the sacrificial nature of Jesus's death in the Pauline writings, he does not explicitly state that Martyr Theology shaped Paul's conception of Jesus's death. Rather, Daly argues that Paul simply presents the suffering of Christians in light of martyrdom and sacrifice (cf. 2 Maccabees 7 and 4 Maccabees 13 with 2 Cor 2:10–11; Gal 2:20; Phil 2:17.).[52]

Otfried Hofius argues that the provenance of the Pauline theme of reconciliation was not Paul's Hellenistic environment, Hellenistic traditions, the liturgy of the Hellenistic community,[53] or ancient Judaism. Paul's background was instead the LXX, the writings Paul so intensely studied. Isaiah 53 informed Paul's description of the redemptive act of God in Jesus, but he did not receive his reconciliatory language from Isaiah. It came to him already fixed from Hellenistic Judaism. Second Macc 1:5; 5:20; 7:33, and 8:39 affirm this.[54]

Christopher A. Davis suggests that Eleazar's death in 4 Macc 6:28–29 had a sacrificial element to it. Martyr Theology was not the only background behind Paul's conception of Jesus's death, but Paul "sets Christ apart from other human beings who had been unjustly executed by attaching special purgative significance to his death—much as the LXX singles out the deaths of the Servant of the Lord and Eleazar as somewhat unique and unprecedented events." Paul does not emphasize Jesus's death

51. Marshall, "Reconciliation," 117–32, esp. 120–21, 129–30.

52. Daly, *Christian Sacrifice*, 236–50.

53. Käsemann, "Erwägungen zum Stichwort," 47–59.

54. Hofius, "Erwägungen," 186–99.

as a vicarious or substitutionary atonement when he uses the ὑπερ-formula, although he may offer faint echoes of these concepts.[55]

Seyoon Kim argues that the origin of Paul's reconciliation motif was not Martyr Theology, but the Damascus-Road experience. He admits that it is possible that Martyr Theology shaped Paul's concept of reconciliation. Nevertheless, Kim argues that theories about the origin of the motif in Paul must be able to explain both the means by which Paul applies the καταλλάσσειν-terminology to God's salvation accomplished in Jesus and the reason for which he designates his ministry as a διακονία τῆς καταλλαγῆς ("ministry of reconciliation"). Even if Martyr Theology offers a satisfactory explanation to the first question, Kim argues that it does not answer the second.[56]

Paul Barnett states that 2 Maccabees is "the only major parallel" with Paul's reconciliation motif in 2 Cor 5:18–20. He contends that this assertion is important since the pertinent texts in 2 Maccabees are closer to NT times than any other parallel. Barnett does not forcefully argue that Martyr Theology was the background behind Paul's conception of Jesus's death, but he simply acknowledges the parallels and differences between Martyr Theology and Paul's conception of Jesus's death.[57]

Thomas R. Schreiner states that Martyr Theology possibly shaped Paul's conception of Jesus's death in Rom 3:25. Against Stuhlmacher, Schreiner argues that Martyr Theology should not be rejected so quickly since ἱλαστήριον is primarily a cultic term and other cultic terms in Rom 3:25 apply to the martyrs in 2 and 4 Maccabees. However, Schreiner cautiously warns that any reference to Martyr Theology in Rom 3:25 should not preclude Paul's dependence on Leviticus 16. The term ἱλαστήριον probably refers to the mercy seat in Rom 3:25 in light of the many other similarities that Rom 3:25–26 has with the Yom Kippur ritual. Although Schreiner affirms that Martyr Theology possibly shaped Paul's conception of Jesus's death, he offers the following caveat with regard to 4 Maccabees' influence on Rom 3:25: "any relationship with 4 Maccabees would be excluded if D.A. Campbell's proposal for a date between AD 135–235 is accepted."[58]

55. Davis, *Structure*, 120–24.

56. Kim, "2 Cor 5:11–21," 360–84, esp. 361–66; idem, *Origin*.

57. Barnett, *Second Corinthians*, 303 n. 10.

58. Schreiner, *Romans*, 192 n. 24; also 192–95. Cf. Haacker, *Römer*, 90–92.

In his commentary on Romans, James D.G. Dunn asserts that "it is possible that Paul was aware of the same language being used to describe the significance of the Maccabean martyrs' deaths" in Rom 3:25. He further states that Paul possibly alludes to Martyr Theology in Rom 3:25, but it is more likely that 4 Macc 17:21–22 and Rom 3:25 are "parallel extensions of the same cultic language and show how sacrificial imagery used to describe the death of a human being (rather than an animal) would have been readily understood in the Diaspora Judaism of Paul's time." However, in his Pauline Theology, although Dunn acknowledges that Martyr Theology appears to have shaped Paul's conception of Jesus's death, he does not think that Martyr Theology's impact on Paul matters. Dunn argues that the martyr texts apply the same sacrificial metaphors to the martyrs that appear in the OT cult. Therefore, it makes little difference whether Martyr Theology shaped Paul's conception of Jesus's death.[59]

Scot McKnight offers an analysis of the death of the historical Jesus. McKnight's main objective is not to discuss the background behind the NT's presentation of Jesus's death, but to present insight into how Jesus envisioned his own mission and death. McKnight concludes as a result of his investigation that Jesus anticipated his own death, that he believed that his death was a sacrifice of atonement, and that the atoning significance of his death was integral to Jesus's mission to protect his followers from God's judgment. McKnight appeals to Martyr Theology to demonstrate that belief that an individual's vicarious death for others would atone for sin was not altogether foreign to Jews and Judaism. McKnight does not explicitly address whether Martyr Theology shaped Paul's conception of Jesus's death as an atoning sacrifice or as a saving event for Jews and Gentiles.[60]

L. Arik Greenberg explores the various roles and formulations of the afterlife in early Christian martyrdom. The afterlife and personal immortality were closely connected to the theme of noble death in Hellenistic and early Jewish literature. The noble death was God's reward for martyrdom. Regarding Paul's conception of Jesus's death, Greenberg argues that he reflects Platonic and pre-Constantian ideas of martyrdom.[61]

---

59. Dunn, *Romans*, 1:170–72, 180, esp. 171, 180; idem, *Theology*, 207–33, esp. 215; idem, "Paul's Understanding," 125–41, esp. 131–32; idem, "The Death of Jesus," 35–56, esp. 40–42; idem, Dunn, *Jesus Remembered*, 1:796–824.

60. McKnight, *Jesus and His Death*.

61. Greenberg, "God's Reward." Cf. Brandon, "Atonement through Suffering," 282–92.

While Robert Jewett acknowledges that Martyr Theology could have influenced Paul's conception of Jesus's death in Rom 3:25, he asserts that many researchers have overlooked that the scope of the martyrs' deaths was limited to their nation. However, Paul suggests in Romans 3 that God provides atonement for humanity. Even if Martyr Theology influenced Paul's conception of Jesus's death, Jewett agrees with those scholars who have argued that the mercy seat imagery of the OT cult was foundational to Paul's use of ἱλαστήριον in Rom 3:25. Fourth Maccabees offers a precedent for Paul to present Jesus's blood as a new institution of atonement, just as the martyrs' deaths replaced the Yom Kippur ritual in 2 and 4 Maccabees.[62]

Background, but not Sacrificial

Sam K. Williams is the most important scholar prior to 1976 who argues that Martyr Theology shaped Paul's conception of Jesus's death. His work focuses on the background behind the early church's interpretation of Jesus's death as a saving event. He argues that the early church interpreted Jesus's death through already existing traditions: viz., Greco-Roman ideas of the effective death of a righteous human. With the possible exception of 4 Maccabees, Williams argues that vicarious, expiatory suffering and death are seldom found (if at all) in the OT and in intertestamental literature. Instead, the effective suffering and death of a human are found in Hellenistic literature. Fourth Maccabees contains the themes of effective suffering and death, but this is due to Greek-Hellenistic ideas, which provided a catalyst for the author of 4 Maccabees to interpret the martyrs' deaths. Greek-Hellenistic ideas also provided new Christians with a needed interpretation of Jesus's death. The message of Jesus's effective death spread from Antioch and was widely accepted as central to the gospel. Romans 3:21–26 is the central text regarding Martyr Theology's influence on Paul. No one understood the martyrs' deaths to be vicarious prior to the writing of 4 Maccabees, which Williams labels as an early Christian document composed in Antioch. Paul instead adopted a pre-Pauline Christian formula that interpreted Jesus's death as an expiation for sin.

According to Williams, 2 Maccabees does not teach vicarious atonement. Furthermore, not even 4 Maccabees clearly teaches expiatory death. The deaths of the martyrs were not deaths *qua* deaths in 4 Macc

62. Jewett, *Romans*, 286–87.

6:28–29 or 17:21–22, but 4 Maccabees provided the background behind Paul's conception of Jesus's death in Rom 3:25–26. Similar to his view of 4 Maccabees, Williams likewise argues that Paul does not present Jesus's death as a death *qua* death in Rom 3:25–26. The available evidence (i.e., OT, Greek-Hellenistic, and NT) suggests that the early church interpreted Jesus's death as a saving event in light of the Greco-Roman ideas of the effective death of a human. That Jesus's death was a saving event arose as an apologetic response to the problem of his death. Jesus's death was not a vicarious, atoning sacrifice for the sins of the nations, but early Christians interpreted his death as such in light of 4 Maccabees and other Greco-Roman literature in order to provide a solution to his tragic death.[63]

Similar to Williams, David Seeley investigates the historical influences behind Paul's interpretation of Jesus's death. The theme of noble death influenced Paul, and this background was Hellenistic and Roman. Seeley gives five components of noble death that he finds in Paul. Seeley suggests that each component occurs in 4 Maccabees: (1) obedience, (2) the overcoming of physical vulnerability, (3) military setting, (4) vicariousness, and (5) sacrificial metaphors. Paul, says Seeley, especially follows Martyr Theology when he presents Jesus's death as vicarious for others. By vicarious, Seeley means that Jesus's death was an example for his followers to imitate. Furthermore, the temple cult and the OT played no role in shaping Paul's conception of Jesus's death.[64]

---

63. Williams, *Jesus's Death*, 39–41, 165–202, 233–54. Williams is not always overtly clear as to whether Jesus's death should be understood as an atoning sacrifice. On the one hand, he asserts that Jesus's death is expiatory in Rom 3:25, just as the martyrs' deaths in 4 Macc 6:28–29 and 17:21–22. On the other hand, Williams argues quite arduously that the martyrs' deaths should not be understood as expiatory atonement in 4 Macccabees (165–202). Yet, he concludes that 4 Maccabees served as an important backdrop behind why early Christians interpreted Jesus's death as a saving event (233–54). Based on his thesis that 4 Maccabees provides the background behind an early Christian interpretation of Jesus's death as a saving event and based on his exegesis of 4 Maccabees in chapter 5 of his monograph, I think it is fair to say that Williams himself rejects the belief that Jesus's death was an atoning sacrifice for sin, because he argues that the NT authors' presentation of Jesus's death derived from the influence of 4 Maccabees and because he argues that 4 Maccabees does not teach vicarious atonement. See also Wengst, *Christologische Formeln*, 59 n. 11, 63; Stowers, *A Reading of Romans*, 206–13; Versnel, "Making Sense of Jesus's Death," 213–94. However, Wengst affirms that 2 Macc 7:32–38 and 4 Macc 6:28–29 teach that the martyrs were atoning sacrifices (59 n. 11, 63).

64. Seeley, *Noble Death*.

Background, but Sacrificial

David Hill argues that Martyr Theology (particularly 4 Macc 17:21–22) was Paul's background in Rom 3:25. Hill agrees that ἱλαστήριον refers to the mercy seat in Heb 9:5 and many times in the canonical LXX. However, the Yom Kippur ritual, the context within which ἱλαστήριον mainly occurs in the canonical LXX, was not the provenance of Paul's comments in Rom 3:25. Instead, Martyr Theology was the source for Paul's presentation of Jesus's death as a propitiatory sacrifice, because (1) both 4 Macc 17:21–22 and Rom 3:25 speak of God's wrath. (2) Both texts speak of the shedding of blood at the expense of one's life. (3) Death for sin occurs in both texts. (4) Both texts declare that death was the means by which God's mercy and deliverance came to the transgressors. (5) Both the death of the martyrs and Jesus's death were vicarious sacrifices in the respective texts. (6) God initiates atonement in both texts, and (7) since 4 Maccabees speaks of the existence of the Second Temple, it could have been written prior to AD 70, which means Paul could have known 4 Maccabees as a source.[65]

J.C. Beker comments on Paul's conception of Jesus's death as a means of developing a larger thesis: Paul's theology is mainly apocalyptic. Hellenistic-Jewish Christianity applied atoning significance to Jesus's death. The concept of a human atonement for the sins of others was a foreign concept to Jews, but it eventually gained acceptance by them via Diaspora theology. Wisdom of Solomon emphasizes that the deaths of the righteous sufferers benefit others, but 2 and 4 Maccabees alone highlight the atoning value of such deaths. Paul received the creedal formulation of Martyr Theology (1 Cor 15:3; Rom 4:25) from the Jewish-Hellenistic church, from which he also inherited the interpretation that Jesus's death was a sacrificial offering (Exod 12:13; 1 Cor 5:7), an expiation (Rom 3:25), and a covenant sacrifice (Exod 24:4–8; 1 Cor 11:23).[66]

As Baumeister before him, John S. Pobee undertakes a similar task: viz., to construct a Jewish theology of martyrdom. He concludes from his investigation that a Jewish Martyr Theology existed, not a Maccabean Martyr Theology. He identifies martyrdom as theodicy in the relevant Maccabean texts. He suggests the following components of a Jewish Martyr Theology: (1) the nation suffered because of its sin. (2) God unleashed his wrath upon the martyrs to propitiate his wrath. (3) God judged

65. Hill, *Greek Words and Hebrew Meanings,* 36–48, esp. 38–48.
66. Beker, *Paul the Apostle,* 182–212, esp. 191, 203–05.

the martyrs through suffering in order to avert his eschatological wrath away from them. (4) Israel's persecution validated a cosmic war, and (5) suffering was the means by which the war was manifested. Pobee extends his discussion of Martyr Theology beyond the Maccabean literature. He interacts with all Jewish writings from the fourth century BC through the rabbinic period. He affirms that there was a late Jewish Martyr Theology in Second Temple Judaism and that Martyr Theology was the background behind Paul's conception of Jesus's death.[67]

Warren Joel Heard searches for the antecedents to Martyr Theology. He argues that the studies of Stauffer and Baumeister prior to his dissertation did not engage in an exegesis of specific texts and that no one prior to his work had ever investigated the antecedent traditions behind Martyr Theology. His study is certainly profitable. He mainly focuses on three components of Martyr Theology: (1) its early formulation, (2) its origin, and, (3) its application to the earliest soteriological interpretation of Jesus's death. He suggests that Martyr Theology was the background behind Paul's conception of Jesus's death.[68]

Gerhard Barth investigates scholarly discussion of Jesus's death. Whether Jesus's death should be understood as vicarious expiation is the most elaborate section of his work. After investigating the OT cult and Isaiah 53, Barth concludes that the OT does not adequately explain Paul's presentation of Jesus's death. Martyr Theology was his background. In Paul, Jesus's death expiated the sins of all believers, and, consequently, believers have been judged in his death.[69]

Joseph A. Fitzmyer argues that in the Greco-Roman world, reconciliation spoke of the restoration of broken relationships. When used religiously, it spoke of the reconciliation between the gods/God and humans (e.g, Sophocles, *Ajax* 744; 2 Macc 1:5; 7:33; 8:29). Since Hebrew does not have a specific word for reconciliation, Fitzmyer insists that (1) the Greco-Roman world and its Martyr Theology were the sources of Paul's reconciliatory language. (2) Paul applies Martyr Theology to the Christ-event, and (3) Paul uses Martyr Theology in his own way.[70]

67. Pobee, *Persecution and Martyrdom*.

68. Heard, "Maccabean Martyr Theology."

69. Barth, *Der Tod Jesus Christi*, 37–71.

70. Fitzmyer, *Gospel*, 164–66.

Stephen Anthony Cummins argues that Martyr Theology shaped Paul's conception of Jesus's death in Rom 3:25. He also asserts that the historical and theological significance behind the Antiochean incident in Gal 2:11–12 would gain clarity when viewed in relation to a Maccabean martyr model of Judaism, just as Paul demonstrates this model through his ministry. Martyr Theology provided early Christians with an application for the earliest soteriological interpretation of Jesus's death.[71]

Daniel G. Powers argues that Martyr Theology's influence on Paul's conception of Jesus's death is evident. He specifically focuses on the participatory language in Paul's soteriology. As a means of arguing his thesis (that believers participate in Christ's fate on account of their participation in Christ), Powers defends that Martyr Theology influenced both Paul's interpretation of Jesus's death and the interpretation of early Christians. This influence came from 2 Maccabees, Judith, Assumption of Moses, and the additions of Daniel.[72]

N. T. Wright argues that Martyr Theology shaped Paul's conception of Jesus's death in Rom 3:25. The martyrs and other Jews understood the deaths of the martyrs as atoning sacrifices for Israel and that the Lord would save Israel from his wrath through their deaths (4 Macc 6:28–29). The Yom Kippur ritual and Isaiah 40–55 also served as a background behind Rom 3:25. Paul, then, presents Jesus's death as an atoning sacrifice for sin by using cultic language from Leviticus 16, Isaiah's Servant- Songs, and Martyr Theology.[73]

Primary Background, but Sacrificial

Eduard Lohse was one of the first scholars to speak of the martyrs' deaths as vicarious atonement. He argues for the importance of Jewish Martyr Theology for early Christians and (to some extent) for Paul's conception of Jesus's death. From the outset of his work, he excludes Hellenism and Hellenistic Judaism from being the possible background behind Martyr Theology. To defend this, he endeavors to prove that the concept of martyrdom in 2 and 4 Maccabees was due to Palestinian Jewish thought. In the latter, the earliest examples of martyrdom occur. Lohse also contends

---

71. Cummins, *Paul and the Crucified Christ.*

72. Powers, *Salvation through Participation.* Powers (*Salvation through Participation,* 199–211, esp. 210) rejects that 2 Maccabees teaches vicarious, substitutionary atonement.

73. Wright, *People of God,* 272–79.

that the Hellenistic background behind 2 and 4 Maccabees was not critical since these works were more indebted to Palestinian Judaism.

In addition, expiatory death is not explicitly stated in 2 Maccabees,
but representation is more evident. Fourth Maccabees teaches vicarious
atonement. This tradition influenced Paul. In his 2003 commentary on
Romans, Lohse argues that the Martyr Theology in 4 Macc 17:21–22 was
Paul's background for his presentation of Jesus's death in Rom 3:25, but
that Paul conflated Martyr Theology with OT cultic language.[74]

Martin Hengel was not likely familiar with Williams' work (*Jesus's
Death*) since he does not specifically mention it. Hengel, however, indirectly counters Williams' thesis. Hengel argues that Greco-Roman literature was a crucial background behind the early church's understanding
of the saving significance of Jesus's death. Jesus, not the early church,
was the first person to interpret his death as an atoning sacrifice. The OT
background alone is insufficient to explain the soteriological categories
that the NT applies to Jesus's death. Hellenistic religious ideas were very
influential on Jewish writers and Paul.[75]

Marinus de Jonge investigates the earliest formulations of Jesus's
death for others. He argues that the deaths of the martyrs in 2 and 4
Maccabees should be understood as substitutionary atonement. Greek,
Hellenistic, and Roman ideas influenced these works. The martyrs' deaths
were the means by which God averted his wrath away from the nation and
peace came to Israel. The effective prayer of the martyrs before their deaths
echoes various OT texts (Exod 32:30–34; Ps 106:16–23; Numbers 25; LXX
Dan 3:38–40). The martyrs' deaths helped early Christians understand the
conception of Jesus's death in Paul and in early Christian confessional
formulas. De Jonge does not dismiss the influence of the OT on Paul, but
he argues that his primary background was Martyr Theology.[76]

Since Williams in the 1970s and Hengel in the 1980s, J.W. van Henten
is arguably the most important scholar who has written about Martyr
Theology's influence on the NT authors. His work on 2 and 4 Maccabees

74. Lohse, *Märtyrer*, 37–78, 150–52; idem, *Römer*, 134–35. See also Surkau, *Martyrien*.

75. Hengel, *The Atonement*. Hengel states that it is unlikely that Paul was familiar with
4 Maccabees. Cf., however, Hengel and Schwemer, *Paul between Damascus and Antioch*,
191–96.

76. de Jonge, "Jesus's Death for Others," 142–51; reprinted in *Jewish Eschatology*,
125–34; idem, *Christology*; idem, *Jesus, the Servant-Messiah*, 37–48; idem, *God's Final
Envoy*, 12–33.

is a detailed exegesis of both books. He argues that the Maccabean martyrs were exemplars of noble death. The deaths of Eleazar, the unknown mother, and her seven sons were idealized stories and representative of specific religious, political, and philosophical ideas. The deaths of the martyrs in 2 Macc 7:32–38 were vicarious. Fourth Maccabees is a spiritualized book that highlights the deaths of the martyrs and the vicarious aspect of their deaths. The authors of both works probably borrowed the concept of vicarious atonement from Greco-Roman traditions. Van Henten does not dismiss the OT's influence on Paul, but he argues that Martyr Theology was the primary background behind Paul's conception of Jesus's death.[77]

David DeSilva argues that Martyr Theology influenced the early church's understanding of Jesus's death. Paul and other Christians attributed the same soteriological value to Jesus's death as the authors of 2 and 4 Maccabees to the martyrs' deaths. Just as Eleazar's death (4 Macc 6:28–29), Jesus's death was purification, atonement for sin, sacrificial, propitiatory, vicarious, and acceptable to God (Rom 3:25; 5:19; Phil 2:5–11).[78]

Udo Schnelle argues that Paul's "Christ died for us" statements did not emanate from the OT sacrificial system. Instead, they came from the Greek idea of the voluntary death of the righteous whose death offers expiation for sin. The same concept also occurs in Martyr Theology (2 Macc 7:37–38; 4 Macc 6:27–29; 17:21–22). The Eucharistic tradition together with LXX Isa 53:11–12 likewise influenced the early church's idea of the vicarious death of the righteous. Paul borrowed these traditions to develop a vicarious understanding of Jesus's death. The OT cult was the main influence behind Paul's presentation of Jesus's death as an atoning sacrifice.[79]

Stephen Finlan devotes one chapter to Maccabean martyrdom. He agrees with van Henten and others that martyrdom was the most prominent model behind Paul's conception of Jesus's death, but he suggests that Paul borrowed from the OT cultic context to convey his martyrological ideas. Paul employs the martyr formula in many places

---

77. Van Henten, *Maccabean Martyrs*; idem, "The Tradition-Historical Background," 101–28; idem, "Prolegomena, 381–90; idem, "Datierung und Herkunft," 136–49; idem, "Das jüdische Selbstverständis," 127–61; idem, "The Martyrs as Heroes," 303–22; idem, "2 Makkabeeën," 853–67; idem, "Die Martyrer als Helden des Volkes," 102–33; idem, "Martyrdom and Persecution Revisited," 59–75; idem, "Jewish Martyrdom and Jesus's Death," 139–68.

78. DeSilva, *4 Maccabees* (1998); idem, *4 Maccabees* (2006).

79. Schnelle, *Apostle Paul*, 443–51, esp. 446–51.

(Rom 5:6, 8; 1 Thess 5:10; 1 Cor 8:11). Each occurrence reflects substitutionary atonement. Paul diverges from Martyr Theology in his teaching of propitiation. He does not describe God as needing appeasement, for God and Jesus took the initiative in his dying for the ungodly (Rom 5:5–6).[80]

CONCLUSION

As the history of research demonstrates, many scholars have discussed whether Martyr Theology had an informative impact on Paul's conception of Jesus's death. However, this monograph offers a more detailed investigation of Martyr Theology's influence on Paul than antecedent scholarship. To my knowledge, no scholar has ever written a major exegetical monograph in which the key texts were analyzed and compared in order to argue the thesis that Paul conceived of Jesus's death both as an atoning sacrifice and as a saving event for Jews and Gentiles, because Martyr Theology shaped his conception of Jesus's death. The major contributions of this monograph are listed as follows: (1) It provides evidence that Martyr Theology shaped Paul's conception of Jesus's death. (2) It argues that Paul presents Jesus's death both as an atoning sacrifice and as a saving event for Jews and Gentiles because Martyr Theology shaped his conception of Jesus's death.

---

80. Finlan, *Atonement Metaphors*, 193–224.

2

Martyrdom in 2 and 4 Maccabees

INTRODUCTION

THIS CHAPTER INVESTIGATES THE key texts in 2 and 4 Maccabees. I argue that the authors of 2 and 4 Maccabees present the martyrs as atoning sacrifices and as a saving event for Israel. The thesis is argued by an exegetical analysis of key texts in 2 and 4 Maccabees.[1] Before I analyze the key texts, I first set forth the background behind the composition of 2 and 4 Maccabees and the background behind their motif that humans died as atoning sacrifices and as a saving event for others.

---

1. Although different authors wrote 2 and 4 Maccabees for distinct purposes and although several years possibly separate the composition of each work, this chapter investigates 2 and 4 Maccabees as a body of literature. This method is plausible since the author of 4 Maccabees possibly depended on 2 Maccabees when he composed his work. Several scholars have argued for such a literary dependency. For example, see Schlatter, "Der Märtyrer," 229–10, esp. 275–76; Dupont-Sommer, *Le Quatrième Livre des Machabées*, 27–32; Hadas, *The Third and Fourth Books of Maccabees*, 92–95; van Henten, *Maccabean Martyrs*, 70–73; DeSilva, *Introducing the Apocrypha*, 355; idem, *4 Maccabees* (2006), xxx–xxxi. Van Henten (*Maccabean Martyrs*, 70) asserts that a literary dependency is evident from the way that 2 and 4 Maccabees describe the martyrdoms of Eleazar, the mother, and her seven sons (2 Macc 6:18–31 with 4 Maccabees 6; 2 Maccabees 7 with 4 Maccabees 9–12 and 14:11–17:1). Contra Freudenthal, *Die Flavius,* 72–90. He posits that both 2 and 4 Maccabees were dependent on the lost history of Jason of Cyrene (cf. 2 Macc 2:23). This, argues Freudenthal, explains the differences between 2 and 4 Maccabees. Both authors offer different interpretations of and distinct interests in Jason's lost history. DeSilva (*4 Maccabees* [1998], 29–32) rejects Freudenthal's theory and considers it to be superfluous on the basis of 4 Maccabees' purpose and its use of historical narrative.

AN INTRODUCTION TO 2 AND 4 MACCABEES

2 Maccabees (ca. 134–63 BC)

Second Maccabees does not state the identity of its author(s),[2] but only that composers edited and abridged Jason of Cyrene's five-volume work about the Maccabean revolt (2 Macc 2:23–42). Evidence, however, of a singular authorship exists in the text of 2 Maccabees (2 Macc 15:37–38), but the book neither discloses the identity of its author nor the identity of its composers. As to the date of 2 Maccabees, determining the exact time of composition is not easy. Some scholars date 2 Maccabees either during the reign of John Hyrcanus (134–104 BC)[3] or circa 63 BC.[4]

Regarding the purpose of writing, 2 and 4 Maccabees were not sequels to 1 Maccabees.[5] Whereas 1 Maccabees focuses on the historical events surrounding the inception and culmination of the Maccabean revolt, the authors of 2 and 4 Maccabees wrote for different purposes. The author of 2 Maccabees, for example, wrote to report selective events from Jewish history from the reign of Nicanor, King Seleucus IV (187–175 BC), and the reign of Onias III as high priest until the defeat of the Seleucid king at the hands of Judas Maccabeus in 161 BC.[6] The reign of the Seleucid kings was indeed variegated and complex (cf. 2 Macc 2:19–15:39). It was a time of Hellenization and intense Jewish persecution at the hands of Antiochus (ca. 175–167 BC). The reign of the Seleucids was also a time in which Jews experienced liberation from their suffering.[7]

---

2. Henceforth author.

3. Goldstein, *2 Maccabees*, 71–72.

4. DeSilva, *Introducing the Apocrypha*, 268–69. Similarly Evans, *Ancient Texts*, 21. For arguments in favor of dating 2 Maccabees prior to 63 BC, see van Henten, *Maccabean Martyrs*, 51–56.

5. First Maccabees highlights religious zeal. This zeal provoked many Jews to fight and to die for the Torah (1 Macc 2:50–51). First Maccabees suggests that one should relentlessly fight against all forms of Hellenism (1 Macc 2:41–48, 68; cf. 1 Macc 2:23–26, 31–38; 3:2–11).

6. So Vanderkam, *Early Judaism*, 65–69.

7. Van Henten, *Maccabean Martyrs*, 17–18. For a detailed discussion of the high priesthood during Second Temple Judaism, see Vanderkam, *From Joshua to Caiaphas*; Brutti, *High Priesthood*.

4 Maccabees (ca. 30 BC–AD 135)

Regarding the authorship of 4 Maccabees, neither the text of 4 Maccabees nor Christian tradition discloses the author's identity. Eusebius (*History* 3.10.6) ascribed authorship to Josephus, but most scholars reject Josephan authorship.[8] The original readers of 4 Maccabees could discern at least two things about the author: (1) he was immersed in Hellenistic culture, and (2) he was a pious Jew (4 Macc 1:1–6:29).[9]

Suggested dates for the composition of 4 Maccabees range anywhere from circa 30 BC–AD 135.[10] Scholars have offered compelling arguments both in favor of and against an early date. Regarding an early date, scholars have argued that first if the author of 4 Maccabees depended on 2 Maccabees (ca. 134–63 BC), 4 Maccabees was certainly written after the composition of 2 Maccabees. Since 4 Macc 4:1 asserts that the high priesthood could formerly be held for a lifetime, 4 Maccabees may have been written shortly after this practice had ended.[11] The explanation in 4:1 would have been unnecessary prior to 63 BC, because the high priesthood was not a lifetime position after the cessation of the Hasmonean dynasty in 63 BC.[12] Second, scholars suggest that the presence of the words θρησκεία ("cult, service") and νομικὸς ("expert in the law") may support an early date, because ancient authors did not commonly use these words until Augustus' reign (ca. 30 BC–AD 14) during the Roman period.[13] Additionally, the author of 4 Maccabees specifically calls Eleazar a νομικὸς (4 Macc 5:4) instead of a γραμματεύς ("scribe," 2 Macc 6:18).[14] Thus, the

8. For example, Townshend, "The Fourth Book of Maccabees," 656–57; Anderson, "4 Maccabees," 531–64; DeSilva (1998), *4 Maccabees*, 12–14.

9. So Anderson, "4 Maccabees," 532–34, esp. 532; DeSilva, *Introducing the Apocrypha*, 355.

10. For dating, see Robert, *Etudes épigraphiques et philologiques*, 219–35, esp. 226–35; Bickerman, "The Date of IV Maccabees," 275–81; DeSilva, *Introducing the Apocrypha*, 355–56; Dupont-Sommer, *Le Quatrième Livre des Machabées*, 75–85; Breitenstein, *Beobachtungen zu Sprache*; Collins, *Between Athens and Jerusalem*, 203–04; DeSilva (2006), *4 Maccabees*, xiv-xvii.

11. Cf. DeSilva (2006), *4 Maccabees*, xiv.

12. Anderson, "4 Maccabees," 533.

13. Bickerman, "The Date of IV Maccabees," 275–81; Robert, *Etudes épigraphiques et philologiques*, 219–35, esp. 226–35; DeSilva, *Introducing the Apocrypha*, 355.

14. So Bickerman, "The Date of IV Maccabees," 275–81.

author uses the particular Roman nomenclature of his time when Syria and Cilicia were united as a singular territory.[15]

Third, 4 Maccabees calls Apollonius (a Seleucid-appointed adminis-trator) a governor (στρατηγός) over Syria, Phoenicia, and Cilicia (4 Macc 4:2). This title is different from his jurisdiction in 2 Maccabees (2 Macc 3:5).[16] The latter states that he was the governor over Coelesyria and Phoenicia.[17] Syria, Phoenicia, and Cilicia became one administrative unit under Roman rule (ca. AD 18–54).[18] The administrative union in 4 Maccabees may sug-gest that 4 Maccabees may have been written during the Roman period at some point between 64 BC (when the high priesthood was not a tenured position) and AD 54. Fourth, the author of 4 Maccabees appears to assume that the temple was still standing even as he writes (4 Macc 4:20). If the temple was standing when the author composed the work, this would sup-port at the latest a date of AD 70 or a date prior to AD 70 since the temple was destroyed in AD 70.[19] Fifth, since there are specific points of contact between 4 Maccabees, the NT, and the Apostolic Fathers, an early date in the first half of the first century AD is possible.[20]

Scholars have offered a number of counter arguments against an ear-ly date of 4 Maccabees. First, one cannot decide the date of 4 Maccabees based on vocabulary, style of writing, or references to administrative unions,[21] because the term στρατηγός (interpreted by some to mean governor) in 4 Macc 4:4 could simply refer to a military person instead of a reference to the governor of a province.[22] Furthermore, although an administrative union existed between Syria and Cilicia during the first century of the Christian era, both literary and epigraphical evidence dem-

---

15. Anderson, "4 Maccabees," 534.

16. Ibid.

17. Ibid.

18. Ibid.

19. Ibid.

20. Cf. DeSilva, *Introducing the Apocrypha*, 355–56.

21. So Campbell, *Rhetoric*, 221–28; van Henten, "Datierung und Herkunft," 136–49; idem, "Martyrdom and Persecution Revisited," 59–75. Van Henten argues in the latter work that 4 Maccabees was a response to early Christian glorifications of martyrdom in the late second or third centuries AD. For van Henten's most recent summary of this thesis, see "Jewish Martyrdom and Jesus's Death," 143–45.

22. Campbell, *Rhetoric*, 221–24.

onstrates that Vespasian ended this union only in AD 72.[23] This would put the composition of 4 Maccabees late in the first century AD. Once more, the names Syria, Phoenicia, and Cilicia likely refer to specific areas in 4 Maccabees, not to a single administrative unit.[24] This would extinguish the possibility that 4 Maccabees was written early in the Roman period.

Second, that the author of 4 Maccabees alludes to a specific historical situation (i.e., the existence of the temple) does not mean that he composed the source during the period to which he alludes.[25] Instead, the author's reference to the temple could simply suggest that 4 Maccabees may have been written either during or after the situation to which he alludes.[26] Moreover, whether the temple actually has an important role in 4 Maccabees is questionable since the references to it primarily occur when the author describes the historical context of martyrdom (4 Macc 3:20–4:26).[27] Third, the literary form of 4 Maccabees exhibits a style similar to post AD 70 rabbinic passages that speak of martyrdom.[28] Fourth, the vocabulary in 4 Maccabees closely reflects the vocabulary in the Apostolic Fathers, who wrote late in the first century AD and beyond.[29] Fifth, NT authors either allude to or quote 2 Macc 6:18–7:42, but they never refer to 4 Maccabees.[30]

Regarding the dating of 4 Maccabees and its influence on Paul, I admit that some scholars would quickly dismiss my thesis in this work on methodological grounds since many have ascribed a late date to 4 Maccabees (ca. 30BC-AD135).[31] If, however, the arguments in favor of a late date for 4 Maccabees are more trustworthy than those, espoused

---

23. Van Henten, *Maccabean Martyrs*, 74.

24. Ibid., 74–75.

25. Ibid.

26. Ibid., 74.

27. Ibid., 75.

28. Ibid., 76.

29. Ibid., 77.

30. Ibid.

31. For example, Schreiner (*Romans*, 192–95, esp. 192 n. 24) affirms that Martyr Theology was possibly the background behind Paul's conception of Jesus's death in Rom 3:25, but cautiously warns that "any relationship with 4 Maccabees would be excluded if D.A. Campbell's proposal for a date between AD 135–235 is accepted." For a late date of 4 Maccabees, see Campbell, *Rhetoric*, 219–28; van Henten, "Datierung und Herkunft," 136–49; idem, *Maccabean Martyrs*, 73–78, esp. 78; idem, "Martyrdom and Persecution Revisited," 59–75.

by Elias Bickerman and others,[32] for an early date, my thesis that Martyr Theology shaped Paul's conception of Jesus's death as an atoning sacrifice and as a saving event is still plausible, because I argue that the Martyr Theology represented in 2 and 4 Maccabees shaped Paul's conception of Jesus's death. I do not argue that 2 and 4 Maccabees *per se* shaped his conception of Jesus's death. Thus, if scholars are correct to attribute a late date to 4 Maccabees, a late date would aid the viability of my thesis in this monograph, because it would suggest that a Martyr Theology tradition existed during Second Temple Judaism (STJ) before the composition of 4 Maccabees and was available for Paul when he wrote his letters since a Martyr Theology occurs elsewhere in Second Temple Jewish texts (STJT) and since each of these STJT either definitely or possibly pre-dates Paul if he died ca. AD 64–65. These STJT would include the Epistle of Jeremiah (ca. 317–306 BC), Wisdom of Solomon (3.6 [ca. 220BC-AD100]), Daniel (MT Dan 11:32–35 [if dated ca. 165BC], 2 Maccabees (2 Macc 5:1–8:5 [ca. 134–63 BC), LXX additions of Daniel (Dan 3:38–40 [i.e., Prayer of Azariah and Song of The Three Young Men, 3–18], [ca. 100BC]), possibly 1QS (1QS 1:1–3:10 [ca. 100BC]),[33] and Assumption of Moses (As. *Mos.* 9.6–10.10 [ca. 168BC-AD135]).[34] Therefore, I understand 4 Maccabees to be further developing an already existing Martyr Theology that preceded Paul.

In addition, scholars agree that the author of 4 Maccabees composed the book in the Diaspora since the work lacks references to Jerusalem, the temple, and specific political institutions.[35] Some scholars likewise have argued that 4 Maccabees was written in Alexandria.[36] Other scholars argue that the author possibly lived in Antioch in light of his use of Greek rhetoric.[37] J.W. van Henten has especially argued that the provenance of 4 Maccabees was likely Asia Minor.[38] Although the provenance could

32. Bickerman, "The Date of IV Maccabees," 1:275–81.

33. I say possibly because 1QS states that a human's death atones for sin and saves the community from God's judgment, but 1QS is not clear that atonement occurs in the context of martyrdom.

34. Dates for the above STJT come from Charlesworth, *The Old Testament Pseudepigrapha*, 2:920; Schreiner, *Romans*, 3–5, esp. 3; DeSilva, *Introducing the Apocrypha*, 131–33, 216–17, 225–26; Vermes, *The Complete Dead Sea Scrolls in English*, 97; Evans, *Ancient Texts*, 17.

35. Van Henten, *Maccabean Martyrs*, 78.

36. Ibid., 78 n. 90.

37. Ibid., 78 n. 91.

38. Ibid., 80–81.

aid in determining whether the book is a Christian or a non-Christian document and whether an early or a late date should be accepted, the evidence in 4 Maccabees is nevertheless insufficient to determine with absolute certainty either the origin or date of the book. However, even if 4 Maccabees was written by a Christian within a Christian community after Paul composed his earliest letters, it is still possible that the Martyr Theology in 4 Maccabees informed Paul's understanding of Jesus's death since a late date and a Christian origin would support that the Martyr Theology in 4 Maccabees contains ideas that were part of Paul's culture prior to or during the composition of 4 Maccabees, prior to or during Paul's composition of his letters, and ideas that were available for the Christian community contemporaneous with Paul.

Regarding the purpose of 4 Maccabees, the author states in the introduction that his purpose for writing was to demonstrate that pious reason was absolute master over the passions (4 Macc 1:1–4:1). He develops this thesis by presenting the steadfast devotion of many pious Jews to their God and to his law. These Jews were resilient in their commitment to their religion, even in the face of persecution and death. Neither Antiochus' tortures nor his threats of death caused them to abandon their allegiance to God (4 Macc 5:1–6:30).[39]

GRECO-ROMAN IDEAS OF HUMAN SACRIFICE AND THE MARTYRS

In contrast to 1 and 3 Maccabees, a prominent feature in both 2 and 4 Maccabees is Jewish martyrdom. Second Maccabees 2:19–15:39 and 4 Macc 5:1–17:22 contain stories and commentary that highlight the martyrdom of Eleazar, an unknown mother, and her seven sons. As I argue below, together these stories in both books teach that God used Antiochus to judge the nation for its religious apostasy (1 Macc 1:16–63; 2 Macc 6:12–7:38; 4 Macc 5:1–6:8). As the martyrs suffered at the hands of Antiochus and his successors, they voluntarily offered themselves to God as sacrifices for the nation (4 Macc 6:28–29; cf. 2 Macc 7:32–38).[40]

---

39. Jewish resiliency in the face of persecution and death also appears in Daniel, History of Susanna, and Bel and the Dragon.

40. Shepkaru ("The Evolution of Jewish Martyrdom," 22–25) argues that Antiochus was not the fundamental initiator of the edicts against the Jews regarding their conformation to the Greek way of life. Nor was his goal to eradicate Judaism. Instead, the contention between Greek and Jewish culture began as an internal struggle. The issue at

However, the sacrificial death of a human for the benefit of others was not a novel concept to the writers of 2 and 4 Maccabees. In fact, this practice was ubiquitous in the Greco-Roman world.[41] Both tragedies and philosophical writings of certain Greco-Roman authors demonstrate that humans voluntarily offered themselves to the gods in death as sacrifices for the benefit of others, and such sacrifices afforded salvation for those whom they died in that their deaths achieved the mercy of the gods. The salvation that these human sacrifices achieved in the literature was often victory for the city-state in war, deliverance from death, and atonement for sins.

Euripides (480–406 BC) demonstrates that humans died as atoning sacrifices for the salvation of others. Their deaths were often the means by which the gods granted favor to Greece. In his play *Iphigeneia among the Tauri*,[42] some citizens thought that the father of Iphigeneia slew Tyndareus and presented her to Artemis (the goddess of light) "for the sake of Helen" (*Iphigeneia in Tauri* 3–10). Consequently, Calchas told king Agamemnon (captain of the Grecian army) that he would not win the crown of victory in battle until he offered his daughter (Iphigeneia) to Artemis as a sacrifice (*Iphigeneia in Tauri* 11–20). The goddess, then, said that Clytemnestra must give birth to a child whom she must sacrifice to the gods (*Iphigeneia in Tauri* 21–24), because the gods would not permit Agamemnon to achieve victory in battle unless he presented his daughter as an atoning sacrifice.

---

stake for Israel was not whether one should be a Jew, but instead exactly how one should be a Jew. Jason and Menelaus, according to Shepkaru, were fundamentally concerned with advancing Jewish society. They thought the best way to do this was to embrace the new way of life offered by the Greeks. Therefore, Jason and Menelaus sought to persuade their fellow Jews to embrace this new way (cf. 1 Maccabees 1).

41. Hengel, *The Atonement*, 6–32; van Henten and Avemarie, *Martyrdom and Noble Death,* 9–41); and Versnel, "Making Sense of Jesus's Death," 227–56 pointed me to the Greco-Roman texts that I discuss in this chapter. In addition, by accentuating the importance of human sacrifice, I do not mean to imply that animal sacrifices were not also a common practice in the Greco-Roman world. Rather, my point is that human sacrifice for the benefit of others was integral to Greco-Roman society. See Yerkes, *Sacrifice,* 61–63, 68–75. He lists many Greco-Roman texts that affirm that the ancients sacrificed animals to the gods. For archaeological evidence that supports the importance of human sacrifice in the Greco-Roman world, see Hughes, "Human Sacrifice in Ancient Greece." Wengst (*Christologische Formeln*, 63 n. 11) argues that the notion of a vicarious death of a human is a Greek idea, but 2 Macc 7:32–38 provides the earliest example where the vicarious death of a human actually accomplishes atonement.

42. Also known as *Iphigenia in Taurica*.

This sacrifice would have achieved the mercy of the gods for the people (*Iphigeneia in Tauri* 21–24; cf. 1368–1401; *Phoenissae* 968–75).[43]

In *Alcestis*, Euripides asserts that a human's sacrificial death for others could benefit those for whom the death was offered. Alcestis was ready to die for Admetus (her husband). Death is personified in the play and beckons for Admetus. Death speaks to Admetus and states that it would spare him from dying only if he would exchange (διαλλάξαντα) another human life for his (*Alcestis* 14).[44] After a long search, however, Admetus could not find anyone who would give his life as a substitute for him, except his wife who was willing to die for Admetus and whose death would save him from death (*Alcestis* 1–36; cf. *Iphigeneia at Aulis* 1553–556; *Hecuba* 38–41, 367–78, 484–582; *Heraclides* 501–50; Plato *Symposium*, 179b).[45]

Plato (428–348 BC) presents Socrates' death in a similar manner. Socrates praises those who died for Athens in battle (*Menexenus* 237a; cf. 243a, 246b; Hor. *Odes* 3.19.2). He describes their deaths as atoning sacrifices that achieve soteriological benefits for the city-state when he asserts that those who died for the city "have accepted death in exchange for the salvation of the living" (τὴν τελευτὴν ἠλλάξαντο ἀντι τῆς τῶν ζώντων σωτηρίας). Socrates' statement reveals sacrificial and soteriological language in three ways: (1) he suggests that humans voluntarily died for others. (2) He suggests that their deaths were vicarious. (3) He suggests that their deaths provided salvation for those for whom they died, because their deaths brought victory to the Greeks in battle.[46]

The Roman *devotio* was a form of self-sacrifice in the Greco-Roman world.[47] The *devotio* basically refers to a human's voluntary and sacrificial

43. Iphigeneia did not die in the end, but the goddess Artemis placed a deer on the altar before she was sacrificed.

44. For various meanings of διαλλάσσω in classical Greek literature, see Liddell and Scott, *A Greek-English Lexicon*, 1:401.

45. For more texts in *Alcestis* that support that the vicarious deaths of humans benefited others, see also 178, 280–82, 339, 383, 434, 524, 620, 644, 649, 682, 690, 698, 701, 710, 716, and 1002.

46. For a more detailed investigation of the pertinent Greco-Roman texts that speak of humans who voluntarily died to atone for the sins of others, see O'Connor-Visser, *Human Sacrifice in the Tragedies of Euripides*; Heard, Jr., "Maccabean Martyr Theology." Gnilka ("Martyriumsparänese und Sühnetod," 223–46) argues that those who died in battle for the city did not achieve spiritual salvation for the city. Their deaths simply achieved deliverance from physical distress. *Pace* Hengel, *The Atonement*, 11–28.

47. For a survey of the Roman *devotio*, see Versnel, "Two Types of Roman Devotio," 365–410.

death that he dies for the benefit of others or for the benefit of an important cause. The *devotio* was an act whereby members of the military dedicated themselves to the gods and to anonymous deities. The Romans believed that this death was the climactic act that provided victory for the soldiers in battle.[48]

Livy (59 BC–AD 17) explains the *devotio* in his history of Rome. The commander of the Roman army would dress himself in the *devotio* toga; he would place a covering on his head, stand on a spear, and place his hand against his chin while awaiting the priest to articulate a *devotio* formula/prayer. After this formula, the commander would pursue death in battle against the enemy (*History of Rome* 8.9.4–9). The *devotio* sacrifices voluntarily gave themselves on behalf of the army and the empire; their sacrifices served as an atonement to the gods, and they brought salvation to the people for whom they died (*History of Rome* 8.9.9–10; 10.28.18). The death of the first Publius Decius Mus illustrates the function of the *devotio* sacrifice.[49]

Circa 340 BC, Decius voluntarily offered himself to the gods on behalf of Rome in battle against the Latins. That he voluntarily offered himself as an atoning sacrifice and that his sacrifice was a saving event for Rome (i.e., provided victory in battle and appeasement of the wrath of the gods) are evident from Livy's description of the event.

> At first, both armies fought with equal strength and equal determination. After a time the Romans on the left, unable to withstand the insistency of the Latins, retired behind the principles. During the temporary confusion created by this movement, Decius exclaimed in a loud voice to Valerius: 'Valerius, we need the help of the gods! Let the Pontifex Maximus dictate to me the words in which I am to devote myself for the legions.' The Pontifex made him veil his head in his toga praetexta, and rest his hand, covered with his toga, against his chin, then standing upon a spear to say these words: 'Janus, Jupiter, Father Mars, Quirinus, Bellona, Lares, you Novensiles and Indigetes, deities to whom belongs the power over us and over our foes, and you, too, Divine Manes, I pray to you; I do reverence you; I crave your grace and favor that you will bless the Roman people, the Quirites, with power and victory, and visit the enemies of the Roman people, the Quirites, with fear and dread and death. In like manner, as I have uttered this prayer, so do

---

48. So van Henten and Avemarie, *Martyrdom and Noble Death*, 19–20.
49. Ibid.

I now on behalf of the commonwealth of the Quirites, on behalf
of the army, the legions, the auxiliaries of the enemy, together with
myself to the Divine Manes and to the Earth.' After this prayer, he
ordered the lectors to go to Manlius and at once announce to his
colleague that he had devoted himself on behalf of the army. He,
then, girded himself with the Gabinian cincture, and in full armor
leaped upon his horse and dashed into the middle of the enemy.
To those who watched him in both armies, he appeared something
awful and superhuman, as though sent from heaven to expiate and
appease all the anger of the gods and to avert destruction from his
people and bring it on their enemies . . . (italics mine).[50]

At least four statements in Livy's citation support that the humans who died
as part of the *devotio* ritual were atoning sacrifices and that their deaths
were a saving event. The onlookers who watched Decius offer himself in
death for the army declared that he resembled a superhuman whom the
gods sent (1) to expiate, (2) to appease their anger, (3) to avert destruction
from Rome, and (4) to turn anger toward the enemies of Rome (*History of
Rome* 8.9.13–14; cf. 2 Macc 4:20–7:38; 4 Macc 6:28–29; 17:21–22).[51]

THE OT CULT AND THE MARTYRS

In addition to Greco-Roman ideas, the OT cult was also an important
background behind the authors of 2 and 4 Maccabees, because they
(especially 4 Maccabees) apply OT cultic language to the deaths of the
martyrs. Thus, they seemingly take a Greco-Roman pagan idea (i.e., the
achievement of salvation for another through a human's self sacrifice) and
conflate this idea with OT cultic language and thereby make the original
Greco-Roman pagan idea a religious, Jewish one. Below I discuss Leviticus
16 and Isa 53 in order to provide examples that the OT cult (in addition to
Greco-Roman ideas) provided a background behind the authors of 2 and
4 Maccabees with regard to their presentation of the martyrs' deaths.

The Martyrs and the Cult

When devout Jews in Jerusalem refused to obey the pagan reforms of
Antiochus and his successors, the Greeks seized the holy city, desecrated
the temple, pilfered the holy vessels, left the temple void, and departed from

50. So Livy, *History of Rome* 8.9.

51. Contra Yerkes, *Sacrifice*, 59–64, esp. 61. He argues that the *devotio* sacrifice was
offered to the gods.

Jerusalem (1 Macc 1:1–63).[52] Their plundering devastated Jews throughout the city (1 Macc 1:25–28; cf. 2 Macc 5:11–16). Two years later, Antiochus deceived the Jews into thinking that he would extend peace to them. He sent a messenger to Judea to execute this deception. The Jews, unfortunately, believed that Antiochus' offer of peace was sincere. His deception enabled him to overtake Jerusalem a second time (1 Macc 1:29–32).

After conquering Jerusalem a second time, Antiochus eventually gained power over the temple and its sanctuary. Once he controlled the temple, he desecrated it again, destroyed the law, and demanded Judea to offer sacrifices to him and to engage in pagan worship. He promised to kill any Jew who obeyed God's law and who refused to yield allegiance to him. As a result, many Jews fled the city (1 Macc 1:33–50; cf. 4 Macc 4:20, 23).[53] Antiochus' abolishment of the law and his desecration of the temple meant that the Jews could no longer offer sacrifices of atonement as prescribed by God in the OT and that they could no longer celebrate Yom Kippur (1 Macc 1:41–64; 2 Macc 1:5; 5:4, 35). The temple was integral to the religious life of every pious Jew (cf. Ezra-Nehemiah; Haggai 1–2), for it was essential for communion with God, and it symbolized that he dwelt with his people.[54] Thus, the end of temple worship meant not only an end to sacrifices, but also the very end of the religious life of the Jews, central to which was the sacrificial system and the Yom Kippur ritual (cf. Ezra-Nehemiah, Haggai 1–2; 4Q508; 11QTemple 25:10–27:10).[55]

Prior to Antiochus seizing Jerusalem and desecrating the temple, Jason (who purchased the high priesthood from Antiochus for money) had already begun to Hellenize his fellow Jews (2 Maccabees 4). Consequently, the priests neglected their service at the altar and failed to offer the necessary sacrifices for Israel (2 Macc 4:11–13). This neglect precluded the Jews from offering the necessary sacrifices as atonement as God commanded in the Torah (cf. Leviticus 1–16). Not all Jews embraced

52. When Antiochus defiled the temple, it was useless in the eyes of pious Jews. There is evidence in Second Temple Qumranic Literature that many Jews would have rendered the temple an inadequate place for God to dwell and an inadequate place for them to offer sacrifices once it became defiled by immorality. For an analysis of this literature, see Klawans, *Purity, Sacrifice, and the Temple*, 145–74.

53. Cf. 1 Macc 1:36–2:13; 4 Macc 1:11; 17:22.

54. See Klawans, *Purity, Sacrifice, and the Temple*.

55. Similarly Pobee, *Persecution and Martyrdom*, 22. Sacrifice was important to the OT concept of atonement. As early as Genesis, the OT employs sacrificial language (Gen 3:21; 22:3, 5, 7–10; Exod 12:1–50; 24:7–8; 29:11–23, 36; 30:10; 32:30–35).

Antiochus' Hellenistic reforms, but instead many rebelled against him and faced his judgment, which resulted in death (1 Macc 2:1–38; 2 Macc 2:21–7:38; 4 Macc 5:4–17:22).[56]

Antiochus' seizure of the temple and his abolishment of sacrifices ended the yearly practice of the Yom Kippur ritual (2 Macc 4:1–14; cf. 1 Macc 1:41–64). As Yahweh prescribed in Leviticus 16,[57] the priests would atone for all of their personal transgressions, the transgressions of the people, and the impurities of the holy place because of the impurities of the people (Lev 16:3–28; cf.1 Maccabees 1).[58] Yahweh commands Aaron to offer specific animals as atonement for sin, so that it would be purified and cleansed (Lev 16:3–34; cf. 11QTemple 25:10–27:10).[59] After Yahweh tells Moses how Aaron should perform the Day of Atonement, he asserts that this day should be celebrated every year for the cleansing of sin (Lev 16:29–30). This cleansing through the offering of blood symbolized God's forgiveness (Lev 16:29–30; 1 QS 3:4).[60]

Some scholars question whether bloody sacrifice actually satisfied God's wrath.[61] Nevertheless, the evidence in Leviticus 16 answers the

56. The refusal of some Jews to eat unclean foods and their willingness to continue circumcising their children was the impetus behind Antiochus' persecution (e.g., 2 Maccabees 2–8).

57. Various source critical complexities exist in Leviticus 16 (e.g., authorship, etc.). For source critical discussion, see Elliger, *Leviticus,* 202–10; Noth, *Leviticus,* 118; Scullion, "A Tradition-Historical Study," 28–29.

58. Ben Ezra (*Yom Kippur,* 115–18) argues that Leviticus 16 and the Yom Kippur ritual were instructive for the vicarious deaths of the martyrs in 4 Maccabees.

59. See Hartley, *Leviticus,* 241. House (*Old Testament Theology,* 137) asserts that atonement in Leviticus 16 provided expiation for all sin except blasphemy against God.

60. These sacrifices were not efficacious in and of themselves. The author of Hebrews in his post-cross and post-resurrection interpretation of the OT cult emphatically states that OT sacrifices neither provided forgiveness of nor atonement for sin (Heb 10:1–11). God did not receive Israel's sacrificial offerings unless they offered them with a pure heart (cf. Psalm 51). Some critical scholars have, therefore, argued that the sacrificial system was not a means by which God would allow Israel to remain in a covenantal relationship with him and that certain OT texts that speak of God rejecting Israel's sacrifices contradict statements in the Pentateuch (e.g., Amos 5:21–22; Hos 6:6; Isa 1:10–17; Mic 6:6–8; Jer 7:21–23). Cf. Rowley, "The Unity of the Old Testament," 5–7; Oesterly, *Psalms,* 1:274. Although it is true that some OT texts speak rather negatively about the sacrificial system, the fundamental reason God rejects Israel's sacrifices in those texts was because of the nation's unrepentant heart (1 Sam 15:22–23; Psalm 51; Isa 1:10–17). Waltke ("Atonement in Psalm 51," 51–60) convincingly argues this point from Psalm 51. For a connection between Israel's sacrifices and repentance, see Milgrom, *Cult and Conscience.*

61. For example, Dodd, *Bible and the Greeks,* 82–95.

question in the affirmative. Leviticus 16 begins by stating how one should offer sacrifices before Yahweh. Yahweh commands Moses to warn Aaron that he should not enter the holy place haphazardly, lest he should die, for Yahweh himself would appear in the holy place above the mercy seat (Lev 16:1–4). The author states that Yahweh commands Moses to speak to Aaron "after the death of the two sons of Aaron, when they brought strange fire in the presence of the Lord, and they died" (Lev 16:1–2). The sons of Aaron died, because they offered an unauthorized sacrifice before Yahweh (Lev 10:2). Immediately after Aaron's sons offered this sacrifice, Yahweh consumed them with fire. The fire represents Yahweh's judgment and wrath that he would dispense to all who disobeyed his sacrificial stipulations (Lev 16). Yahweh's response to the sons of Aaron contrasts with his response to Aaron and Moses after they offered their sacrifices to Yahweh exactly as he had prescribed (Lev 9:1–24; cf. Lev 1:1–13). Instead of revealing his wrath by consuming Moses and Aaron with fire, Yahweh revealed his glory and consumed their sacrifices (Lev 9:23–24). Leviticus 16:1, therefore, suggests that Yahweh would display his wrath and judgment against disobedience. Aaron's obedience to Yahweh spared him and the nation from being the objects of his wrath (cf. 4QpPs 2:9–11).[62]

The authors of 2 and 4 Maccabees conflate the Greco-Roman idea that a human's self-sacrifice could save those for whom he died and the Jewish idea of cultic atonement, and they applied both concepts to the Jewish martyrs. The martyrs were humans (not animals). The authors of 2 and 4 Maccabees suggest that these humans died for the sins of others in order to save them from God's judgment (2 Macc 7:32–38; 4 Macc 6:28–29). The authors ascribe both soteriological and cultic language to the martyrs' deaths. For example, the authors assert that the martyrs died for Israel's sin in order to reconcile the nation to God (2 Macc 5:1–8:5),

---

62. Contra Gray, *Sacrifices in the Old Testament*, 95. Gray asserts that Israel often offered sacrifices with feelings of joy rather than fear or contrition. The truthfulness of Gray's claim, though, does not necessarily extinguish the reality that Israel also offered sacrifices in accordance with Yahweh's prescriptions to appease his wrath. Dodd (*The Bible and the Greeks*, 82–95) and Scullion ("A Tradition-Historical Study," 147–52) offer lexical arguments against propitiation in the OT cult. They both argue that God's wrath is not personal. The latter premise seems antithetical to many OT texts. For example, see Exod 4:24–26; 32:1–34:9; Deut 4:25–31; 9:1–10:22; 30:1–10; Josh 7:1–26; Judg 2:10–23; 3:7–15; 4:6–8, 10–12; 1 Sam 7:2–14; 12:8–11; 2 Sam 12:7–23; 21:1–9; 24:1–25; 1 Kgs 8:22–53; 21:17–29; 2 Kgs 13:1–7; 22:14–20; 1 Chr 21–22; 2 Chr 6:12–42; 7:12–16; 12:1–12; 15:1–15; 29:1–32:33; 34:20–28. See also Watson, "Wrath and Reconciliation."

to purify the land (4 Macc 6:28–29), and that their deaths accomplished salvation for the nation (4 Macc 17:21–22).

ISAIAH 53 AND THE MARTYRS

In addition to Greco-Roman ideas and the OT cult, Isaiah 53 could have played a role in 2 and 4 Maccabees' presentation of the martyrs' deaths.[63] Similar to the pious Jews who remained steadfast to the law in the face of persecution and death (2 Macc 6:18–7:41; 4 Macc 6:28–29), the Servant of Isaiah 53 was righteous/pious (Isa 53:7, 9, 11). He[64] suffered at the hands of his enemies (Isa 53:3, 7–8); he suffered divine judgment (Isa 53:4, 6, 10), and he suffered because of sin (Isa 53:3–5, 8, 10–12).[65]

The Righteous Servant and Suffering

Similar to the Jewish martyrs in 2 and 4 Maccabees, the Servant's suffering was a gratuitous act. He was innocent. There was neither deceit in his mouth nor violence in his deeds (Isa 53:7, 9), but he was righteous (Isa 53:11; cf. 2 Macc 3:1; 4 Macc 5:18, 31). Isaiah 52:13–15 begins the Fourth Servant Song by speaking of the Servant's exaltation. According to the author, the Servant will prosper (Isa 52:13). He will be highly exalted (Isa 52:13). Surprisingly, though, the author digresses in his comments about the Servant by speaking of his defective appearance (Isa 52:15). Isaiah 53:3 states that the Servant was despised and rejected with respect to men. The author subsequently explicates this statement by stating that the Servant was acquainted with sorrows and grief (Isa 53:3). Finally, the author states that the Servant was oppressed and afflicted (Isa 53:7–8). In light of Isaiah 53:3, this affliction in part came from the Servant's enemies (cf. 1 Maccabees 1; 2 Macc 5:1–7:41; 4 Maccabees 5–6).

---

63. Isaiah 53 is one of the most contested chapters in the Hebrew Bible. I offer a more detailed analysis of Isaiah 53 in chapter 3 of this monograph. The goal in this chapter is to demonstrate the similarities between the Servant's death in Isaiah 53 and the deaths of the martyrs in 2 and 4 Maccabees.

64. By calling the Servant a he in the above sentence, I do not mean to suggest at this point that the Servant was an individual male figure.

65. Although Hengel's recent essay ("The Effective History of Isaiah 53," 75–146) does not investigate 2 and 4 Maccabees, he argues that Isaiah 53 influenced some authors of pre-Christian texts.

Divine Judgment against Sin

Similar to the authors' statements in 2 and 4 Maccabees about the martyrs' deaths (2 Macc 6:16–17; 7:35; 12:40–42; 4 Macc 6:28–29; 17:21–22; cf. Ep. Jer. 2; Song of the Three Young Men 1–8, 13; As. *Mos.* 9.1–10.10), Isaiah 53 asserts that the Servant's suffering was God's act of judgment against sin. After stating that men despised and rejected the Servant, the author states that Yahweh afflicted him (Isa 53:4) and that he was pleased to crush and inflict him with grief (Isa 53:10). Yahweh afflicted the Servant with grief, because he judged the nation's iniquity in the Servant (Isa 53:4, 6, 10; cf. 2 Macc 7:33; 4 Macc 6:28–29).

Death for Sin

Isaiah 53 states that the reason for which the Servant suffered was sin. The author expresses that the Servant bore the suffering and sorrows of others (Isa 53:4). He also states that the Servant was pierced and crushed because of the transgressions of others and that Yahweh made the Servant to be an אשם ("guilt-offering") for others (Isa 53:10; cf. Lev 5:14–6:7; 7:1–6). Isaiah 53:4–5 and 53:8–12 jointly support that the grief and sorrows carried by the Servant were the result of sin. The author expresses Yahweh's judgment of the Servant because of sin when he asserts that Yahweh judged and cut off the Servant from the land of the living on account of the sins of others (Isa 53:5, 8–10; cf. 2 Macc 7:32). Because the Servant bore the sin of others, those for whom he suffered received Yahweh's mercy (Isa 53:11–12).[66] Second and 4 Maccabees likewise assert that the martyrs died as servants because of the nation's sin (2 Macc 7:32–33). Thus, in addition to Greco-Roman ideas and the OT cult, Isaiah's Servant could have been part of the background behind Martyr Theology's presentation of the martyrs' deaths as atoning sacrifices and as a saving event for Israel.[67]

66. I credit Pobee (*Martyrdom and Persecution*, 37) for showing me the connection between Martyr Theology and Isaiah 53. Some scholars (e.g., Childs, *Isaiah*, 418; Orlinsky, "The So-Called Servant of the Lord," 56) argue that Isaiah 53 does not speak of atonement since the text is not cultic. Childs (*Isaiah*, 410), though, rightly asserts that Isaiah 53 presents the Servant as the means by which God would forgive Israel's sin. Oswalt (*Isaiah*, 386) is more specific and argues that Isaiah 53 is cultic. Regardless of an explicitly cultic context, my above discussion of Isaiah 53 at least suggests that the author of the Fourth Servant Song applies cultic language (e.g., guilt-offering) to the Servant's suffering and death for others.

67. Van Henten (*Maccabean Martyrs*, 185) asserts that it is possible that the author of 2 Maccabees conflated Greco-Roman ideas about sacrificial death with biblical traditions

MARTYRDOM AS AN ATONING SACRIFICE
AND A SAVING EVENT

The Martyrdom of Eleazar

The authors of 2 and 4 Maccabees present the deaths of the Jewish martyrs as atoning sacrifices and as a saving event for Israel with similar language that appears in the antecedent Greco-Roman and OT cultic traditions. These similarities between 2 and 4 Maccabees and the traditions that preceded these books were the inevitable result of Hellenism.[68] Contrary, however, to the pertinent Greco-Roman texts, the martyrs did not die to appease multiple gods or anonymous deities as in the plays of Euripides, the dialogues of Plato, or the Roman *devotio*. In addition, contrary to the OT cult, the martyrs did not offer animals as atoning sacrifices to deal with the nation's sin as in the Yom Kippur ritual (Leviticus 16). Instead, similar to Isaiah 53, the martyrs died for Israel to atone for their sin and to save the nation from God's wrath.

The martyrdom of Eleazar is the chief example that supports that the martyrs died as atoning sacrifices and that their deaths were a saving event for the nation.[69] Eleazar was a religious man from a religious family (2 Macc 6:18; 4 Macc 5:4, 35). He was an expert in the Torah (4 Macc 5:4). Antiochus tried to compel him to eat unlawful foods (2 Macc 6:18–22; 4 Macc 5:6). Instead of eating and preserving his life (2 Macc 6:21–22; 4 Macc 5:5–13), Eleazar chose death since he believed to do otherwise would have dishonored God (2 Macc 6:19–31; 4 Macc 5:16–6:30). As a result of his disobedience, Antiochus tortured and subsequently executed him (2 Macc 6:28–31; 4 Macc 6:1–30).

Shortly before his tortures culminated in death (4 Macc 6:1–27, 30), Eleazar asked God to provide salvation for Israel through his death (4 Macc 6:28–29). This is evident in that he asked God to use his death to

---

of Moses, Phinehas, and other mediators who appeased God's wrath. Finlan (*Atonement Metaphors*, 198–99) argues that this notion harmonizes with other biblical texts where a mediator acts on behalf of another to avert God's wrath (Ps 106:23; cf. Num 25:11, 13).

68. For discussion of Hellenism, the Maccabeans, and Second Temple Judaism, see Moore, *Judaism*; Farmer, *Maccabees, Zealots, and Josephus*; Tcherikover, *Hellenistic*; Bickerman, *The God of the Maccabees*; Segal, *Other Judaisms*; Bowersock, *Hellenism in Late Antiquity*; Hengel, *Judaism and Hellenism*; idem, *The Zealots*; Sacchi, *History*; Collins, *Jewish Cult and Hellenistic*; Feldman, *Judaism and Hellenism Reconsidered*.

69. Similarly DeSilva, *4 Maccabees* (2006), 147.

be the means through which he would impart (1) mercy (ἵλεως γενοῦ; 4 Macc 6:28), (2) satisfaction (ἀρκεσθεὶς; 4 Macc 6:28), and (3) purification (καθάρσιον; 4 Macc 6:29) to the nation. That Eleazar requested that his death would achieve the nation's salvation is further evident because he expressed that his death was God's judgment against the nation (4 Macc 6:28) and because he requested that God would use his death as a ransom for the nation (4 Macc 6:29).[70]

God's Mercy for and Judgment against Israel

In the first part of his prayer in 4 Macc 6:28, Eleazar urged God to be merciful to Israel through his death: "Be merciful to your nation." Eleazar especially prayed that God would deliver the nation from his wrath through his death, because 1, 2, and 4 Maccabees show that God was judging Israel through Antiochus on account of the fact that many Jews abandoned the Torah as a way of life (1 Maccabees 1; 2 Macc 4:1–6:31; 4 Macc 5:4–6:40). In addition, other uses of the adjective merciful (ἵλεως), the author's preferred word for mercy in 4 Macc 6:28, in 4 Maccabees affirm that when Eleazar asked God to be merciful to the nation through his death, he was essentially asking God to save the nation from his wrath through his sacrificial death for the nation.

For example, before Antiochus tortured the seven sons, he urged them to provide mercy for themselves by eating unclean meat (4 Macc 8:14). If they would have heeded to Antiochus' commands, they would have ensured deliverance from his judgment. While one of the seven sons endured many tortures, he encouraged his brothers to follow his example of godliness, because God would be merciful to the nation through his death (4 Macc 9:24). After the seventh son refused to obey Antiochus (4 Macc 12:4–16), he hurled himself into the fire while praying that God would be merciful to the nation through his death (4 Macc 12:17).

Once more, the canonical LXX's uses of ἵλεως further supports that Eleazar's request for mercy (ἵλεως) in 4 Macc 6:28 was a request that God would be merciful to the nation by delivering Israel from his wrath through the martyrs' deaths, and these uses could provide additional evidence that Eleazar's death was an atoning sacrifice and a saving event for Israel. In Exod 32:12, Moses asked God to be merciful (ἵλεως

---

70. Pobee (*Persecution and Martyrdom*, 36–38) states that the deaths of the martyrs were atoning sacrifices both for themselves and for others.

γενοῦ) to Israel when he urges him not to judge the nation for idolatry (cf. Exod 32:33; Numbers 14). In Deut 21:8, Moses exhorts the nation to pray for God's mercy (ἵλεως γενοῦ) when an unknown member of the community wrongly sheds innocent blood (cf. Deut 21:1–8). LXX Deut 21:8 is especially pertinent for my argument, because the translators rendered ἵλεως from the Hebrew root כפר (cf. MT Deut 21:8). The latter root often refers to atonement in the OT. Since the context of Deut 21:8 is arguably cultic, the LXX's translation supports that a close connection existed between God's mercy, sacrificial atonement, and forgiveness in STJ. This connection is also evident from the LXX's ἐξιλασθήσεται ("it will be cleansed") in LXX Deut 21:8, which is translated from MT Deut 21:8 from the root כפר. The LXX's ἐξιλάσκομαι occurs in several places in the LXX to refer to the forgiveness that occurs as a result of sacrificial atonement (cf. Exod 30:10; Lev 16:20; Num 5:8; 25:13; 1 Kgs 3:14; Ps 105:30). Finally, in 2 Chr 6:25, Solomon requests that God would look from heaven and be merciful (ἵλεως) to Israel and forgive the nation of its sin (cf. 2 Chr 6:27, 39; 7:14).[71]

Additional support regarding the sacrificial and soteriological nature of Eleazar's request is evident when he prayed that God would be satisfied with the martyrs' deaths for the nation (ἀρκεσθεὶς · τῇ ἡμετέρᾳ ὑπὲρ αὐτῶν δίκῃ). Eleazar's words "on behalf of them" (ὑπὲρ αὐτῶν) in 4 Macc 6:28 suggests that he died for Israel as a provision for God's mercy because of the nation's sin and that he hoped that his death would save the nation from God's wrath. That is, since Eleazar asked God to be satisfied with the martyrs' judgment for the nation in 4 Macc 6:28 and since he asked God to make his blood to be a ransom for the nation so that the nation would be purified from its sin in 4 Macc 6:29, the preposition ὑπὲρ ("for/on behalf of") suggests that Eleazar offered himself as a vicarious, atoning sacrifice for Israel (cf. 1 Macc 2:50).

Moreover, even the grammatical structure of 4 Macc 6:28 affirms these observations. For example, in light of τῷ ἔθνει ("the nation") in the first part of Eleazar's prayer in 4 Macc 6:28 (ἵλεως γενοῦ τῷ ἔθνει σου), αὐτῶν ("their") should be taken as a reference to Israel, and the phrase τῇ ἡμετέρᾳ ("our") should be understood as a reference to the martyrs. The phrase ὑπὲρ αὐτῶν ("for them") is embedded between τῇ ἡμετέρᾳ

<hr/>

71. For other connections in the LXX between God's mercy and forgiveness of sins, see Amos 7:2; Jer 5:1, 7; 27:20; 38:34; 43:3.

δίκη ("our judgment") in a context where the author states that a human died in the place of another to satisfy God's judgment against the one for whom the human died. Thus, the phrase τῇ ἡμετέρᾳ ὑπερ αὐτῶν δίκη makes the prepositional phrase descriptive of the judgment ("with respect to our on behalf of them judgment)."[72]

Regarding Eleazar's death as the satisfaction of God's wrath, the participle (ἀρκεσθεὶς: "having been satisfied") suggests that Eleazar's martyrdom was an atoning sacrifice and a saving event for Israel, because the participle demonstrates that Eleazar wanted God to use his death to remove his wrath away from the nation. That Eleazar offered this prayer to God while the entire nation faced his judgment supports this assertion (4 Macc 6:28; 17:22; cf. 1 Macc 6:60). In addition, the propitiatory nature of Eleazar's death is bolstered by the occurrence of δίκη ("judgment") in 4 Macc 6:28, for the latter term consistently refers to God's judgment throughout both 2 and 4 Maccabees (2 Macc 8:11, 13; 4 Macc 4:13, 21; 8:14, 22; 9:9, 15, 32; 11:3; 12:12; 18:22).

Israel's Purification

The third part of Eleazar's prayer in 4 Macc 6:28 suggests that his death was an atoning sacrifice and a saving event for Israel, for Eleazar urged God to make his blood to be Israel's purification (καθάρσιον αὐτῶν ποί ησον τὸ ἐμὸν αἷμα).[73] The presence of blood in this text reveals a connection with the OT cult (Lev 16:16, 30; 17:11). In the cult, the shedding of the animals' blood was a crucial ingredient for Israel's atonement and forgiveness (Lev 16:30), and the blood that was spilt represents the life that was taken from the animal on behalf of the nation (Lev 17:11). With this request in 4 Macc 6:28, then, Eleazar urged God to make his death an atoning sacrifice and a saving event for Israel (cf. Lev 16:16, 30; 17:11), because he asked God to use his "blood" to be the means by which he would cleanse the nation from its sin (2 Macc 5:17–18; 6:15; 7:32; 12:42; 4 Macc 5:19; 17:21; cf. Lev 16:16, 30).[74]

---

72. For more uses of the ὑπέρ-formula in atonement texts, see the LXX of Exod 21:20; Lev 26:25; Deut 32:41, 43; Mic 7:9; Wis 1:8; 14:31; 18:11; cf. 1 Macc 5:32; 2 Macc 1:26; 3:32; Rom 5:6–11; 8:32; 1 Cor 1:13; 11:24; 15:3; 2 Cor 5:14–15, 21; Gal 1:4; 2:20–21; 3:13; 1 Thess 5:10.

73. I take αἷμα as a reference to death (cf. 4 Macc 7:8; 17:22; Rom 3:25; 5:9; 1 Cor 10:16; 11:27; Eph 2:13). Eleazar's request resembles LXX Lev 16:15.

74. Contra Seeley, *The Noble Death*, 97–98. He argues that Eleazar's death was not sac-

Besides 4 Macc 6:29, καθάρσιον ("purification") occurs nowhere else in the LXX. [75] However, καθαρισμὸς ("purification"), a cognate of the former term, occurs in the LXX and in the NT to refer both to the purification of Israel and to Christians. In the respective Jewish-Christian texts, purification comes through sacrificial atonement (Exod 29:36; 30:10; cf. 2 Pet 1:9), ritual cleansing (Lev 14:32; 15:13; cf. Mark 1:44; Luke 2:22; 5:14; John 2:6; 3:25), God's forgiveness (Num 14:18), the cleansing of holy utensils (1 Chr 23:28), the purification of the temple (2 Macc 1:18; 2:16, 19; 10:5), or through godliness (4 Macc 7:6). [76] Since Eleazar was a priest, an expert in the Torah, and from a priestly family, he understood the OT background behind purification (2 Macc 6:18; 4 Macc 5:4, 35; Lev 1–27). In addition, since Antiochus abolished the sacrificial system and killed anyone who yielded allegiance to the Torah (1 Macc 1:41–64; 2 Macc 5:4, 35), Eleazar thought that his death and the deaths of the other martyrs replaced the sacrificial system as the means of purification for Israel's sin. If this is a correct reading of Eleazar's prayer, this would mean

---

rificial, but only an example for the nation to follow. The author of 4 Maccabees attaches sacrificial language to his death to note his endurance and the exemplary nature of his death. Purification came to the nation because the martyrs' endurance of suffering forced Antiochus to leave the land (cf. 4 Macc 17:11–24). In response to Seeley, Eleazar's death has striking similarities with many OT texts in which the authors employed sacrificial language in reference to actual cleansing, not exemplary suffering. See Exod 30:10, 15–16; 32:30; Lev 1:4; 4:20, 26, 31, 35; 5:6, 10, 13, 16, 16, 26; 6:23; 7:7; 8:15, 36; 9:7; 10:17; 12:7, 8; 14:18, 19, 20–21, 29, 31, 53; 15:15, 30; 16:6, 10–11, 16, 20, 24, 27, 30, 32–34; 17:11; 19:22; Num 5:8; 6:11; 8:12, 19, 21; 15:25, 28; 17:12; 28:22, 30, 30; 29:5, 11; 1 Sam 3:14 (LXX 1 Kgs 3:14); 1 Kgs 6:3; 1 Chr 6:34; 2 Chr 29:24.

75. Besides καθάρσιον in 4 Macc 6:29, the only other place where purification is connected to the purification of sins via the death of a human is Heb 1:3. There the author states that Jesus "made purification for sins" (cf. Heb 8:1–10:39; Rom 3:25; 5:9; Eph 1:7; Col 1:20).

76. Examples occur in the DSS that state that God provides purification through the obedience of the godly within the community with language that echoes the OT cult (cf. 1QS 1:1–3:10). In fact, salvation and atonement came to those in the community who perfectly obeyed God's precepts according to 1QS. Garnet (*Salvation*, 80–81) argues, however, that 1QS does not speak of individuals as vicariously dying for others. Hence, the community did not regard itself in a "Suffering Servant role." Instead, the members of the community bore the punishment of their own transgressions in fulfillment of Leviticus 26. Yet, Garnet (*Salvation and Atonement*, 81) acknowledges that those within the community who bore their own transgressions benefited others in the community in that their deaths had a "saving effect upon the rest of Israel by constituting a foundation upon which future penitents could be built. These penitents, of course, would need to accept their own punishment as an essential ingredient in their repentance."

that Eleazar thought that the martyrs' deaths replaced the Yom Kippur ritual, because (1) Antiochus controlled the temple (1 Maccabees 1). (2) The temple was no longer available for cultic worship in compliance with the Torah because of Antiochus' Hellenistic policies (1 Maccabees 1). (3) Antiochus restricted the Jews from offering sacrifices to their God (1 Maccabees 1). (4) Pious Jews would have considered the temple to be defiled and unfit for cultic worship because of Antiochus' desecration of it (1 Macc 4:36–58; cf. Tob 1:4; 4Q395; Jub 22:16–18; Ep. Arist. 152–53; Pss Sol 2:2; Acts 21:27–30). (5) Eleazar asked God to use his "blood" to be the means by which he would bring purification to the nation (4 Macc 6:28–29).[77] Therefore, Eleazar could have likely thought that Yom Kippur was insufficient to provide atonement for Israel's sin and to achieve the nation's purification (1 Macc 1:41–61).

A Ransom for Israel

In the final part of his prayer, Eleazar asked God to receive his death as a ransom for the nation (4 Macc 6:29): "and receive my soul to be their ransom" (καὶ ἀντίψυχον αὐτῶν λαβὲ τὴν ἐμὴν ψυχήν). The καὶ in 4 Macc 6:29b connects the last portion of Eleazar's prayer with the preceding clause in 4 Macc 6:29a ("make my blood their purification," καθάρσιον αὐτῶν ποίησον τὸ ἐμὸν αἷμα), for the request in 4 Macc 6:29b develops the petition in 4 Macc 6:29a. The term ἀντίψυχον[78] ("ransom") in 4 Macc 6:29b also occurs in 4 Macc 17:21. In the latter text, the term expresses that the martyrs' deaths were a ransom for Israel, because the author of 4 Macc 17:21 connects ἀντίψυχον with the martyrs' deaths and with Israel's purification and salvation. The author conveys by his use of ἀντίψυχον in both 4 Macc 6:29 and 17:21 that the blood of the martyrs was the required price paid to achieve Israel's purification and salvation. This interpretation is supported by Eleazar's earlier request that God would purify Israel and satisfy his judgment against the nation by means of his death for the nation (4 Macc 6:29; cf. Exod 33:12–34:9; Lev 9:1–10:2; 16:1–34) and by the author's statements in 4 Macc 17:21–22

---

77. The OT speaks of the Lord as purifying the land. Cf. Williams, *Jesus's Death*, 83–88. Williams argues that purification of the land in the OT does not speak of the cleansing of sin, but of the slaughtering of Israel's enemies (cf. Deut 32:36).

78. In post-NT literature, ἀντίψυχον refers to Christian martyrs. For example, see Ign. *Ant. Eph.* 21:1; *Smyrn.* 10:2; *Poly.* 2:3; 6:1. Patristic citations come from Lohse, *Märtyrer*, 70 n. 6.

that the martyrs' deaths were the means by which Israel was purified, God's wrath was removed, and salvation came to the nation. Therefore, when Eleazar asked God to receive his death as an ἀντίψυχον for Israel in 4 Macc 6:29b, Eleazar prayed that God would accept his death and the deaths of the other martyrs as sufficient payment for the nation's sin (cf. Exod 33:12–34:9; Lev 9:1–10:2; 16:1–34; 2 Macc 5:20–7:38; 4 Macc 6:28–29; 7:8; 17:10; 17:21–22; 18:4; cf. As. *Mos.* 9:6–7; 10:2–10).[79]

THE MARTYRDOM OF THE MOTHER
AND HER SEVEN SONS

Reconciliation

Just as the author of 4 Maccabees presents Eleazar's death as an atoning sacrifice and a saving event for Israel, the author of 2 Maccabees presents the martyrdoms of the mother and her seven sons as atoning sacrifices and a saving event for Israel (2 Macc 7:32–38).[80] After killing Eleazar in 2 Maccabees 6, Antiochus tried to compel a mother and her seven sons to eat unlawful foods (2 Macc 7:1). Faced with the same tortures and punishment as Eleazar if they disobeyed, each of the seven sons and their mother refused to obey Antiochus. As a result, each suffered a torturous death (2 Macc 7:2–41). When encouraged by his mother to trust God in death (2 Macc 7:28–29), the seventh son stated that Antiochus would not escape God's judgment, "for we suffer because of our own sins" (2 Macc 7:32; cf. 2 Macc 5:17).[81] The seventh son also uttered that although God

79. Similarly DeSilva 4 *Maccabees* (2006), 148–49. Kraus (*Der Tod Jesu*, 38–39) argues that 4 Maccabees does not suggest that the martyrs were atoning sacrifices for the nation. Likewise, Williams (*Jesus's Death*, 176–79) rejects that the martyrs' deaths were vicarious, expiatory deaths in 4 Maccabees. He argues instead that their deaths should be understood as effective for the nation, because the author of 4 Maccabees does not speak of the removal of the nation's sin as forgiveness of personal wrongs, but as the reversal of a situation. The land was purified in that Antiochus left it. Only in this sense one can speak of the expiatory deaths of the martyrs.

80. Collins (*Daniel, First Maccabees, Second Maccabees*, 310–11) asserts that the martyrdoms of the mother and her seven sons were legendary fables used to elaborate a Martyr Theology. The legendary character of Jewish martyrdom is supported by the appearance of stories about seven sons in other STJT (e.g., Assumption of Moses, Joseph *Ant.* 14.15.5). Cf. Schiffman, "2 Maccabees," 906.

81. The above is a confession that sin is the basis of the martyrs' suffering. Similarly Kraus, *Der Tod Jesu*, 35. However, Kraus argues against a cultic background behind 2

was angry with the nation, "he will be reconciled [καταλλαγήσεται] again to his servants" (2 Macc 7:33; cf. 2 Macc 1:5; 7:37–38; 8:29).

Before the seventh son's statements, the author placed a panegyric speech in the mouth of Eleazar in 2 Maccabees 6 and in the mouths of the mother and her seven sons in 2 Maccabees 7. Prior to these speeches, the author lucidly asserts that the sin for which the Jews suffered torturous death was the nation's rebellion against the Torah (2 Macc 5:20–7:32; cf. 1 Macc 1:11–15). The respective martyr texts in 2 and 4 Maccabees do not overtly state that the martyrs themselves actually violated the Torah along with the rest of the nation. Nevertheless, the "we" in "we suffer because of our sins" (2 Macc 7:32) includes the martyrs along with apostate Israel, for the martyrs were part of the nation for which they suffered (cf. 2 Macc 7:16, 30, 30–32, 38). That is, the martyrs were pious Jews who suffered along with the apostate Jews who rebelled against the Torah (cf. 2 Macc 6:12–17). When the seventh son stated that God would be reconciled to his servants (2 Macc 7:33), this expression refers to Israel as a nation but includes the martyrs, because when a few in the nation sinned against God and suffered the consequences of their sin, it was as though the entire nation (including the martyrs) sinned and suffered the consequences (cf. Num 25:11; Isa 1:1–26). The martyrs were not sinless, but they were innocent of individual religious apostasy. Therefore, they offered themselves to God as atoning sacrifices for Israel to pay for the nation's sin, which also became a payment for their sin by virtue of their corporate solidarity with the nation (cf. 2 Macc 7:32).[82]

The nation's rebellion against God's law resulted in a dishonoring of the temple (2 Macc 5:27–6:6). When Antiochus and Menelaus (an apos-

Macc 7:32–38.

82. Contra Williams, *Jesus's Death*, 79 n. 29; Seeley, *The Noble Death*, 87. In response to Wengst (*Christologische Formeln*, 69), Seeley argues against understanding the martyrs' suffering as vicarious for the nation, for the martyrs stated that "we suffer for our own sins." Seeley contends that "it is true that the author is probably not suggesting the martyrs themselves have sinned. Nonetheless, there is no hint of a special representative function being played by the martyrs here. Rather, 7:32 seems to point to a form of group solidarity. It is portraying not the martyrs' special status as representatives of the people, but the extent to which they are at one with the people." In comparison to Seeley, see de Jonge, 181–82; Kellermann, "Zum traditionsgeschichtlichen," 63–83, esp. 69. Van Henten (*Maccabean Martyrs*, 137) rightly states that the martyrs were in solidarity with the people and they died for the nation's sin. O'Hagan ("The Martyr in the Fourth Book of the Maccabees," 94–120, esp. 108) argues that the martyrs were sinful. Baumeister (*Die Anfange*, 41–42) argues to the contrary.

tate Jewish high priest) entered the temple in Jerusalem, they profaned it (2 Macc 5:15–16). Consequently, Antiochus was joyful on account of his seizing of the temple, for he did not understand that God was using him to judge Israel on account of the nation's sin (2 Macc 5:17–18; cf. 7:32). To eradicate God's judgment against the nation, the seven sons voluntarily offered themselves as atoning sacrifices for the nation.[83]

The seventh son was confident that God would be reconciled again to the nation through the martyrs' deaths. He asserted that God "will be reconciled again to his servants" (2 Macc 7:33). God fulfilled the seventh son's prophecy by becoming reconciled to the nation through the martyrs' deaths. Second Maccabees 8:1–5 supports the latter point. (1) The text states that God was reconciled to the nation (2 Macc 8:1–5). (2) The author of 2 Maccabees connects the nation's reconciliation with the martyrs' suffering and death (2 Macc 7:32–33). (3) The author connects the nation's reconciliation with sin and God's wrath (2 Macc 7:32–38). (4) Nothing in context of the seventh son's statement regarding reconciliation in 2 Macc 7:33 suggests that God would become reconciled to the nation in any way except through the martyrs' deaths.[84] (5) The context neither denies that God would become reconciled to the nation.[85] (6) Second Maccabees 5:20 and 8:5 affirm that the seventh son's prophecy was fulfilled because God indeed became reconciled to Israel once again (2 Macc 5:20–8:5; cf. 2 Macc 1:5; 4 Macc 1:11; 18:4).[86]

83. Similarly Lohse, *Märtyrer und Gottesknecht*, 67–69; Gnilka, "Martyriumsparänese," 223–46; J. Downing, "Jesus and Martyrdom," *JTS* 14 (1963): 279–93, esp. 288–89; van Henten, *Maccabean Martyrs*, 140–44. Williams (*Jesus's Death*, 82–88) has perhaps been the most influential adversary of a vicarious reading of this text. Likewise, Goldstein (*2 Maccabees*, 316) asserts that there is nothing in 2 Macc 7:32–38 about vicarious atonement. Instead, the martyrs suffered along with Israel, and they hoped that their deaths would begin the turning point for the nation. Seeley (*The Noble Death*, 87–91, 145) acknowledges that the martyrs' deaths were vicarious in a mimetic sense. In this respect, he follows Williams. Recently in 2005, Versnel ("Making Sense of Jesus's Death," 258–59; originally appeared as "Quid Athenis et Hierosolymis?" 162–96) recapitulates Williams' view.

84. Similarly van Henten, "Tradition-Historical Background", 117. He states that "the only possible means by which this reconciliation could have come about in the context of 2 Maccabees is the death of the martyrs, although the text does not state explicitly in 7:33." Cf. also van Henten, "Tradition-Historical Background," 117–21.

85. Ibid.

86. Ibid. Contra Williams, *Jesus's Death*, 88–89. Williams thinks that nothing in Judas' prayer in 2 Macc 8:1–4 suggests that the martyrs were the means by which peace came to Israel, because there is no "cause and effect between the death of the martyrs and the deliverance and purification of Israel." God accomplished purification through the

Regarding the preceding point, the seventh son said to Antiochus that the Lord was only temporarily angry with the nation and that the nation would escape his wrath since he would be reconciled again to it (2 Macc 7:33). On the other hand, Antiochus would momentarily escape suffering in this life, but he would not be saved from God's wrath (2 Macc 7:34–36). After the seventh son spoke of God's future judgment of Antiochus, he stated that he, just as his brothers, offered his life to God with the prayer that he would be merciful to the nation through their deaths (2 Macc 7:37). Subsequent to the author's presentations of the martyrdoms of Eleazar, the mother, and her seven sons (2 Macc 6:18–7:42), the author immediately discusses the response of pious Jews to the martyrs' deaths.

In 2 Maccabees 8, Judas Maccabaeus reappears in the narrative (Israel's leading guerilla fighter). He and other pious Jews asked God to be merciful to the martyrs, the temple, and the city (2 Macc 8:2–3). They also prayed that the Lord would hear the blood of the martyrs, that he would remember the destruction of the innocent babies, that he would remember the blasphemies against his name, and that he would hate all of the evil committed against Israel (2 Macc 8:4).[87] That the blood for which Judas prayed refers to the martyrs' blood is certain, because of the context of 2 Macc 5:20–8:5. In the latter unit, righteous Jews prayed for mercy; the martyrs died to achieve God's mercy, and God granted mercy by means of their deaths. The prayers of the faithful Jews were effective. Immediately after the prayer, Judas organized his army, and the Gentile rebels could no longer prevail against him, because God's wrath against the nation turned to mercy toward the nation (2 Macc 8:5). The prayer of these pious Jews preceded God's mercy, but God's wrath against Israel did not end only because of the prayer itself. Rather, God answered Judas' prayer, because he received the martyrs' blood as a sufficient payment to end his wrath (2 Macc 5:1–8:3).[88]

Maccabean warriors (89). However, commenting on 4 Macc 17:21, Williams states that this purification should not be seen in terms of expiatory death, but in Antiochus leaving Jerusalem (176). This is what Williams means when he asserts that there was not a cause and effect relationship between the deaths of the martyrs and the purification of Israel.

87. Some argue since Judas mentions more than the blood of the martyrs in his prayer, his prayer must not have been for the vicarious effect of the martyrs' deaths. For example, see Williams, *Jesus's Death*, 85–90; Seeley, *The Noble Death*, 88.

88. Cf. Kellermann (*Auferstanden in den Himmel*, 54–55) argues that prayer accomplished atonement in 2 Macc 7:37–38. Contra Williams, *Jesus's Death*, 88.

For example, the author introduced the deaths of the martyrs in 2 Macc 5:20 by stating that God was reconciled to the nation. Second Maccabees 5:21–6:11 speaks of Antiochus' deception, seizure of the temple, and his persecution of the Jews in Israel. In 2 Macc 6:12–17, the author interrupts his explanation of Antiochus' evil deeds with a short exhortation to his readers. He explains to his readers why God brought suffering to the nation through Antiochus, and he encourages them not to be discouraged by what they have just read or what they would read regarding the suffering of their fellow Jews. The author follows his exhortation by highlighting the martyrdoms of Eleazar, the mother, and her seven sons (2 Macc 6:18–7:41). In 2 Macc 8:1–4, the author records that Judas Maccabeus asked God to be merciful to the nation. He demonstrates that Judas' prayer (and the prayers of all pious Jews) was answered, because the text asserts that God used his prayer to provide salvation for Israel through the martyrs' deaths and that he received their deaths as payment for the nation's sin (2 Macc 7:32–8:5). God's provision of salvation was the answer to Judas' request for mercy in 2 Macc 8:5. Both the prayers of the pious Jews and the deaths of the martyrs achieved the reconciliation of which the author speaks in 2 Macc 5:20. God, therefore, was merciful to the nation; he answered the prayers of the pious Jews; he received the deaths of the martyrs as atoning sacrifices, and he relieved the nation from wrath and reversed his judgment against the Gentiles by means of the martyrs' deaths for Israel (2 Macc 7:32–8:5; cf. Eur. *Iphigeneia in Tauri* 3–1401; *Phoenissae* 968–75).[89]

The Cessation of God's Wrath

The final element of the seventh son's prayer in 2 Macc 7:37–38 supports that the martyrs were atoning sacrifices and a saving event for Israel. The most important part of the prayer in 2 Macc 7:37–38 for my thesis are the words ἵλεως ταχὺ τῷ ἔθνει γενέσθαι ("to be merciful quickly to the nation") in 7:37 and ἐν ἐμοὶ δὲ καὶ τοῖς ἀδελφοῖς μου στῆσαι τὴν τοῦ παντοκράτορος ὀργήν ("to end the wrath of the almighty in me and in my brothers") in 7:38. The former series of words form an infinitive

89. Similarly Cummins, *Paul and the Crucified*, 88. Although his essay is primarily about the development of holy war in ancient Israel, STJ, and the NT, Brown ("Holy War," 287–88) states that "Judas and his men are asking God to accept the present national suffering as sufficient, not only to atone for the nation's sins, but as sufficient to invoke his wrath upon the Syrian armies."

clause. It is similar to the construction in 4 Macc 6:28 where Eleazar asked God to provide mercy for the nation through his death (ἵλεως γενοῦ τῷ σου). Moreover, just as Eleazar's prayer in 4 Macc 6:28–29, each portion of the seventh son's request in 2 Macc 7:37–38 supports both a sacrificial and a soteriological understanding of the martyrs' deaths. That is, the final elements of the prayer suggest that the seventh son voluntarily gave his life to God, that he prayed that God would be merciful quickly to the nation through his death, and that God would end his wrath by means of both his martyrdom and the martyrdoms of his brothers.[90]

However, Scholars have debated exactly how to interpret the seventh son's statement that God's wrath would end "in me and in my brothers" (2 Macc 7:38). Sam K. Williams argues that the death of the seven sons did not avert God's wrath away from the nation. The phrases "in me and in my brothers" do not suggest the means by which the wrath of God was averted, but the point at which the wrath of God was averted. The seventh son simply affirmed that the wrath of God would end with him and his brothers.[91] Williams maintains his view partly because he rejects that 2 Maccabees teaches vicarious atonement. According to him, 2 Maccabees only presents the martyrs as exemplars and their deaths as exemplary for fellow Jews to imitate in the face of persecution and death. Williams asserts that their deaths did not atone for sin.[92]

Williams is partially correct. The suffering and deaths of the martyrs in 2 Maccabees were exemplary (2 Macc 6:28, 31; cf. 2 Macc 6:24–31). The author states that Eleazar's death was an example of nobility for the entire nation (2 Macc 6:28, 31). Moreover, even 4 Maccabees, in which the sacrificial and the soteriological natures of the martyrs' deaths are more explicit, speaks of the martyrs' deaths in exemplary terms (4 Macc 6:18–21; 9:23; 10:3, 16; 11:15; 12:16; 13:8–18; 17:23). However, the exemplary nature of the martyrs' deaths in 2 and 4 Maccabees does not preclude them from also being atoning sacrifices and a saving event for the nation (cf. 1 Pet 2:21–24).[93]

Williams and others speciously sever the exemplary, sacrificial, and soteriological aspects of the martyrs' deaths. As a result, they wrongly con-

90. Cf. van Henten, *Maccabean Martyrs*, 143–44.

91. Williams, *Jesus's Death*, 83–88.

92. Ibid.

93. First Peter 2:21–24 is the closest biblical parallel where the death of a human is referred to both as exemplary and vicarious for others.

clude that the exemplary aspect of their deaths in 2 Maccabees cancels the
sacrificial and the soteriological natures of their deaths. To the contrary, 2
and 4 Maccabees do not teach only exemplary suffering or only sacrificial
atonement, but both exemplary suffering and sacrificial atonement. Thus,
2 and 4 Maccabees suggest that the martyrs' deaths were atoning sacrifices
and a saving event for Israel. Fourth Maccabees simply emphasizes atoning sacrifice and salvation more explicitly than 2 Maccabees.

In addition, Williams is correct to note that the preposition ἐν in the
statement "to end the wrath of the almighty *in* me and *in* my brothers"
can convey a variety of meanings (i.e., "in," "with," "by means of," etc.).
However, it likely conveys instrumentality in 2 Macc 7:38 (i.e., "by means
of"), because the preceding meaning occurs elsewhere in 2 Maccabees (2
Macc 1:28; 5:20; 7:29; 15:11; cf. 4 Macc 9:22; 16:15),[94] and it occurs in close
proximity of 2 Macc 7:38 in 2 Macc 7:29. If the translation "by means of"
is correct in 2 Macc 7:38, then the seventh son prayed that the wrath of
God would end "by means of" him and "by means of" his brothers. The
seventh son wanted his death and the deaths of his brothers to satisfy
God's wrath against the nation (cf. 4 Macc 6:28–29).[95]

H.W. Surkau argues that 2 Macc 7:32–38 affirms that the martyrs'
deaths were atoning sacrifices and a saving event for Israel. Yet, he appears to go beyond the textual evidence when he asserts that the author
of 2 Maccabees intentionally presents the martyrs' deaths in light of Deut
32:32–43 so that his readers would recall this text to mind when they read
his presentation of the martyrs' deaths (cf. 2 Macc 7:6). Deuteronomy
32:32–43 (esp. 32:43) teaches that Yahweh would avenge the blood of his
servants by taking vengeance on their adversaries. According to Surkau,
the prayers of the righteous martyrs induced God to use the martyrs'
deaths as expiation and vicarious atonement for the nation's sin with
similar language found in Deuteronomy 32.[96]

Williams rejects Surkau's arguments for the expiatory function of
the martyrs' deaths in 2 Macc 7:32–38. He offers three rebuttals. (1) Even
if the author knew that Deuteronomy 32 consisted of the song of Moses,
this knowledge does not require the belief that the author intended his

---

94. For other examples where ἐν conveys means or instrumentality, see Robertson,
Grammar, 589–91; Smyth, *Greek Grammar*, 376–77. Also, instrumentality can be expressed in the dative case without the preposition (e.g., 2 Macc 7:33b).

95. Contra Williams, *Jesus's Death*, 88.

96. Surkau, *Märtyrien*, 59.

readers to recall any part of Deuteronomy 32. (2) Even if the deaths of the martyrs induced God to provide salvation, nothing in the text suggests that the martyrs' deaths actually achieved atonement. (3) Even if Surkau is correct to assert that the author intended his original readers to recall Deut 32:43 when interpreting the martyrs' deaths, Surkau's interpretation of Deut 32:43 (that the blood of God's servants expiates sin) does not necessarily follow.[97]

Regardless of how one understands the preposition in 2 Macc 7:38 and regardless of the arguments put forth both by Surkau and Williams, the contextual evidence in 2 Maccabees strongly supports that the martyrs' deaths were atoning sacrifices and a saving event for Israel, because their deaths (along with the prayers of pious Jews) were the means by which God was merciful to the nation, the means by which the wrath of God ended against Israel, and the means by which peace came to Israel (2 Macc 5:1–8:5). Furthermore, regardless of whether Deut 32:43 teaches expiatory atonement or whether the author wanted his readers to interpret the expiatory function of the martyrs' deaths in light of Deuteronomy 32, Surkau's general point should be accepted: Martyr Theology teaches that the martyrs were atoning sacrifices and a saving event for Israel,[98] because God demonstrated his mercy to the nation by becoming reconciled to the nation once again (cf. 2 Macc 7:32–8:5). There is compelling contextual evidence in 2 Macc 5:1–8:5 to support these suggestions.

While Antiochus was invading Egypt a second time, he heard that Judea was in revolt (2 Macc 5:1–11). He immediately left Egypt and seized Jerusalem while he commanded his soldiers to kill anyone whom they met along the way (2 Macc 5:11b-14). Dissatisfied with the slaughtering, Antiochus entered the holy temple and profaned it, for he was oblivious that God was using him to defile the temple because he was angry with

---

97. So Williams, *Jesus's Death*, 82–84. Similarly Seeley, *The Noble Death*, 83–91. According to Seeley, the deaths of the seven brothers in 2 Maccabees were not vicarious, expiatory deaths, but simply evidence of Israel's suffering and discipline (88–89). Yet, argues Seeley, Eleazar's death was vicarious in that he died mimetically as an example for the people, not as an expiatory sacrifice to cancel sin (89).

98. It is possible, though, that Deuteronomy 32 provided the martyrs with hope that God would indeed avenge the nation through their deaths. Much like the martyrs possibly interpreted their suffering in light of Isaiah 53, they too could have interpreted their suffering in light of Deuteronomy 32 where God promised to avenge Israel from its enemies (cf. 2 Macc 5:1–8:5; 4 Macc 6:18–31; 17:20–22, and 18:6–19 with Deuteronomy 32 and Isaiah 10 and 53).

Israel (2 Macc 5:17–18). God chose the temple for Israel and, therefore, it suffered his wrath because of the nation's sin (2 Macc 5:19).

Just as the temple suffered pollution and judgment because of the nation's sin, it also experienced God's blessings when he pardoned the nation (2 Macc 5:20a; cf. Lev 16:16, 30). Second Maccabees 5:20b states that God's wrath ended, and the glory of Israel was restored "by means of the reconciliation of the Great Lord" (2 Macc 8:5; cf. Lev 9:1–10:2). The reconciliation for which the seventh son asserted that his death would achieve for the nation became a reality for Israel through the martyrs' deaths, and God's glory was again restored to both the temple and the nation through their deaths (cf. 2 Macc 5:20–8:5; 4 Macc 17:21–22).

After the author describes the other abominations that Antiochus and his companions committed (2 Macc 5:21–6:11), he subsequently explains why the Jews suffered so severely. He offers this explanation immediately before he wrote about the martyrdoms of Eleazar, the mother, and her seven sons (2 Macc 6:18–8:2). In 2 Macc 6:12–17, the author urges his readers not to be discouraged by the grave calamities that had befallen the nation by asserting that God provided the calamities for the nation's benefit. The author also states that God would soon judge the impious nations when they reached the full measure of their sins, but he would not deal with Israel in this way. Instead, God judged Israel in the calamities that had befallen the nation through Antiochus, and the deaths of the martyrs were representative of his divine judgment. The author explains that God did not, therefore, relinquish his mercy from his people nor did he forsake them (2 Macc 6:13–16). The author, then, highlights the deaths of the martyrs in 2 Macc 6:18–8:2 to demonstrate how God's mercy was achieved for the nation (2 Macc 5:20; 8:5–7). God reveals his mercy to Israel by his reconciliatory acts toward the nation, and this is the mercy of which the author speaks in 2 Macc 5:20 and 6:12–16, and the mercy for which Judas prays in 2 Macc 8:1–4.[99]

Therefore, the text of 2 Macc 7:32–38 teaches that the martyrs' deaths were an atoning sacrifice and a saving event for Israel in at least five ways: (1) the seventh son and his brothers suffered and, eventually, died because of the nation's sin (2 Macc 7:32). (2) They offered their lives to God in death to achieve reconciliation for the nation (2 Macc 7:37). (3) The seventh son asserted that God would again be reconciled to the nation

---

99. Contra Seeley, *The Noble Death*, 87–88.

through his death (2 Macc 7:37b). (4) The seventh son prayed that God would deliver the nation from his wrath through his death and through the deaths of his brothers (2 Macc 7:38).[100] (5) God was reconciled to the nation once again by means of the martyrs' deaths (2 Macc 5:1–8:5).

4 Maccabees' Interpretation of the Martyrs' Deaths

In 4 Macc 17:21–22, the author interprets the significance of the martyrs' deaths.[101] His interpretation suggests that the martyrs died as atoning sacrifices and as a saving event for Israel. He states that "the tyrant was punished, and the homeland was purified, as they became a ransom for the nation's sin, and divine providence saved Israel, who was beforehand mistreated, through the blood of these pious ones and through their propitiatory death" (cf. 4 Macc 1:11).[102]

---

100. So Moule, *Origins*, 114. Similarly van Henten, *Maccabean Martyrs*, 143–44. Contra Williams, *Jesus's Death*, 83–88.

101. Contra Williams, *Jesus's Death*, 177–78; Seeley, *The Noble Death*, 97.

102. The adverb ὥσπερ ("as"/"just as") in 4 Macc 17:21 causes Williams (*Jesus's Death*, 179–82), followed by Seeley (*The Noble Death*, 97), to argue that the author of 4 Maccabees metaphorically refers to the martyrs' deaths as a ransom for sin. According to Williams, although this adverb might not illumine the meaning of the text, it could also suggest something very important about the martyrs' deaths. God received their deaths "just as" (ὥσπερ) he received sacrifices, because he deemed their deaths as an act of expiation. In reality, however, they were not expiatory. In response to Williams, first, even if ὥσπερ is a metaphor in 4 Macc 17:21, a metaphorical use does not dismiss the fact that the martyrs' deaths actually accomplished salvation for the nation. Both 2 and 4 Maccabees incontrovertibly affirm that God actually brought salvation to the nation, a point with which even Williams would agree. Second, Williams' metaphorical reading of the adverb ὥσπερ and, thus, of the cultic vocabulary in 4 Macc 17:21–22 indirectly contradicts his understanding of the effective deaths of the martyrs. On the one hand, he asserts that the martyrs were not sacrificial victims for the nation, because the cultic language in 4 Macc 17:21–22 is metaphorical. On the other hand, he defends that the martyrs' deaths provided purification for the nation in that Antiochus left Jerusalem. Williams seemingly uses metaphor one way when he argues that the martyrs' deaths actually achieved purification for the nation, but restricted his metaphor when arguing that the cultic terms in 4 Macc 17:21–22 that describe the effectiveness of the martyrs' deaths were not sacrificial. Third, Williams only attributes metaphorical language to the cultic vocabulary in 4 Macc 17:21–22, not to the actual salvation that the cultic vocabulary describes. This seems arbitrary since he does not consider the language that describes the suffering and deaths of the martyrs, the punishment of Antiochus, or Israel's salvation as metaphorical. The preceding language occurs in the same text along with the cultic vocabulary that Williams deems as metaphorical. Fourth, cultic vocabulary occurs in 4 Macc 17:21–22 in an important section of the book: after the deaths of the martyrs. It is likely that the author of 4 Maccabees interpreted his presentation of the martyrs' deaths for his readers as atoning sacrifices and as a saving

There are four sacrificial elements in 4 Macc 17:21–22 within three soteriological statements. The sacrificial elements are purification, vicarious suffering for sin, blood, and death. The three soteriological statements are as follows: (1) the author states that the martyrs' deaths purified the homeland (4 Macc 17:21). (2) He states that the martyrs were a ransom for the nation's sins (4 Macc 17:22). (3) He states that God saved Israel through the martyrs' blood and through their pro-pitiatory (ἱλαστήριον) deaths (4 Macc 17:22).[103] Since I have already discussed three of the above sacrificial metaphors during my discussion of 4 Macc 6:28–29 and since ἱλαστήριον introduces a specific lexical connection between Martyr Theology and Paul (cf. Rom 3:25), I limit my discussion here to ἱλαστήριον.[104]

Ἱλαστήριον

The author of 4 Macc 17:21–22 asserts that the martyrs' deaths provided purification and salvation for Israel. He attributes atoning significance to the martyrs' deaths after he discusses their steadfast devotion to their religion (4 Macc 6:18–14:20). He highlights the steadfast devotion of the mother to

event since he has presented in detail the martyrs' suffering and the reason for it in the antecedent chapters (cf. 4 Macc 17:1–18:5). Fifth, a metaphorical use of ὥσπερ does not necessarily diminish the sacrificial element of the martyrs' deaths. For example, Jesus was not really a Passover Lamb, but NT authors present his death as such to accentuate the sacrificial aspect of it (cf. 1 Cor 5:7).

103. Similarly Kim, "Atonement in 1 John," 92–94. Williams (*Jesus's Death*, 169–170, 176) argues that the martyrs' deaths *per se* did not avert God's wrath in 4 Maccabees, but their endurance did. The issue in 4 Maccabees is not "death *qua* death that was effective, but the martyrs' steadfastness, their endurance, to the point of death itself." Williams appeals to 4 Macc 11:24–25, 17:2, 17:20–22, and 18:4–5 to support his claim. To his credit, 4 Maccabees emphasizes the martyrs' faithful endurance of suffering. Against him, however, their godly obedience was the reason for which God received their deaths as atoning sacrifices and a saving event for the nation and as a key element that averted his wrath (cf. Isa 53; Heb 12:2–11; esp. 12:2). Fourth Maccabees 6:28–29 and 17:21–22 support this in that these texts do not emphasize the martyrs' endurance, but the atoning value of their deaths.

104. With reference to ἱλαστήριον, there is an important textual variant in 4 Macc 17:22. Alexandrinus and Venetus have τοῦ ἱλαστηρίου θανάτου αὐτῶν ("their propi-tiatory death"), whereas Rahlfs follows Sinaiticus and reads as ἱλαστήριου τοῦ θανάτου αὐτῶν ("their death, namely, propitiation." Klauck (*4 Makkabäerbuch*, 753), van Henten ("The Tradition-Historical Background," 123), and DeSilva (*4 Maccabees* [2006], 250) follow the reading of Alexandrinus and Venetus. I follow Rahlfs, but I am not currently convinced that the textual variant matters in determining the meaning of ἱλαστήριον in 4 Macc 17:22 since both variants could support that the martyrs' deaths were atoning sacrifices and a saving event for Israel.

her God in the face of her own torturous suffering while she concurrently observed the execution of her sons (4 Macc 15:1–17:6). The author asserts that both man and God would honor the martyrs because of their endurance in their religion (4 Macc 17:7–20), but God especially honors them by sanctifying them as atoning sacrifices for the nation (4 Macc 17:20). The martyrs' deaths prevented their enemies from being victorious over Israel (4 Macc 17:20). This salvation is seen in part when God turns Antiochus' judgment away from the nation against Antiochus and his companions (4 Macc 17:21). Through their deaths, God saved Israel, cleansed the nation of its sin, and ended his wrath against the nation (4 Macc 17:22).[105]

To my knowledge, 4 Macc 17:22 and Rom 3:25 are the only places in extant literature where an author applies ἱλαστήριον to a human's self sacrificial death for the sins of another person or people.[106] The term occurs in the canonical LXX often as a reference to the mercy seat (Lev 16:14–15). It does not occur in the non-canonical LXX apart from 4 Maccabees. In the canonical LXX, it occurs in both cultic contexts (Exod 25:17–37:8; Lev 16:14–15) and in non-cultic contexts (Amos 9:1). The term also appears in Heb 9:5. In the latter text, ἱλαστήριον adopts the OT's use of mercy seat.[107] The major concern regarding ἱλαστήριον in 4 Macc 17:22 is whether it refers to the mercy seat/Day of Atonement,

---

105. So also O'Hagan, "The Martyr," 103, 119; DeSilva (1998), 4 *Maccabees*, 138.

106. In NT scholarship, ἱλαστήριον has been the subject of much debate. As early as Origen, interpreters have argued that ἱλαστήριον refers to the mercy seat. In the 1800s, Deissmann (*Bible Studies*, 124–35; idem, "ἱλαστήριος," 193–211) challenged this thesis. In 1945, Manson ("ἱλαστήριον," 1–10) wrote an influential article in which he revived the thesis that ἱλαστήριον refers to the mercy seat in Rom 3:25. In the 1930s, Dodd argued that ἱλαστήριον and related terms refer to expiation (*The Bible and The Greeks*, 82–95). Cf. Hofius, "Erwagungen," 186–99. As a result of Dodd's bold thesis, the ἱλαστήριον-debate again gained the interest of scholars in the 1950s. In response to Dodd's work, scholars did not altogether abandon the discussion of the referent of ἱλαστήριον in the NT, but they focused especially on the singular question whether the term means expiation or propitiation. Nicole ("C. H. Dodd and the Doctrine of Propitiation," 117–57) challenged Dodd's attacks against propitiation. Likewise, Morris (*Apostolic Preaching*; idem, *The Cross*) argued that ἱλαστήριον refers to propitiation. In the 1960s, Hill (*Greek Words and Hebrew Meanings*, 23–48) also offered a sharp critique of Dodd's thesis in which he argued in favor of propitiation. Bailey ("Mercy Seat,") refocused scholarly attention on the referent of ἱλαστήριον by arguing that it refers to the mercy seat in Rom 3:25, but not in 4 Macc 17:22. Bailey's doctoral thesis is the most exhaustive work on ἱλαστήριον.

107. The Lord appeared over the mercy seat, the place at which the priest sprinkled blood for atonement (Lev 16:13–15).

means of atonement, or a propitiatory offering that was similar to the offerings presented to offended deities to propitiate their wrath.

Daniel P. Bailey's recent doctoral thesis challenges the NRSV's rendering "atoning sacrifice" and suggests that ἱλαστήριον in 4 Macc 17:22 takes the common pagan meaning instead of the biblical imagery mercy seat (cf. Lev 16 LXX). Bailey carefully argues the thesis that Paul's use of ἱλαστήριον in Rom 3:25 and the author's use in 4 Macc 17:22 are distinct.[108] Paul uses the term consistent with its occurrence in the biblical world (i.e., mercy seat), and the author of 4 Macc 17:22 uses the term consistent with its occurrence in the Hellenistic world (i.e., propitiatory).[109] To argue that ἱλαστήριον refers to an atoning sacrifice in 4 Macc 17:22 is a mistake. After reviewing the evidence in the relevant Hellenistic literature that supports reading the term as "propitiatory," Bailey argues that various inscriptions affirm that ἱλαστήρια were offered either to propitiate the wrath of offended deities or to ensure favors from them.[110] He also argues that -τήριον words do not regularly refer to actions, but to places.[111] Bailey concludes that the meaning of ἱλαστήριον in 4 Macc 17:22 as it relates to the martyrs' deaths "should be sought against a non-sacrificial background."[112] According to Bailey, 4 Maccabees nowhere states that the martyrs died as atoning sacrifices for Israel's sin.[113]

Bailey's lexical analysis is certainly helpful.[114] Furthermore, he is correct to assert that the occurrence of the same term in different texts (i.e.,

---

108. I am grateful to Daniel P. Bailey for kindly e-mailing me a copy of his dissertation.

109. Bailey, "Mercy Seat," 5–12, esp. 11–12.

110. For the above analysis and summary of Bailey's view, see DeSilva (2006), *4 Maccabees*, 250–51, who cites Bailey ("Mercy Seat," 31–75).

111. Finlan, *Atonement Metaphors*, 200–03, who cites Bailey, "Greek Heroes," 6–7; idem, "Mercy Seat," 1, 4, 12, 237–38. For Bailey's examples, see my history of research in chapter 1.

112. The above quote comes from DeSilva (2006: *4 Maccabees*, 251), who summarizes Bailey's view.

113. DeSilva (2006: *4 Maccabees*, 251) agrees with Bailey in part, but DeSilva asserts that "the effect of the propitiatory gift is, however, fundamentally the same as the sacrifice of atonement: on the basis of the martyrs' loyalty to God unto death, God's anger turns away from Israel, and God turns again to Israel with a favorable disposition so as to deliver her from her enemies (2 Macc 7:37–38; 8:5)." Contra to Bailey, DeSilva argues that the author used the cultic language from the Yom Kippur ritual to describe the effect of the martyrs' deaths (250–51).

114. See Finlan, *Atonement Metaphors*, 123–35.

4 Macc 17:22 and Rom 3:25) does not necessitate that the term should be translated the same way. Nevertheless, Bailey's arguments seem to pit his lexical analysis against the context within which ἱλαστήριον occurs in 4 Macc 17:22. He, therefore, prevents the metaphors of the-τήριον word-group from conveying their contextual themes.[115] For example, 4 Macc 6:28–29 speaks of the martyrs' deaths in the context of blood, purification, and ransom. Likewise, 4 Macc 17:21–22 speaks of the martyrs' deaths in the context of purification, ransom, blood, and salvation.[116] Therefore, the contextual evidence in 4 Macc 6:28–29 and 17:21–22 does not support Bailey's reading of ἱλαστήριον in 4 Macc 17:22: viz., that it should be understood as a pagan reference to a non-cultic background.

Instead, together 4 Macc 6:28–29 and 17:21–22 jointly affirm that the martyrs offered themselves to God as atonement for Israel's sin to achieve the nation's salvation, because these texts state that the martyrs' deaths purified the homeland and provided salvation for the people by turning God's wrath away from Israel (cf. 1 Macc 1:11; 2 Macc 5:1–8:5; 4 Macc 17:20–22).[117] The context supports the latter in spite of the fact that ἱλαστήριον could be translated differently in 4 Macc 17:22 and in Rom 3:25. Thus, since the author of 4 Maccabees describes the martyrs' deaths with cultic vocabulary, as the means by which God forgives the nation's sin, and as the means by which God extends salvation to the nation, their deaths should be understood both as atoning sacrifices and as a saving event for Israel (2 Macc 5:1–8:5; 4 Macc 17:21–22; 18:4–5; cf. 4 Macc 6:28–29).[118]

Therefore, to distinguish between the translations mercy seat, means of atonement, or propitiatory in 4 Macc 17:22 creates unnecessary distinctions.[119] Since the occurrence of ἱλαστήριον in 4 Macc 17:22 appears in

---

115. For a similar critique, see also Finlan, *Atonement Metaphors*, 200.

116. Ibid., 202.

117. Ibid., 202–3. Cf. also van Henten, *The Maccabean Martyrs*, 142. Contra Bailey, "Greek Heroes," 6; idem, "Mercy Seat," 237–38.

118. Similarly de Jonge, "Jesus's Death for Others," 142–51, esp. 150–51.

119. DeSilva (2006: *4 Maccabees*, 251) agrees with Bailey in part, but the former adds that "the effect of the propitiatory gift is, however, fundamentally the same as the sacrifice of atonement: on the basis of the martyrs' loyalty to God unto death, God's anger turns away from Israel, and God turns again to Israel with a favorable disposition so as to deliver her from her enemies (2 Macc 7:37–38; 8:5)." Contra to Bailey, DeSilva argues that the author used the cultic language from the Yom Kippur ritual to describe the effect of the martyrs' deaths (250–51). Cf. 4 Macc 17:20–22.

the same context as several atonement concepts found in the OT cult (e.g., judgment, purification, ransom, vicarious death, sin, and blood), it should likely be understood as a reference to both the expiatory and propitiatory accomplishment of the martyrs' deaths. Thus, the occurrence of ἱλαστή ριον on abstract monuments that were erected to appease angry deities in the ancient world should not determine the meaning of the term in 4 Macc 17:22,[120] for the author's point in 4 Macc 17:21–22 with his use of ἱλαστή ριον is that God saved Israel from his wrath by means of the martyrs' blood and that their blood was an atoning sacrifice for Israel (4 Macc 17:21–22; 18:4–5; cf. 2 Macc 5:1–8:5; 4 Macc 6:28–29).

CONCLUSION

The authors of 2 and 4 Maccabees suggest that the martyrs' deaths were atoning sacrifices and a saving event for Israel. First, the martyrs suffered and died because of sin (2 Macc 7:18, 32; 12:39–42; 4 Macc 4:21; 17:21–22; cf. Lev 1:1–7:6; 8:18–21; 16:3–24; Song of the Three Young Men 3–16). Second, the martyrs' blood was the required price for the nation's salvation (2 Macc 7:32–38; 4 Macc 6:28–29; 7:8; 17:21–22). Third, the martyrs' deaths provided purification and cleansing for the nation (4 Macc 6:28–29; 17:22; cf. Lev 16:16, 30; Isa 53:10). Fourth, the martyrs' deaths ended God's wrath against the nation (1 Macc 1:1–64; 2 Macc 7:32–38; 8:5; 4 Macc 17:21–22). Fifth, the martyrs' deaths spared the nation from suffering the penalty for their own sin in the eschaton (2 Macc 5:1–8:5; cf. 2 Macc 7:1–14). Sixth, the martyrs died vicariously for the nation (2 Macc 7:18, 32; 4 Macc 4:21; 17:21–22). Seventh, God judged sin and granted forgiveness through the martyrs' deaths (2 Macc 6:12–7:38; 4 Macc 17:21–22).

120. Contra Bailey, "Mercy Seat," 31–75.

3

Martyrdom in the Old Testament

INTRODUCTION

THIS CHAPTER INVESTIGATES GENESIS 22, Exodus 32, Numbers 25, and Isaiah 53 to see if these texts could have provided the background behind Paul's conception of Jesus's death.[1] Since each of these OT texts mentions human sacrifice and since three of the four texts seem to suggest that a human's death served as an atoning sacrifice and a saving event for Israel, I limit my investigation to these specific OT texts. The thesis argued in this chapter is that with the possible exception of Isaiah 53, the sort of human sacrifice that atones for sin and saves others, which is present in Martyr Theology and in Paul, is not present in these OT texts.

GENESIS 22

Genesis 22 is a well-known text. It records Abraham's offering of Isaac as a sacrifice on Mount Moriah.[2] The story is somewhat paradoxical since

1. Daniel 3, 6, and 11 have appeared in some of the literature as important martyr texts since Daniel 3 and 6 closely reflect the Maccabean situation and since Daniel 11 speaks of the righteous purifying the land (Dan 11:32–35).

2. Henceforth "Mt. Moriah." Because of the binding of Isaac in Genesis 22, scholars have posited a theory about his sacrifice known as the *Akedah Hypothesis*. No scholarly consensus exists regarding the meaning of this hypothesis. The hypothesis has generally argued that the sacrifice of Isaac was vicarious and had an atoning significance for Israel and that this legend influenced the NT authors' conception of Jesus's death. Geiger ("Erbsünde und Versöhnungstod," 166–71) was one of the earliest scholars to consider whether the *Akedah Hypothesis* was instructive for early Christian thought on the atonement. He argued that the legend was conceived in a Syrian-Christian context. Schoeps ("The Sacrifice of Isaac," 385–92) was the first NT scholar to provide a defense of this legend in the English language. He offered a modified version of Israel Levi's theory ("Le Sacrifice d'Isaac," 161–235), who argued that the Father and the Son initiated redemption

Isaac was Abraham's promised son (Genesis 12, 15; LXX of Gen 22:2, 12, 16).[3] God promised Abraham[4] that he would make him a great nation and bless him, that he would make his name great, and that all the nations of the earth would be blessed through him (Gen 12:2–3; cf. 15:1–5; 17:1–6; 18:18). Several years elapsed before God fulfilled his promise to Abraham. Added to the lapse of time, Sarah[5] was barren, and both Abraham and Sarah were increasing in age (Gen 16:1; 17:1; 18:11). Old age and barrenness, therefore, made it less likely that God would fulfill his promise to Abraham. Nevertheless, God fulfilled his promise (Gen 21:1–8), but shortly after God blessed Abraham with Isaac, he commanded Abraham to offer him as a sacrifice.

The Sacrifice of Isaac

Abraham obeyed God's command and made the necessary preparations to offer Isaac as a burnt-offering (Gen 22:6, 9–10). Once they arrived at

---

in Paul's conception of atonement (e.g., Rom 8:32; Gal 1:4) and that Paul's conception of atonement has both Jewish and Hellenistic roots. Perhaps the most important work on the *Akedah Hypothesis* is that of Spiegel ("Meaggadot Ha-Akedah," 471–547). Spiegel suggests that a connection exists between Isaac's sacrifice and the Passover in Exodus Rabbah 15. Lerch (*Isaaks Opferung*), however, inferred different conclusions from Spiegel after investigating the evidence. He specifically challenges the redemptive merit of the *Akedah Hypothesis*. Daniélou (*Sacramentum*, 102–03) agrees with Lerch and contends that Genesis 22 was the background behind Paul's conception of atonement, but Daniélou denies that Paul intentionally borrowed from Genesis 22. In 1954, Goodenough (*Jewish Symbols*) basically espoused Spiegel's view (that both the *Akedah Hypothesis* and Christian soteriology were indebted to Hellenism and Judaism). For other important works on the *Akedah Hypothesis* and its influence on the early Christian or Pauline conception of Jesus's death, see Ginzberg, *Legends*; Bossmann, "In Christ;" Vermes, "Redemption and Genesis xxii," 193–227; Wilken, "Melito, The Jewish Community at Sardis," 53–69; Daly, "The Soteriological Significance," 45–75; Davies, "Passover and the Dating of the Akedah," 59–67; Chilton, "Isaac and the Second Night," 78–88; Meile, "Isaaks Opferung," 111–28; Hayward, "The Present State of Research," 127–50. For a rejection of both the *Akedah Hypothesis* and its influence on Pauline soteriology, see Heddoric, "An Investigation." For a recent assessment of the evidence for the *Akedah* as an expiatory and redemptive act for Israel in Qumran literature, see Fitzmyer, "The Sacrifice of Isaac," 211–29. Cf. also the account of Gen 22:1–19 in Jubilees 17–18 and 4Q225 (4Q-Pseudo Jubilees).

3. Genesis 22 emphasizes that Isaac was Abraham's first-born since he had already sent Hagar and Ishmael into the wilderness of Beer-Sheeba (Gen 21:8–21) and since the latter was not his promised-son (Gen 12–18). Similarly Fitzmyer, "The Sacrifice of Isaac," 213. See Brandscheidt, "Das Opfer," 1–19.

4. Abram until Gen 17:5.

5. Sarai until Gen 17:15.

Mt. Moriah, Isaac became curious as to the location of the animal that Abraham would sacrifice (Gen 22:6). Abraham responded in Gen 22:6: "My son, God will see to it, the young lamb, for a burnt-offering." Abraham seemingly knew that he would not actually sacrifice his son, but that God would instead provide a substitute. When Abraham was about to sacrifice Isaac, God acknowledged Abraham's devotion to him and provided a lamb for him to sacrifice in the place of Isaac (Gen 22:11–13).

The paradox of God's command is seen in that Isaac was Abraham's promised son, whom he loved, whom God promised, for whom Abraham and Sarah waited so long to receive, and through whom all the nations of the earth would be blessed (Gen 22:2; cf. Gen 12:2–3; cf. 15:1–5; 16:1; 17:1–6; 18:11, 18). Nevertheless, God expected Abraham to offer him as a burnt-offering. Genesis 22:1 and 22:12 confirms, however, that God did not command Abraham to sacrifice Isaac as a burnt-offering in order to atone for sin, but to test him. Therefore, no textual evidence exists in the MT of Genesis 22 that warrants the interpretation that Isaac's sacrifice atoned for sin.[6] On the other hand, evidence suggests that the goal of this sacrifice was simply to test him in order to prove the validity of Abraham's faith (Gen 22:1, 12; cf. Jas 2:21–24).[7]

Summary

Human sacrifice in Genesis is an explicit conceptual similarity between the sacrifice of Isaac, Martyr Theology, and Paul's conception of Jesus's death since each of the preceding asserts that a human dies as a sacrifice (Gen 22:2; cf. 2 Macc 7:32–38; 4 Macc 6:28–29; 17:21–22; Rom 3:24–26; 1 Cor 5:7). Still, there are palpable differences between the sacrifice of Isaac, Martyr Theology, and Paul's conception of Jesus's death.[8] The most notable difference is that both Martyr Theology and Paul suggest that humans died as atoning sacrifices and as a saving event for others. To the contrary, Genesis 22 does not state that Isaac died.[9] Rather, the text em-

---

6. Cf. Segal, "Jesus, Paul, and the Akedah," 169–84, esp. 176–77.

7. James states that the goal of Isaac's sacrifice was to prove that Abraham's works justified him in that they proved that he was justified by faith (Jas 2:21–24).

8. Contra Schoeps, *Paul*, 148–49; Vermes, "Redemption and Genesis xxii," 193–227.

9. Later Jewish rabbis especially argued that Isaac was actually sacrificed and that his ashes were used to atone for Israel's sins. For a discussion of the Jewish texts and for a bibliography, see Mathews, *Genesis 11:27–50:26*, 300–06. Mathews rejects that the *Akedah Hypothesis* was a viable background behind Paul's soteriology (*Genesis 11:27–50:26*, 306).

phasizes that God intervened so that Abraham would not sacrifice his son (Gen 22:12).[10] Furthermore, unlike the deaths of the martyrs and Jesus, Isaac's death did not atone for sin (Gen 22:1; cf. Fragment-Targums of the Pentateuch, esp. Tg. Neof. Gen 22:1–19).[11]

Therefore, the differences between Isaac's sacrifice, the martyrs' deaths, and Jesus's death are greater than any one similarity with Genesis 22.[12] First, Abraham did not actually sacrifice Isaac (cf. 4 Macc 17:20–22; Rom 3:25).[13] Second, there is no explicit connection in Genesis 22 between Isaac's death, atonement, and salvation for Israel resulting from Isaac's death (cf. 2 Macc 5:1–8:5; 4 Macc 6:28–29; 4 Macc 17:20–22; Rom 3:21–11:32). Third, Isaac's sacrifice was a means through which God tested the genuineness of Abraham's faith (cf. 4 Macc 17:20–22; Rom 5:9–11).

EXODUS 32

Exodus 32 is another important text in determining the background behind Paul's conception of Jesus's death, because this text (unlike Genesis 22) expresses that a human's death could atone the nation's sin and provide salvation for it.[14] In Exodus 32, Israel committed idolatry while they awaited Moses' return from Sinai. As Yahweh's mediator for Israel, Moses went before him to receive instruction for the nation (Exod 19:3–40:16). Frustrated with Moses' slackness in returning from Sinai, the people urged Aaron to make an object of worship for them (Exod 32:10). Aaron obliged the people's request and joined with them in committing idolatry against Yahweh (Exod 32:2–6; cf. 20:2–6). Yahweh saw Israel's sin and became angry as a result of the nation's disobedience (Exod 32:7–9; cf. 1 Maccabees 1).

After Yahweh became angry, Moses immediately entreated him not to destroy Israel in spite of the nation's sin (Exod 32:11). As reasons for

Cf. Segal, "Jesus, Paul, and the Akedah," 169–84, esp. 176–77.

10. Contra the *Akedah Hypothesis*.

11. Ibid.

12. Cf. Levenson (*The Death and Resurrection*), who argues that a father's sacrifice of his first-born child in the Hebrew Bible was foundational for the early church's interpretation of Jesus's death.

13. The above is one reason why the *Akedah Hypothesis* must be rejected as an instructive background behind Paul. Rightly Reventlow, *Opfere deinen Sohn*, 82.

14. For a recent monograph that analyzes Moses' dialogue with Yahweh in Exodus 32–34, see Suomala, *Dialogue*. For a detailed exegesis of Exodus 32–34 in light of Paul, see Hafemann, *Paul, Moses, and the History of Israel*, 189–459.

which Yahweh should not destroy his people with his wrath, Moses appealed to the great power that Yahweh demonstrated to Egypt and to the nations when he delivered Israel from slavery, and he appealed to Yahweh's promise to Abraham and to the patriarchs that he would bless the nations through them and through their seed (Exod 32:11–13). Yahweh was compassionate to his people in that he answered Moses' request and did not immediately destroy Israel as he had initially promised (Exod 32:14).[15]

Moses subsequently returned to Israel at the bottom of Sinai only to hear and to see the nation lauding the golden calf with the worship that the people should have exclusively given to Yahweh (Exod 32:15–18). Moses became angry and shattered the tablets, which symbolized that Yahweh's covenant between him and Israel had been broken. Moses also destroyed the golden calf and rebuked Aaron for allowing the people to become negligent in their devotion to Yahweh (Exod 32:15–26). Afterwards, Moses summoned all of the servants of Yahweh from amongst the people, from which came forth the sons of Levi (Exod 32:26). He commanded the sons of Levi to kill everybody in the camp in order to purify the people, and he urged the people to purify themselves before Yahweh (Exod 32:28–29; cf. Numbers 25).

Moses told the people that he would return to the mountain to see if he could possibly atone for their sin (Exod 32:30). Once he returned to Yahweh, he admitted to him that the people had greatly sinned against him (Exod 32:31). He asked Yahweh to forgive Israel of its sins and instead to blot his name out of his book (Exod 32:31–33). Yahweh responded by saying that he would punish those who sinned against him (Exod 32:33; cf. 32:34–35; 33:12–34:35).[16]

After Israel committed idolatry, Moses returned to Yahweh on Sinai with the hope that he could atone Israel's sin and achieve the nation's salvation by offering himself as Israel's sacrifice. His self-sacrifice would have fulfilled the request of his earlier prayer in Exod 32:11–13 (that Yahweh would not destroy Israel, but instead would recreate them as his holy nation).[17] He was not certain, however, whether Yahweh would accept his atonement for the people. This is clear from his statement "perhaps I will atone [אֲכַפְּרָה] for your sin" (Exod 32:31).

15. For a recent dissertation that investigates early rabbinic interpretation of Exod 32:7–14, see Jerrow, "Arguing with God."

16. For a concise discussion of the unity of Exodus 32–34, see Stuart, *Exodus*, 659.

17. Ibid., 683.

Exodus 32:30–32 supports that Moses voluntarily offered himself to Yahweh as an atoning sacrifice and as a saving event for the nation. The relationship between Moses' statements in Exod 32:30–31 (that Israel had greatly sinned and that he would perhaps offer atonement for them), his request to Yahweh that he would pardon the sins of the people, and his request that Yahweh would blot his name out of his book if he would not pardon Israel's sins support that Moses would die as a sacrifice for the nation's sin to achieve the people's salvation (Exod 32:32).[18] Furthermore, Yahweh's response to Moses supports the above interpretation: "But Yahweh said to Moses: whoever has sinned against me, I will blot him out of my book" (Exod 32:33).[19] Yahweh rejected Moses' request and asserted that the one who sinned against him would bear the judgment of his own sin in death (cf. Exod 32:34–35; Ezek 18:20; Jer 31:30).[20]

Summary

Exodus 32 more closely parallels Martyr Theology and Paul's conception of Jesus's death than Abraham's sacrifice in Genesis 22. First, Israel suffered because of sin (2 Macc 7:32; Rom 4:25). Second, Moses represented the nation (cf. 2 Macc 7:32–38; 4 Macc 6:28–29; Gal 3:10). Third, Moses vicariously offered himself to Yahweh as an atoning sacrifice and as a sav-

18. Similarly Durham, *Exodus*, 432. Contra Stuart, *Exodus*, 684–85, esp. 685 n. 72. Stuart does not assert that Moses was a vicarious atonement, but that he was willing to forfeit his eternal life. Moses did not offer his life instead of Israel as a substitute, but he offered his life along with the nation, for Moses wanted Yahweh to judge him along with the transgressors. Yahweh had already honored Moses (Exod 32:10). Moses was likely saying to Yahweh, "If you kill them, you ought to kill me too, even though you have already supported me so strongly. In other words, Moses could be understood at most here to mean, if you do kill off Israel, you will lose me too by rights. But that is not the same thing as saying let me die in their place, so only one person will die and all the rest may go on as your people." Cf. also Moberly (*At The Mountain of God*, 44–115, esp. 57), who interprets Moses' request to mean that he wanted to die along with Israel, not as a substitute. According to Moberly, since Moses was Israel's mediator, he declined a future for himself that did not include the nation. Hafemann (*Paul, Moses, and the History of Israel*, 205) states that Moses stood in the presence of Yahweh as the faithful one among the unfaithful Israelites and that Moses prayed for his own eventual punishment. However, Hafemann does not explicitly assert that Moses vicariously offered himself in Exod 32:32 to Yahweh as an atoning sacrifice for Israel's sin.

19. To be blotted out of Yahweh's book would also entail loss of eternal life (Ps 69:28; Isa 4:3; Ezek 13:9. So also Stuart, *Exodus*, 685–88.

20. Cf. MT and LXX Exod 32:32–33.

ing event for Israel (cf. 2 Macc 7:32–38; 4 Macc 6:28–29; 17:21–22; Rom 3:24–25; Gal 1:4).

Nevertheless, the above parallels between Exodus 32, Martyr Theology, and Paul's conception of Jesus's death are not enough to support that Exodus 32 was Paul's background. First, no explicit soteriological connections exist between Exodus 32, Martyr Theology, or Paul. Second, Paul mainly pits Jesus's ministry against Moses' ministry in his letters and presents Moses' ministry as inferior to Jesus's ministry (2 Cor 3:1–18). Third, since Moses did not die, he did not atone for the nation's sin and thereby was not the means by which Yahweh saved Israel from his wrath. Instead, Yahweh rejected Moses' request (Exod 32:34–35; cf. 2 Macc 5:1–8:5; 4 Macc 17:20–22; Rom 3:24–26). To the contrary, Martyr Theology and Paul suggest that the deaths of humans for others actually accomplished salvation for those whom they died (cf. 2 Macc 5:1–8:5; 4 Macc 6:28–29; 17:21–22; Rom 3:25–26; 5:8–9). Fourth, Israel paid for its on sin, but Martyr Theology and Paul argue that the martyrs (=Martyr Theology) and Jesus (=Paul) paid for the sin of others with their sacrificial deaths (cf. 2 Macc 5:1–8:5; 4 Macc 6:28–29; 17:21–22; Rom 3:24–26; 2 Cor 5:19, 21).

NUMBERS 25

Numbers 25 is another important text for my thesis,[21] for Numbers 25 contains the idea that a human's death is an atoning sacrifice and a saving event for Israel. While Israel was at Shittim, the people sinned against Yahweh by engaging in sexual relations with the daughters of Moab (Num 25:1).[22] The Moabites worshipped other gods instead of Yahweh. They convinced Israel to offer sacrificial worship to their gods (Num 25:2a; cf. Exodus 32). Unfortunately, Israel consented and joined the Moabites in idolatry (Num 25:2b-3a). As a result, Yahweh's wrath was kindled against the nation (Num 25:3b). He, therefore, summoned Moses to sacrifice all[23] of the leaders from the tribes of Israel in order to avert his wrath away from the nation (Num 25:4).[24]

21. For commentary on Numbers 25, see Gray, *Numbers*, 380–87; Milgrom, *Numbers*; Cole, *Numbers*, 432–46.

22. So Milgrom, *Numbers*, 212.

23. Cf. Cole (*Numbers*, 438–40) for different views of how many people Yahweh slaughtered.

24. The verb that I translated above as sacrifice (הוקע) can mean to crucify in the

Moses summoned the judges of Israel to slaughter those who "attached themselves" to the wickedness of Peor (Num 25:5). Before Israel's judges executed this command, an Israelite man brought a Midianite[25] woman before Moses and the entire assembly (Num 25:6) while Israel stood weeping in front of the tent of meeting. The people were possibly weeping because of Yahweh's imminent wrath and judgment that he would execute against the nation through its judges on account of its sin.[26]

Moses and his fellow Israelites did not immediately judge the Israelite man and the Midianite woman for their sin since the text states that he and the woman entered into a tent together (Num 25:8).[27] They possibly entered into this tent in order to engage in sexual relations as part of their pagan worship.[28] Phinehas[29] (from the priestly lineage of Aaron) was one of those present in the assembly, before whom this Israelite man and the Midianite woman stood. Once he saw the two enter inside of the tent together, his zeal for Yahweh provoked him to enter the tent and to execute them with a spear.[30] As a result, Numbers 25 states in three distinct ways that Phinehas' actions benefited the nation: (1) the plague against Israel was restrained (Num 25:8). (2) The wrath of Yahweh turned from Israel (Num 25:11), and (3) Phinehas' sacrifice of the two atoned Israel's sin (MT: כפר and LXX: ἐξιλάσκομαι) and saved the community from God's judgment (MT and LXX Num 25:13; cf. 25:4, 8).

Summary

As Exodus 32, Numbers 25 has parallels with Martyr Theology and Paul's conception of Jesus's death. Numbers 25 speaks of the sacrifice of hu-

---

hiphil stem. The latter is the form in Num 25:4 (הוקע). Yahweh's command implies that his judgment against Israel represents that the nation was cursed by him and, thus, needed his wrath to be averted in order to remove the curse from Israel, because cursed is everyone who hangs on a tree (Deut 21:23; Gal 3:10–13).

25. Midianites were not only pagans, but they were also Israel's enemies (Gen 37:36; Num 31:2; Judg 7:7).

26. So Cole, *Numbers*, 440.

27. Probably not the tent of meeting (cf. the different terms in MT Num 25:6 with Num 25:8).

28. So Milgrom, *Numbers*, 212; Cole, *Numbers*, 441–42.

29. For a discussion of Phinehas' religious devotion to Yahweh, see Cole, *Numbers*, 440–42.

30. For a recent dissertation that discusses Phinehas' zeal, see Thoennes, "Biblical Theology."

mans for sin (Num 25:1–4, 13; cf. 2 Macc 5:1–8:5; 4 Macc 6:28–29; Rom 3:24–26; Gal 1:4; 2 Cor 5:21), propitiation and reconciliation (Num 25:4, 8, 11; cf. 2 Macc 5:1–8:5; 4 Macc 17:20–22; Rom 3:25–26; 5:9–11; 2 Cor 5:18–21), God's wrath (Num 25:11; cf. 2 Macc 7:32–38; 4 Macc 6:28–29; 17:20–22; Rom 5:9–11), and atonement (Num 25:13; cf. 2 Macc 7:32–38; 4 Macc 6:28–29; 4 Macc 17:20–22; Rom 3:23–26; Rom 5:6–11; 2 Cor 5:21; Gal 1:4). Nevertheless, one cannot extrapolate from the parallels between Numbers 25, Martyr Theology, and Paul's conception of Jesus's death that Numbers 25 was the background behind Martyr Theology and (more importantly) behind Paul's conception of Jesus's death for the following reasons. First, the Israelite man and the Midianite woman did not voluntarily offer themselves to Yahweh as atoning sacrifices to achieve Israel's salvation (cf. 2 Macc 7:32–38; 4 Macc 6:28–29; 17:20–22; Gal 1:4). Although their deaths appeased Yahweh's wrath and saved the community from his judgment, these two simply suffered the consequences of their own sin. Second, those who were slaughtered died for the nation to avert Yahweh's wrath away from the nation, but Numbers 25 nowhere acknowledges that their deaths were voluntary, pious offerings to God (cf. 2 Macc 7:32–38; 4 Maccabees 6–7; Gal 1:4).

ISAIAH 53

The final OT text that is relevant to my thesis is Isaiah 53. Martyr Theology and Paul's conception of Jesus's death at first appear to have parallels with Isaiah's Servant. I readily admit that biblical scholarship has not reached a consensus as to the meaning of the Servant-Songs in Isaiah 42–53,[31] and no scholarly agreement exists whether Isa 52:13–53:12 originally referred to the death of a person or if this person referred to Jesus when the original author penned this song.[32] My goal in this section is not to answer every exegetical and theological question that arises from an analysis of

---

31. In his nineteenth-century commentary on Isaiah, Duhm (*Jesaja*) was the first OT scholar to separate a series of four Servant-Songs (Isa 42:1–4; 49:1–6; 50:4–9; 52:13–53:12). For a discussion of Isaiah 53 and its relation to the NT, see the recent essays in Bellinger and Farmer, *Jesus and the Suffering Servant*; Janowski and Stuhlmacher, *The Suffering Servant*; Childs, *Struggle*.

32. For example, Hooker, *Jesus and the Servant*; Oswalt, *Isaiah*, 109–410; Childs, *Isaiah*, 323–423. See also the histories of research provided by North, *The Suffering Servant*, 6–120; Rowley, "The Servant," 3–60; Whybray, *Thanksgiving*; idem, *Isaiah*, 175; Haag, *Der Gottesknecht*; Sekine, *Identity and Authorship*, 29–56; Ruppert, "Mein Knecht," 1–17.

Isaiah 53, but to note the important issues in the text that relate to my thesis regarding whether Martyr Theology shaped Paul's conception of Jesus's death. I, therefore, limit my discussion in this chapter to both the parallels and differences between Isaiah 53, Martyr Theology, and Paul's conception of Jesus's death. Before engaging in an exegesis of Isaiah 53, I must first discuss the issue of the Servant's identity.

The Servant's Identity

Yahweh and his Servant are the main figures of Isaiah 42–53.[33] In the unit of Isaiah 52–53, the term עֶבֶד ("servant") first appears in Isa 52:13a. Its placement occurs here in a verse that proclaims both the Servant's exaltation and humiliation in death (cf. Isa 52:13–15 with 45:18–25). The Servant's exaltation in Isa 52:13 is subsequent to Isaiah's positive and negative comments about the Servant in Isaiah 42–52.

Speaking positively of the Servant, the author states that Yahweh delights in his Servant (Isa 42:1). He appoints his Servant to be a light to the nations (Isa 42:6) and to bring physical deliverance to the afflicted (Isa 42:7–8). The Servant was Yahweh's chosen witness (Isa 43:22–28; 43:8–10; 44:1–8), and he would bring salvation to both Israel and the nations (Isa 49:1–26). Yahweh helps his Servant in times of affliction (Isa 50:1–11), and he would be highly exalted (Isa 52:13). Speaking negatively of the Servant in chapters 42–53, the author refers to him as spiritually blind (Isa 42:19), as a sinner and as one who needs redemption (Isa 44:21–23; 48:1–22), as the object of Yahweh's wrath (Isa 51:1–23), and as one who is afflicted (Isa 53:3–11; cf. 52:13a).[34]

Collective Israel

Because of the diverse statements that the author attributes to the Servant throughout chapters 42–53, some have argued for two distinct, but related, views of the Servant in these chapters. The arguments can be summarized as follows: First, the author does not employ עֶבֶד to refer to a human

33. For a discussion of the four Servant-Songs, see Budde, *Die sogenannten Ebed-Jahwe-Lieder*; Mettinger, *A Farewell to the Servant Songs*; Hermission, "Voreiliger," 209–22; Laato, *The Servant of YHWH*, 16–21; idem, "The Composition of Isaiah 40–55," 207–28.

34. Whybray (*Isaiah 40–66*, 175) posits that the Servant did not vicariously suffer for the transgressors, but that he either simply identified with Israel in the nation's suffering or he simply received their suffering in exchange for his. Cf. Westermann, *Isaiah 40–66*, 263.

figure in Isaiah 53. Second, if the term refers to a human figure, he is not divine or messianic. Both positions note that the Servant Songs refer to Israel/Jacob as the עֶבֶד on multiple occasions throughout chapters 42–53 (Isa 43:1–13; 44:21; 48:20; 49:3; cf. 41:8–9).[35]

Advocates of the collective interpretation of the Servant in Isaiah 42–53 are partially correct, for the author clearly applies the title Servant to Israel in the Servant Songs (e.g., Isa 48:20). Nevertheless, there are compelling reasons to reject the position that the Servant refers to collective Israel on every occasion in Isaiah 42–53. First, the Servant-Songs state that Yahweh gave his Servant a mission to restore Israel (Isa 49:5; cf. 7:13–16; 9:6–7; 11:1–5).[36] Second, this restoration would result in the salvation of both Israel and the nations (Isa 49:6; 53:11). Third, throughout the Servant-Songs, the songs present the Servant as a blameless sufferer (Isa 42:1, 6; 52:13–14; 53:3–12; cf. 11:1–5), whereas they present Israel as a spiritual harlot (Isa 43:14–25; cf. 1:2–31; 10:1–11). Fourth, the author of Isaiah 53 originally addressed the prophecy to Israel. It is unlikely that the recipient of the prophecy in Isaiah 52–53 would also be the Servant of the prophecy in Isa 52:13a.[37] Fifth, Isaiah 52:13–53:12 highlights the individual suffering of the Servant for the sins of others (Isa 42:1; 44:3–6; 52:13; 53:4–12) and that this suffering provides justification for the transgressors (Isa 53:10).[38]

Could Isaiah's Servant in Isaiah 53 be Israel? The context of the song seems to suggest no. Isaiah 52:14 explicitly speaks of the Servant as undergoing physical suffering by men. By his suffering, he would sprinkle (i.e., cleanse) the nations (Isa 52:15). The author, then, states that the Servant "was rejected and despised by men" (Isa 53:3–4). Additionally, the author's use of the pronouns "we," "us," "our," "his," "him," "them," and his use of

35. Snaith, "Isaiah 40–66," 186–87.

36. Cf. Isa 11:1–5 with 53:10 where the Servant is called the righteous one (cf. Ps 110 with Acts 2, 13).

37. Young, *Isaiah*, 108. Young is specifically commenting on the Servant in Isa 42:1. Of course, as I have already demonstrated, there are places in the Servant-Songs where Yahweh refers to Israel as his Servant (Isa 41:8–9; 42:19).

38. Yahweh calls his Servant (Isa 42:1; 44:3–6; 52:13; 53:11), formed him in his mother's womb (Isa 42:6; 49:5, 8), elects him for favor (Isa 42:1), sustains him (Isa 42:1), equips him and places his Spirit upon him (Isa 42:1), gives him his prophetic instruments (ear: Isa 50:4; mouth: Isa 49:2; 50:4), and afflicts him (Isa 53:2–12). For the preceding, see Heard, "Maccabean Martyr Theology," 302 n. 7. Cf. Hengel, *The Atonement*, 59–60; France, *Jesus and the Old Testament*; Hofius, "The Fourth Servant Song," 163–88, esp. 175–88.

3MS verbs in MT Isa 53:2–12 further suggest that the Servant of Isaiah 53 refers to an individual person, not to Israel.[39] The author's use of these pronouns and verbs more sharply demarcate Yahweh's Servant from the rebellious nation of Israel (cf. Isaiah 1).

The author states that the Servant hides his face "from us" (Isa 53:3b), and "we did not esteem him" (Isa 53:3).[40] He suffers because of "our weakness" (Isa 53:4), "our sorrows" (Isa 53:4),[41] "our transgressions" (Isa 53:5), "our sins" (Isa 53:5), and for "our salvation" (Isa 53:5). Although "we all" have rebelled against Yahweh and his Servant (Isa 53:6), "his punishment" (Isa 53:5) and "his wounds" (Isa 53:5) were for "our healing" (Isa 53:5), because Yahweh places "our guilt" (Isa 53:6) on "his" Servant (Isa 53:6), presents "his soul" as a guilt-offering (Isa 53:10), and delights to "crush him with grief" (Isa 53:10).[42] Yahweh buried his Servant with the wicked (Isa 53:9).[43] Isaiah 53 also suggests that Yahweh would resurrect his Servant by stating that the Servant would see his seed (Isa 53:10), that Yahweh would extend his days (Isa 53:10), and that Yahweh's joy would prosper in his Servant's hand (Isa 53:10).[44] The Servant of Isaiah 53 not only suffered for the transgressors (i.e., for rebellious Israel [Isa 1:2–31; 48:1–11] and for sinful nations [cf. Isa 10:1–19; Isa 13–24; 49:6]),[45] but he also died for them (Isa 53:4, 6, 11–12).[46]

39. For a book on Isaiah's use of pronouns in the Servant-Songs, see Clines, *I, He, We, and They.*

40. So also MT Isa 53:4 (cf. Isa 42:6; 49:6; cf. 42:1, 4). So Oswalt, *Isaiah,* 384 n. 4.

41. I take the מִן as causal in Isa 53:5. Cf. LXX Isa 53:5 for a causal interpretation of the preposition. See also van der Merwe, et al., *Biblical Hebrew,* 289; Brown, et al., *The Brown-Driver-Briggs Hebrew and English Lexicon,* 577. For recent exegesis of Isaiah 53 as it pertains to atonement, see Gentry, "The Atonement in Isaiah's Fourth Servant Song," 20–47.

42. Some have appealed to the exiles' words in Lam 5:7 to rebut the vicarious nature of the Servant's suffering in Isaiah 53. The exiles lament that they carried the sins of their fathers into exile. In Lamentations 5, the text applies the same terms to the exiles who bore their sin in exile as Isa 53:11 applies to the Servant who bore the sin of others. Lamentations 5:7 clearly does not suggest that the exiles' death was beneficial and vicarious on behalf of the fathers' sins since Israel was alive and in exile even as the exiles uttered these words. Thus, critics say: when Isaiah 53 states that the Servant bore the sin of the transgressors, this did not necessarily mean that he died vicariously for them. So Whybray, *Thanksgiving,* 25, 29–76. Against Whybray, see Oswalt, *Isaiah,* 385–86.

43. Whybray (*Isaiah 40–66,* 171–72, 177) denies that the Servant actually died.

44. Other pronouns occur in Isaiah 53 that support my argument. See Isa 53:7–12.

45. Rightly Tidball, *The Message,* 106.

46. Contra Whybray, *Isaiah 40–66,* 171–72, 177; idem, *Thanksgiving,* 29–57. Tidball (*The*

A Non-Messianic, Historical Figure

Because of the problems expressed above with an exclusive collective reading of עֶבֶד in the Servant-Songs, some have interpreted the Servant as an historical, individual figure.[47] Such advocates would agree that the Servant of Isaiah 42–53 does not exclusively refer to collective Israel, but the Servant at times refers to an historical figure.[48] However, this historical figure is not necessarily the Messiah.[49] This view is likewise problematic.

First, although the OT refers to many individuals with the term servant (Ezra 4:15; 5:11; Dan 2:4, 7; 3:26, 28; 6:21), the contexts of these references do not speak of Israel's future salvation. Nor do they speak of those servants as dying as atoning sacrifices and a saving event for others.[50] Second, the author of Isaiah 53 uses the noun עֶבֶד in a technical sense in chapters 42–53 to introduce lengthy discussions of the Servant. These discussions often begin with the vocative עַבְדִּי ("my Servant") (cf. Isa 42:1; 52:13).[51] Third, the phrase עֶבֶד יהוה ("Servant of Yahweh") does not always explain something about the individual to whom the appellation Servant was ascribed (cf. Isa 42:1; 52:13a with Ps 18:1). Fourth, Isa 52:13–14 speaks of the Servant's individual exaltation and humiliation. The Servant received this humiliation because of the nation's sin (cf. Isa 53:4–6, 10–11). Fifth, Isa 53:8–12 suggests that the Servant would suffer, die, and resurrect (cf. Luke 18:31–33).[52] Therefore, in light of the evidence in Isaiah

---

Message, 100) asserts that human sacrifice was practiced by Israel's neighbors, but forbidden in Israel. If Tidball is correct, this might explain why Yahweh rejected Moses' request in Exod 32:32. Cf. Goldingay, *God's Prophet*, 147–48. Childs (*Isaiah*, 422) refuses to separate the Servant in Isaiah 53 from Israel's historical situation. Similarly Whybray (*Thanksgiving*, 25) suggests that the Servant refers to Second Isaiah himself. However, Childs (*Isaiah*, 422–23) assigns a greater theological importance to Isaiah 53 than Whybray.

47. So Whybray, *Thanksgiving*, 25.

48. Following the thesis advocated earlier by Miller ("Prophetic Conflict in Second Isaiah," 77–85), Ceresko ("The Rhetorical Strategy," 42–55) identifies the Servant of Isaiah 53 with a prophet who was killed by the Babylonians for political reasons.

49. Cf. Ceresko, "The Rhetorical Strategy," 42–55.

50. The terms "servant" and "servants" were used of patriarchs (Gen 24:14; 26:24), Levites (Ps 113:1), prophets (1 Kgs 14:18; Isa 20:3), Israel (Jer 30:10; 46:27–28), and kings (2 Sam 3:18; Hag 2:23). So Childs, *Isaiah*, 324. Paul also understood his ministry to the Gentiles in light of Yahweh's Servant (cf. Isa 42:6 with Acts 13:47; Luke 2:32).

51. That the Servant was a divine figure in Isaiah 53 is on occasion seen with certain introductory particles, such as in Isa 52:13a or Isa 42:1. Similarly Oswalt, *Isaiah*, 378.

52. For some of the above objections, see Heard, "Maccabean Martyr Theology," 303.

53, one can say with a high degree of probability that Isaiah's Servant refers to an individual regardless of whether this individual is messianic.

THE SERVANT AS AN ATONING SACRIFICE
AND A SAVING EVENT FOR OTHERS

The following discussion of the sacrificial nature of the Servant's death in Isaiah 53 overlaps some with what I argued above regarding the identity of the Servant.[53] Here I do not offer a detailed discussion of Isaiah's concept of atonement, but I specifically discuss the parallel language in Isaiah 53 with Martyr Theology and Paul's conception of Jesus's death.[54] I exclusively discuss below the statements that the author attributes to the Servant's death.[55]

The Servant's sprinkling of the Nations

Isaiah 52:13 states that the Servant would sprinkle many nations (יַזֶּה גּוֹיִם רַבִּים). This statement occurs in the context of the Servant's exaltation (Isa 52:13). However, it possibly refers to the Servant's death, because Isa 53:2–12 states that the Servant would die for the nations.[56] But, since the root כָּפַר, a common root for atonement in the MT (cf. Exod 32:30), does not occur in Isaiah 53, one could argue that Isaiah 53 is not a sacrificial text and therefore does not refer to atonement. To support this claim, one could appeal to the LXX, which translates the verb יַזֶּה ("he will sprinkle") as θαυμάσονται ("they will marvel"). The latter translation would seem to challenge the belief that Second Temple Jews read Isaiah 53 as a sacrificial text.

Because of the LXX's translation, some scholars have argued that the MT's יַזֶּה does not mean "to sprinkle" in the context of Isaiah 53. Brevard Childs, for example, proposes that (1) the LXX renders the MT differently on account of the semantic range of the Hebrew term. (2) In the hiphil

---

53. Bailey ("Concepts of Stellvertretung," 223–50) prefers the German *Stellvertretung* over the English attempts of representation and substitution to explain the Servant's death for the many.

54. For recent bibliographic work on atonement and other debated issues in Isaiah 53, see Hüllstrung, et al., "A Classified Bibliography," 462–92.

55. Groves' essay ("Atonement in Isaiah 53," 62–89) helped me structure this portion of the chapter.

56. Contra North, *Second Isaiah*, 228–29.

stem, the root נזה never specifies the object of what is sprinkled, but focuses on the application of the blood. (3) To emphasize that Isaiah 53 is a sacrificial context when the text never clearly establishes this point is exegetically incorrect. (4) The astonishment over the Servant likely refers to the nation's experience in seeing and understanding the Servant's suffering (cf. Isaiah 48–51). The interpretive key for the latter is found in Isaiah 48 where Israel is "challenged to hear and to see the new things God is about to reveal to Israel." The ones whose mouths would be shut in Isa 52:15, then, refers to Israel whom God promises would see and understand, and the confession that follows in Isa 53:1–12 comes from those within Israel whom Yahweh would make to understand his will "through their experience with his Suffering Servant."[57]

Childs certainly offers some important arguments. Notwithstanding these arguments, there are some compelling textual reasons to translate the root נזה in Isa 52:15 as "to sprinkle" and to understand this root as a reference to the sacrificial death of the Servant. First, the translators of the LXX did not translate the root נזה to reflect a sacrificial interpretation of the text, but this does not necessarily mean that their translation is correct. Second, except for two, clear instances (2 Kgs 9:33; Isa 63:3), the root נזה usually appears in sacrificial contexts in the LXX. Third, virtually every occurrence of נזה in sacrificial contexts appears in the hiphil stem, refers to sprinkling of some sort, and is translated by the LXX with the various verbs that mean "to sprinkle" (cf. MT and LXX of Exod 29:21; Lev 4:6, 17; 5:9; 6:20; 8:11, 30; 14:7, 16, 27, 51; 16:14–15, 19; Num 8:7; 19:4, 18, 19, 21). Fourth, the translators of the LXX quite possibly rendered יזה as θαυμάσονται on exegetical grounds, because they possibly did not understand the text to explicitly refer to the Servant's death as an atoning sacrifice.[58] Fifth, there are examples of the root נזה in the MT where the object of this root is grammatically specified, either in terms of a direct object (Lev 16:15), a prepositional phrase (Lev 4:6, 17; 8:11, 30; 14:7), which can too function as the direct object of a verbal clause (Lev 5:9;

---

57. Childs, *Isaiah*, 412–13.

58. Groves ("Atonement in Isaiah 53," 62–87) argues that the absence of cultic language is not problematic for Isaiah 53 since atonement is mentioned through the concept of bearing guilt. Rather, the problem in Isaiah 53 is the humanness of the atonement, because the voluntary sacrifice of a human for the benefit of others is unprecedented in the OT.

6:20),[59] or where the object is simply implied from the context (Exod 29:21).

Sixth, Childs' distinction between the object of what is sprinkled and blood is a superfluous dichotomy. In the above examples from MT Leviticus, blood is the object of the verb "to sprinkle." Seventh, since the author of Isaiah 53 employs the root נזה, which usually appears in sacrificial contexts, he possibly understood the Servant's sprinkling[60] of the nations in a sacrificial sense,[61] especially since Isa 53:2–12 refers to the Servant's death. Eighth, the astonishment about which the author speaks in Isa 52:15, the astonishment that would close the mouths of kings, anticipates the universal and eschatological reign of the Servant. The surrounding context of Isaiah 53 supports this assertion. The author mentions Israel's sin (Isa 1:2–31; 6:5), future purification and redemption (Isa 11:11–16; 35:1–10; 43:1–7; 44:21–28; 54:1–55:13; 60:1–62:12; 65:17–25), future judgment (Isa 1:2–31), and the future universal reign of a messianic figure who would bring salvation to the nations (Isa 2:1–22; 7:10–14; 9:6–7; 11:1–11; 65:17–66:2; cf. Deut 32:43; Ps 18:49; 117:1). The kings' astonishment, then, would result from their shock that many would have as they saw the unexpected manner by which Yahweh would reveal his salvation to the nations: viz., through the death of his Servant (cf. 52:13–15).[62]

The Servant's Death and Salvation

Isaiah 53:1 suggests that the report about the Servant proclaimed by Yahweh through the prophet was not universally believed. The report refers to Yahweh's proclamation that he would provide salvation to the nations through his Servant's death. The phrase זרוע יהוה ("arm of Yahweh") in Isa 53:1b supports the preceding point about salvation. At times, Yahweh's arm in the OT relates specifically to his power to save and

---

59. For this specific grammatical point regarding prepositions, see Deut 7:7; Ezek 44:5. See also van der Merwe, et al., *Biblical Hebrew*, 275.

60. In defense of the translation "to sprinkle" for נזה in Isa 52:15, see Young, "נזה," 125–32; Barthélemy, *Critique textuelle*, 2:384–87. Cf. North (*Second Isaiah*, 228–29) who argues that the verb should be translated "to sprinkle," but that the subject of the verb is "nations" and the object is "Servant." The nations sprinkled Yahweh's Servant with their heathenish and crude reactions against him (*Isaiah*, 229).

61. Cultic overtones can occur in a text even when the context is not explicitly cultic (cf. Leviticus 9–10, 16 with Numbers 25).

62. Oswalt (*Isaiah*, 379–80) understands the astonishment to refer to the contrast between the Servant's exaltation and his humiliation.

to deliver his people (Ps 71:18; 77:16; 88:22; 98:1; 136:12) or to his ability to judge and to crush his enemies (Ps 79:11). According to Isaiah 53, Yahweh would save his people and crush his enemies through his Servant (cf. Isa 7, 9, 11 with Ps 2; 110, Joel 2).

In Isa 53:2b-12, the author elucidates the content of the report about the Servant: the Servant would die for transgression to achieve the nations' salvation. The author suggests this by his description of the Servant's suffering. The Servant's appearance would be despised and shameful (Isa 53:2). He would be the object of Yahweh's wrath (Isa 53:4–6, 10). The Servant would bear and carry the sins of the transgressors (Isa 53:4–6, 11–12).

Isaiah 53:4 is the first place in Isaiah 53 where the prophet states that the Servant would bear and carry the sin and guilt of the transgressors.[63] The two clauses "Truly, our sicknesses he carried, and our sorrows, he bore them" (אכן חלינו הוא נשא ומכאבינו סבלם) function as a verbal hendiadys. The hendiadys is evident from the repetition of similar terms in both clauses: the nouns (חלינו/מכאבינו, "our sorrows/our weaknesses") and the verbs (נשא/סבל "he bore/he carried"). When interpreted together with the two nouns, both verbs convey that the means by which the Servant would bear and carry sin would be by dying on behalf of the transgressors.

Furthermore, the syntax of Isa 53:4 supports that the Servant's death would be an atoning sacrifice and a saving event for the nations, because the grammatical structure accentuates the Servant's sacrificial death for others. The author employs (what grammarians call) a *casus pendens construction* in Isa 53:4.[64] First, he places the direct objects of both clauses before their respective verbs (אחלינו הוא נשא ומכאבינו סבלם). Second, he places a particle at the beginning of the first clause (אכן). Third, he attaches a pronominal suffix to the first verb in the second clause to emphasize the sacrificial nature of the Servant's death (סבלם). Another emphatic grammatical construction that accentuates both the sacrificial and soteriological nature of the Servant's death occurs in Isa 53:12: נשא חטא־רבים והוא ("and he, the sin of many, he carries"). Along with Isa 53:4 and 53:7, Isa 53:11–12 teaches that the Servant would vol-

---

63. For a detailed analysis of the syntactical structure of Isa 53:4, 11–12, see Groves, "Atonement in Isaiah," 63–86.

64. For other examples of the emphatic nature of the *casus pendens construction*, see Gen 13:15; 21:13; 28:13; 35:12; 47:21; 1 Sam 25:29; 1 Kgs 15:1; Ps 125:5; Isa 1:7. See also Joüon and Müraoka, *Biblical Hebrew*, 3:586–88.

untarily[65] carry the sins of many as a substitute for them,[66] and that he would intercede for the transgressors for whom he would die.[67]

Yahweh's response to the Servant's intercession for the transgressors appears to be contingent upon the Servant's sacrificial death for them (cf. 2 Macc 7:32–38; 4 Macc 6:28–29), because the Servant's prayer for the transgressors in death perhaps guarantees the atoning efficacy of his death (cf. 2 Macc 5:1–8:5; 4 Macc 6:28–29; 17:20–22).[68] Yahweh offers his Servant for the transgressors to achieve their salvation, and the Servant prays that Yahweh would receive his sacrifice on behalf of them (cf. 2 Macc 5:1–8:5, 4 Macc 6:28–29; 17:20–22).[69] The Servant's sacrificial death, juxtaposed with his intercession for the transgressors, supports the vicarious nature of the Servant's sacrifice.[70]

---

65. Rightly Tidball, *The Message*, 109–10. He states that "the voluntary nature of his [the Servant's] death distinguishes it from all of Israel's animal sacrifices offered up to this point. The victims selected for slaughter had had no choice in the matter. Their complaints would not have been heard or understood by their executioners, even if they could have expressed them. The animals were incapable of understanding what was going on. For all they knew, they might as well have been on their way to new pasture, or to sheering, as to death. Their calmness, if such it was, was the calmness of ignorance rather than of control. But here was a human being in full possession of all his faculties, who knew what the outcome was going to be, yet who permitted others to victimize him and hound him to death" (brackets mine). Following Motyer (*Isaiah*, 336, 433), Tidball continues: "The earlier sacrifices of Israel were good as far as they went, but suffered one 'fatal flaw': '. . . sin involves the will. But this is precisely the point at which animals can only picture the substitute we require and cannot actually be that substitute: they have no consciousness of what is afoot nor of any deliberate, personal, self-submissive consent to it. Ultimately only a person can substitute for people.' Here was a sacrifice that surpassed the earlier guilt of atonement offerings; a sacrifice that exposed the fatal flaw and overcame it in one stroke. Rams, sheep, goats, and bulls had only approximated to our condition. They could do no more than that. But here was a substitute that exactly fitted our need."

66. Rightly Oswalt, *Isaiah*, 384–85.

67. Cf. 2 Macc 7:32–38, 4 Macc 6:28–29.

68. יַפְגִּיעַ ("to intercede") is the same verb that appears in Isa 53:6. The latter refers to Yahweh's placing the sins of the transgressors upon his Servant, whereas Isa 53:13 refers to the Servant's intercession for the transgressors.

69. The Servant's carrying the sins of the transgressors should not be understood in the same way as Ezekiel's statement that he bore the sins of Israel (Ezek 4:4–6) or as the exiles' statement that they bore their own sins (Lam 5:7). The contexts of Ezekiel and Lamentations are entirely different. Ezekiel symbolically represents Israel's imminent exile, and the exiles in Lamentations 5 bore their own guilt by suffering exile. Rightly Spieckermann, "Vicarious Suffering," 2.

70. For a vicarious interpretation of MT Isa 53:12, see LXX Isa 53:12.

Furthermore, Isa 53:5–6 and 53:10–12 affirm that the Servant's death was an atoning sacrifice and a saving event for the transgressors. In Isa 53:5, the participles (נרפא, מדכא, מחלל, "pierced, crushed, restored"), their prepositional phrases (בחברתו, לנו, מעונתינו, מפשענו, and עליו: "on account of our sins," "for us," "by his stripes," "on account of him"), and the author's use of the various terms that refer to purification, sin, transgression, and guilt throughout the book of Isaiah suggests that the Servant's death was superior to and possibly would replace the insufficient OT cult (cf. Isa 1:11–27; 2 Macc 1:5; 7:32–38; 8:29; 4 Macc 6:28–29; 17:20–22; Rom 3:24–26), the cult which could not keep Israel out of exile (cf. Isaiah 1).[71]

Isaiah's description of the Servant's death throughout the rest of Isa 53:6 continues to highlight the atoning efficacy of his death for the nations. Isaiah 53:6b, for example, states: "And Yahweh caused the guilt of all of us to fall on him." The phrase "the guilt of all of us" primarily refers to Israel's iniquity (Isa 1:1–31; 6:5; 43:22–28), but it includes the iniquity of the nations since he states that the Servant sprinkles "many nations" (52:15), that he justifies many (53:11), and that he dies for the transgressions of many (53:12). Isaiah never suggests that the Servant would die for his sin, but exclusively for the sins of others. His death would provide universal salvation for the nations (Isa 49:6). The author describes the universal salvation that the Servant's death would accomplish as an אשם ("guilt-offering") in Isa 53:10.

Even if the author is not specifically calling the Servant a guilt-offering for sin, the occurrence of אשם alludes to the sacrificial cult of the OT, because this is the same term that occurs in cultic contexts in the OT in reference to a guilt-offering (e.g. MT Lev 5:6–7, 15–16, 18–19).[72] Israel presented the אשם to Yahweh to expiate the nation's sin (MT Lev 5:6–7) and to avert Yahweh's wrath away from the nation (MT Lev 9:1–17:11; 1 Sam 6:3–4, 8, 17).[73] The appearance of אשם here affirms

---

71. Similarly Tidball, *The Message*, 110; Groves, "Atonement in Isaiah," 65–67. Groves (67) states that the cult "plays little or no positive role in Isaiah."

72. So Fohrer, "Stellvertretung und Schuldopfer," 24–43; Schenker, "Ascham," 3. Against Reventlow, "Basic Issues," 28–29; Janowski, *Sühne*, 144.

73. Cf. Lev 5:15–16, 18, 25. The OT offerings for sin placated Yahweh's wrath (cf. Lev 9:1–16:34). It is important to note, however, that אשם occurs in non-cultic contexts to refer to the guilt caused by sin (Gen 26:10). Following Janowski (*Sühne*, 144), Reventlow ("Basic Issues," 29) uses Gen 26:10 and 1 Sam 6:3–4, 8, 17 to argue that אשם is not sacrificial in Isa 53:10. Reventlow thinks that the original sense of the term in Gen 26:10 and

that the Servant's death was indeed an atoning sacrifice.[74] The appearance of both sacrificial and soteriological vocabulary in Isaiah (e.g., Isa 49:6; salvation; Isa 52:15 purification; Isa 53:3–6, 10–12: sin; and Isa 53:3–6, 11–12: vicarious death for sin) supports a sacrificial reading of אשם in Isa 53:10 (cf. Targ. Neof. Isa 53:10–12; 1QIs).[75] Unlike Israel's animal sacrifices offered in the cult, however, Yahweh's Servant would voluntarily[76] die for others to atone for their sin and to achieve their salvation.[77] Isaiah 53 states that Yahweh's Servant would be exalted by the nations (Isa 52:13; cf. 45:23–25), but the Servant's path to exaltation leads to his death for the transgressors (Isa 45:23–25; 52:13–53:12).[78]

Summary

The Servant of Isaiah 53 was possibly a human who would suffer injustice and who would die as an atoning sacrifice and as a saving event for Jews and Gentiles, for Isaiah 53 describes the Servant's death with anthropological and sacrificial language. Thus, Isaiah 53 more closely parallels Martyr Theology and Paul's conception of Jesus's death than the other OT texts investigated above. The close parallels with Isaiah 53 and Martyr Theology provide strong evidence that the martyrs possibly interpreted their deaths in light of Isaiah's Servant. In chapter 4, I make the argument

---

1 Sam 6:3–4, 6:8, and 6:17 refers to "restitution of damages due to a misdeed, for which the offender has to give an equivalent."

74. So Oswalt, *Isaiah*, 386, 398–400. Tidball (*The Message*, 106) states that the Levitical cult was the background behind Isaiah 53. For other OT examples where an OT author attributes cultic language to Israel's purification, see Exod 29:36; 32:30; Lev 1:4; 4:20, 26, 31, 35; 5:6, 10, 13, 16, 18, 26, 6:23; 7:7; 8:15, 36; 9:7; 10:17; 12:7–8; 14:18, 19, 20, 21, 29, 31, 53; 15:15, 30; 16:2–28; 17:1–16; Num 5:8; 8:5–22; 6:11; 8:12, 19, 21; 15:25, 28; 17:12; 28:22, 30; 25:10–13; 29:5, 11; 1 Sam 3:14 (LXX 1 Kgs 3:14); 1 Kgs 6:3; 1 Chr 6:34; 2 Chr 29:24. Contra Childs, *Isaiah*, 418; Whybray, *Thanksgiving*, 29–57; Orlinsky, "The So-Called Servant," 56; Spieckermann, "Vicarious Suffering," 3; Janowski, "He Bore Our Sins," 67–70; Hofius, "The Fourth Servant Song," 167.

75. See Schreiner, "Penal Substitution," 67–98, esp. 86.

76. Rightly Spieckermann, "Vicarious Suffering," 5–6.

77. Since some OT texts suggest that Yahweh did not accept Israel's sacrifices as a means of atonement, critical scholars have argued that the various OT texts (e.g., Ps 51:16; 1 Sam 15:22–23; Isa 1:10–17; Jer 7:21–23; Amos 5:21–22; Hos 6:6; Mic 6:6–8) that clearly speak of Yahweh rejecting Israel's sacrifices contradict the Pentateuchal view of atonement. Cf. Oesterley, *The Psalms*, 1:274.

78. For vicarious death in Isaiah 53, see also Motyer, *Isaiah*, 429–43.

that Isaiah 53 interpreted through the lens of Martyr Theology shaped Paul's conception of Jesus's death as an atoning sacrifice and as a saving event for Jews and Gentiles. That is, Martyr Theology's appropriation of Isaiah's Servant to the martyrs and not Paul's independent interpretation of Isaiah 53 shaped Paul's conception of Jesus's death.

However, the following conclusions from my analysis of Isaiah 53 support that there are at least three points of disjunction between Isaiah 53, Martyr Theology, and Paul's conception of Jesus's death. First, Isaiah 53 does not explicitly state that the Servant's death accomplished reconciliation between Yahweh and the transgressors. Isaiah 53 states that both Israel and the nations would be saved (Isaiah 40–66) and that the Servant would be the agent through whom Yahweh would accomplish this restoration (Isaiah 40–66). However, Isaiah 53 does not use the explicit reconciliation language that appears in Martyr Theology or in the Pauline corpus (cf. 2 Macc 5:1–8:5, esp. 7:32–38; Rom 5:9–10; 2 Cor 5:14–21). Second, Isaiah 53 does not explicitly state that the Servant satisfied Yahweh's wrath, whereas Martyr Theology and Paul argue that the deaths of humans remove God's wrath away from those for whom they die (cf. 2 Macc 5:1–8:5; 4 Macc 6:28–29; 17:21–22). Third, Isaiah 53 never calls the Servant a ἱλαστήριον for the nations (cf. 4 Macc 17:22; Rom 3:25).

CONCLUSION

The thesis argued in this chapter is that with the possible exception of Isaiah 53, the sort of human sacrifice that occurs in Martyr Theology and in Paul does not occur in the OT. Both Martyr Theology and Paul speak of human sacrifice with language that closely parallels Isaiah 53. The parallels between the traditions provide the probability that the martyrs possibly understood their deaths in light of Isaiah's Suffering Servant, and Isaiah 53 possibly shaped Paul's conception of Jesus's death in so far as Martyr Theology interpreted the martyrs' deaths in light of Isaiah's Suffering Servant. Chapter 4 considers the key texts in Paul.

4

Martyrdom and Jesus's Death in Paul

INTRODUCTION

Tʜɪs ᴄʜᴀᴘᴛᴇʀ ᴄᴏɴᴄʟᴜᴅᴇs ᴛʜᴇ investigation by examining the key texts in the Pauline corpus. Here I argue that Paul ascribes to Jesus's death language that closely parallels Martyr Theology. I also argue that the parallels with and similarities between Martyr Theology and Paul's presentation of Jesus's death suggest that Paul borrowed from the ideas and concepts in Martyr Theology regarding the death of the righteous for others to present Jesus's death both as an atoning sacrifice and as a saving event for Jews and Gentiles.

MARTYR THEOLOGY AND JESUS'S DEATH

Romans 3:21–26

Romans 3:21–26 is the most important text in the Pauline corpus in the discussion of whether Martyr Theology shaped Paul's conception of Jesus's death.[1] Many scholars agree that Rom 3:21–26 is the central section of the letter.[2] Paul begins this section with an emphatic salvation-historical contrast to what he has argued in Rom 1:18–3:20.[3] The two particles νυνὶ

---

1. See Williams, *Jesus's Death*, 5. For a summary of important exegetical issues in Rom 3:21–26 and for a concise bibliography, see Käsemann, "Zum Verständis," 150–54; Talbert, "A Non-Pauline Fragment," 287–96; van Henten, "Tradition-Historical Background," 101–28, esp. 101–06.

2. For example, Cranfield (*Romans*, 1:199) states that Rom 3:21–26 is "the center and the heart" of the unit to which it belongs. It is "the center and the heart of the whole of Rom 1:16b-15:13."

3. Most scholars agree that the particles νυνὶ δὲ introduce a shift in Paul's argument.

δὲ ("but now") reveal this contrast.[4] Having argued in Rom 1:18–3:20 that all (both Jews and Gentiles) have sinned, are under God's wrath, stand condemned before God, and all are incapable of being justified by the law,[5] Paul offers an antithesis in Rom 3:21–26. His antithesis to humanity's condemnation by law is justification by faith on the basis of Jesus's death for sin.

Paul's argument in Rom 3:21–26 can be summarized as follows: But now (in this new age of salvation-history), God forensically reveals his saving righteousness to Jews and Gentiles apart from obedience to his law since both Jews and Gentiles have sinned and have fallen short of God's glory (Rom 3:21–23). That is, God freely justifies Jews and Gentiles who place faith in Christ[6] by his grace (Rom 3:22–23) through the redemption in Christ Jesus (Rom 3:24),[7] for he offered him to be a sacrifice of atonement for sin to be received by faith (Rom 3:25a). God offered Jesus to be an atoning sacrifice in order to demonstrate his righteousness, because

---

Cf. Campbell, *Rhetoric*, 22–23.

4. Cranfield, *Romans*, 1:201; Käsemann, *Romans*, 92; Dunn, *Romans*, 1:164; Fitzmyer, *Romans*, 344; Schreiner, *Romans*, 180. For examples in Paul where νυνὶ δὲ function as temporal markers, see Rom 6:22; 7:6, 17; 9:30; 15:23, 25; 16:25–26; 1 Cor 15:20; Eph 2:12–13; Col 1:22, 26–27.

5. Schreiner, *Law*, 41–42. Prior to 1977, many NT scholars affirmed that the law demanded perfect obedience. With the publication of E.P. Sanders' monumental works on Paul (*Paul*; idem, *Paul, the Law, and the Jewish People*), scholars began to rethink the traditional Lutheran understanding of the law in Paul. In addition to Sanders' works, see the following works that have been instrumental in challenging the old perspective of the law in Paul: Dunn, *Jesus, Paul, and the Law*; Wright, *Climax*; idem, *Saint Paul*. For recent responses to and critiques of the New Perspective, see Thielman, *From Plight to Solution*; idem, *Paul & the Law*; Seifrid, *Christ, Our Righteousness*; Schreiner, *Law*; Carson, et al., *Justification and Variegated Nomism*; Das, *Paul, The Law, and The Covenant*; Kim, *Paul and the New Perspective*; Gathercole, *Boasting*; Westerholm, *Perspectives*; Sprinkle, *Law and Life*.

6. I read πίστεως᾽ Ἰησοῦ Χριστοῦ ("faith in/of Jesus Christ") in Rom 3:22 as an objective genitive. Paul's argument here is that God justifies Jews and Gentiles by one's personal faith in Jesus apart from one's individual works (cf. Rom 3:20). Against the preceding translation (most notably), see Hays, *The Faith of Christ*. For other representatives of the subjective genitive, see Taylor, "Πίστις Χριστοῦ," 58–76; Howard, "On the 'Faith of Christ,' " 459–65; idem, "Rom 3:21–31," 223–33; idem, "The Faith of Christ," 212–15; Robinson, "The Faith of Jesus Christ," 71–81; Johnson, "Rom 3:21–26," 77–90; Williams, "Again Pistis Christou," 431–47; Hooker, "Πίστις Χριστοῦ," 321–42; Keck, "Jesus in Romans," 443–60; Campbell, *Rhetoric*, 58–69; Longenecker, "Πίστις in Rom 3:25," 478–80. For a recent response, see Yong, "The Faith of Jesus Christ."

7. For a classic study of Paul's atonement terminology, see Morris, *Apostolic Preaching*.

he previously passed over sins in his patience during the old covenant (Rom 3:25b). God previously passed over sins in order to demonstrate his righteousness in this new age of salvation-history by the death of Jesus (Rom 3:25b-26a), so that he would be just (i.e., the one who punishes sin) and the justifier (i.e., the one who forensically declares sinners to be in the right) of the one who has faith in Jesus (Rom 3:26b).

Jesus's Death as a Ransom for Sin

Martyr Theology's influence on Paul's conception of Jesus's death first appears in the unit of Rom 3:21–26 in 3:23–24. In the latter, Paul states that Jesus died as a ransom for sin.[8] In Rom 3:23, Paul asserts that "all have sinned and fallen short of the glory of God."[9] He asserts in 3:20–24 that God justifies Jews and Gentiles by faith, because both groups fail to give God the honor that he deserves and because neither group is capable of being justified by obedience to the law (Rom 1:18–3:20). As a result of humanity's sin-problem, Paul states in Rom 3:24 that God takes the initiative and justifies Jews and Gentiles by his grace (δικαιούμενοι δωρεὰν τῇ αὐτου χάριτι).[10]

The fiercely debated words δικαιοσύνη ("righteousness") and δι–καιόω ("to justify") occur in Rom 3:21–26.[11] Regardless of whether one understands them as forensic terms for justification or God's covenantal faithfulness, these δικ-words nevertheless introduce the concept of salvation into a text where sin, blood, and God's judgment are mentioned.[12]

8. Some scholars affirm that Paul presents Jesus's death as a "vicarious atonement," but reject that he presents his death as a "penal substitute." Cf. Hooker, "Interchange in Christ," 349–61; idem, "Interchange and Atonement," 462–81; Cousar, *Theology*, 79. For recent discussion of penal substitution in the Pauline corpus, see Schreiner, "Penal Substitution," 67–98; Williams, "Penal Substitution," 73–81.

9. The glory of which everyone falls short at least refers to the glory that both Adam and Eve forfeited in the garden as a result of their disobedience (cf. Rom 5:12–21; Gen 3:8–24; As. *Mos.* 21:6). So Cranfield, *Romans*, 1:204; Dunn, *Romans*, 1:168. Against Sanday and Headlam, *Romans*, 85.

10. Since God initiates and effects salvation according to Paul, Fryer ("Hilastērion," 99–116, esp. 103–04) argues that this is one reason why 4 Macc 17:22 was not Paul's background in Rom 3:25.

11. For examples of this debate, see Ziesler, *Righteousness*; Cranfield, *Romans*, 1:202; Moo, *Romans*, 221–22; Schreiner, *Paul*, 193–95, 199–203; Piper, *The Justification of God*, 103; Wright, *Saint Paul*, 119, 122, 124–26, 29; idem, *Justification*; Gundry, "Non-Imputation," 17–45; Vickers, *Jesus's Blood*; VanLandingham, *Judgment & Justification*.

12. Δικαιόω occurs in both legal/forensic contexts and in ethical contexts in the

Moreover, these δικ-words occur in a text where the death of a human provides the solution to humanity's sin-problem (cf. 2 Macc 7:32–38; 4 Macc 6:28–29; 17:21–22). Paul states in 3:21–22 that God reveals his righteousness (a soteriological concept) by faith and in 3:24 that God accomplishes justification (another soteriological concept) and deals with the sin-problem of 1:18–3:23 through the "redemption in Christ Jesus." He clarifies in Rom 3:25 that the price of the justification and the redemption was Jesus's blood when he states that God set forth Jesus to be a ἱλαστή ριον by faith by his blood.

"Redemption" (ἀπολυτρώσις) appears for the first time in Romans in 3:24, and it reveals Paul's first explicit connection with Martyr Theology.[13] The term ἀπολυτρώσις in 3:24 is a synonym for ἀντίψυχον ("ransom") in 4 Macc 6:29b and 17:21, because both terms in their respective contexts suggest that the self sacrifices of humans were both the means by which God dealt with sin and the means by which they achieved salvation for others.[14] Eleazar asked God in 4 Macc 6:28–29 to receive his blood as a ransom for the nation. Fourth Maccabees 17:21–22 states that the martyrs' deaths accomplished salvation for the nation because the martyrs offered themselves as a ransom for the nation and their deaths purified the homeland of its sin.

Paul likewise suggests in Rom 3:24–25 that Jesus's blood paid the price for the redemption and was the means by which justification was accomplished for those who have sinned. Thus, since Paul uses ἀπολυτρώ σις to state that Jesus was the means through which God accomplished justification and redemption for Jews and Gentiles (cf. Rom 3:21–22, 24) and since he refers to Jesus's blood in 3:25, ἀπολυτρώσις likely suggests

---

LXX and in the NT. For examples, see Gen 38:26 (ethical); 44:16 (forensic); Isa 1:17; 5:23; 43:9, 26; 45:25; 50:8; 53:11 (forensic); Isa 42:21 (ethical); Sir 1:22; 7:3; 9:12 (forensic); 18:2 (ethical). In the gospels and Acts, when salvation is in view, δικαιόω is only forensic (Matt 12:37; Luke 10:29; Acts 13:38). In Paul, the majority of occurrences of δικαιόω are forensic (Rom 2:13; 3:3, 20, 24, 26, 28, 30; 4:2, 5; 5:1, 9; 6:7; 8:30, 33, 34; 1 Cor 4:4; 6:11; Gal 2:16–17; 3:8, 11, 24; 5:4; Titus 3:7).

13. See Warfield, "New Testament Terminology," 2:327–98. Warfield contributed much to the debate regarding the meaning of ἀπολυτρώσις in the early 1900s. Warfield argued for a threefold meaning of the term: (1) deliverance as analogous to the Exodus or the Babylonian Exile, (2) ransom, and (3) legal procedure. For a discussion of ἀπολ— υτρώσις, see also Morris, *Apostolic Preaching*, 11–64.

14. See Swallow, "Redemption in St. Paul," 21–27; Hill, *Greek Words and Hebrew Meanings*, 73–74.

in 3:24 that Jesus's death was a payment of ransom for sin and that his payment provided salvation for Jews and Gentiles, just as ἀντίψυχον in 4 Macc 6:29b and 17:21 suggests that the martyrs died as a payment of ransom for sin and that their payment provided salvation for Israel.[15] Paul does not state to whom the ransom is paid in Rom 3:24. However, since he mentions Jesus's blood in Rom 3:25, one can infer that the means by which God's saving righteousness is revealed by faith (3:21–22) and the means by which he justifies all who have sinned (3:24) is Jesus's blood. Moreover, just as the martyrs' deaths, Paul's reference to Jesus's blood in 3:25 implies that the redemption that Jesus achieved was by means of an atoning death and that his death was a saving event.

Jesus's Death, Ἱλαστήριον, and God's Wrath

Martyr Theology's influence on Paul is also evident in Rom 3:25 when he calls Jesus ἱλαστήριον.[16] There is no scholarly consensus as to how one should translate ἱλαστήριον in 3:25,[17] but suggested translations are

15. See Hill, *Greek Words and Hebrew Meanings*, 49–81; Finlan, *Atonement Metaphors*, 164–69.

16. Although van Henten argues that 4 Maccabees was a late second century document and, thus, post-dates Paul, he likewise argues that Paul's formulation in Rom 3:25 "consists of ideas concerning martyrdom." Van Henten surveys both martyrological and Greek pagan traditions to argue his thesis regarding Rom 3:25. He demonstrates that ἱλασ-words occur with αἷμα-words and πίστις-words in sacrificial contexts in martyrological and Greek literature. He suggests that LXX Dan 3:39–40 is the closest parallel to Rom 3:25 in Jewish Literature. See van Henten, "Tradition-Historical Background," 101–28.

17. For example, see Deissmann, *Bible Studies*, 124–35; Sanday and Headlam, *Romans*, 87–88, 91–94; Rashdall, *Atonement*, 130–32; Hanson, "ἱλαστήριον," 1–10; Dodd, *The Bible and the Greeks*, 82–95; Nicole, "C.H. Dodd and the Doctrine of Propitiation," 117–57; Morris, "The Meaning," 3–43; Hill, *Greek Words*, 23–48; Fryer, "Hilastērion," 99–116; Campbell, *Rhetoric*, 107–13; van Henten, "The Tradition-Historical Background," 101–28; Stuhlmacher, *Romans*, 58–61; Moo, *Romans*, 230–40; Schreiner, *Romans*, 164–66; Haacker, *Römer*, 90–92; Bailey, "Mercy Seat;" Knöppler, *Sühne*, 112–17; Wright, *Romans*, 272–79; Williams, *Jesus's Death*, 39–41, 165–202, 233–54; Talbert, *Romans*, 110–15; Ben Ezra, *Yom Kippur*, 198–202; Holland, *Contours*, 157–82; Finlan, *Atonement Metaphors*, 193–224.

mercy seat,[18] propitiation,[19] and expiation.[20] Recent exegesis suggests that the term in 3:25 has nothing to do with expiation or propitiation, but rather it speaks of reconciliation.[21] That is, Paul simply states that Jesus's death provides access to God.[22] Another recent proposal is that Paul uses ἱλαστήριον to state that Jesus was a "revelatory means of atonement."[23] Another is that ἱλαστήριον in 3:25 simply alludes to the Yom Kippur ritual, but it does not specifically refer to the mercy seat.[24]

Moreover, working with the assumption that the Yom Kippur ritual is the background behind Paul's use of ἱλαστήριον in 3:25, Peter Lampe recently argues that Paul does not present Jesus's death as an atoning sacrifice since Paul does not equate Jesus's blood with the animal's blood that was sprinkled over the mercy seat.[25] However, regardless of the plethora of translation options and contrary to Lampe's thesis, Jesus's death in Rom 3:25 should be understood as an atoning sacrifice and as a saving event precisely because Martyr Theology shaped Paul's conception of Jesus's death. That ἱλαστήριον occurs in both 4 Macc 17:22 and in Rom 3:25 along with the cultic concepts of sin, blood, and death support that Martyr Theology influenced Paul's use of the term. Moreover, both 4 Macc 17:21–22 and Rom 3:24–25 implement cultic language in their respective contexts to express the soteriological achievement of a human's sacrificial death for others.[26]

18. Origen, *Romans*, 216–25; Calvin, *Romans*, 75; Barth, *Romans*, 104–05; Manson, "ἱλαστήριον," 1–10; Nygren, *Romans*, 156–62; Lyonnet, "De notione expiationis," 336–52; Bruce, *Romans*, 104–07; Swain, "For our Sins," 131–39; Wilckens, *Römer*, 191–92; Hultgren, *Paul's Gospel and Mission*, 59–60; Schlatter, *Romans*, 99; Byrne, *Romans*, 132–33; Williams, *Paul's Metaphors*, 247, 253 n. 19; Bailey, "Mercy Seat;" Seifrid, "Romans," 618–19.

19. Morris, "The Meaning," 3–43.

20. Dodd, *The Bible and the Greeks*, 82–95; idem, *Romans*, 20–24, 77.

21. Jewett, *Romans*, 286.

22. Ibid.

23. Ekem, "A Dialogical Exegesis," 75–93. Ekem (80) clearly asserts, though, that expiation is the more likely reading of ἱλαστήριον in Rom 3:25.

24. Ben Ezra, *Yom Kippur*, 198–202.

25. Lampe, "Human Sacrifice," 191–209, esp. 194–95. In a series of publications in the 1990s, scholars argued that sacrificial theology was altogether absent from Paul's soteriology. See McLean, "Christ as Pharmakos," 187–207; idem, "The Absence of an Atoning Sacrifice," 531–53; idem, *The Cursed Christ*; Breytenbach, *Versöhnung*. Stuhlmacher ("Cilliers Breytenbachs," 339–54) responds to Breytenbach's thesis.

26. Van Henten, "The Tradition-Historical Background," 101–28.

As I stated in the history of research, an increasing amount of scholars reject that Martyr Theology shaped Paul's conception of Jesus's death as a ἱλαστήριον in Rom 3:25. Tom Holland, for example, argues that Martyr Theology does not adequately explain the soteriological motifs of justification, righteousness, and redemption in Rom 3:21–26.[27] Paul's soteriological motifs in the latter text most closely reflect the New Exodus model of salvation (cf. 1 Cor 5:7).[28] Paul explicitly appeals to the OT as his background with the words law and prophets in Rom 3:21.[29] According to Holland, to affirm that Martyr Theology shaped Paul's conception of Jesus's death reduces his death in his thought to nothing more important than the death of an innocent sufferer.[30] Such a reduction surrenders the substitutionary sufferings of Christ.[31] There is no clear allusion, says Holland, to Martyr Theology in Paul.[32]

Holland raises some important critiques against reading Paul's conception of Jesus's death exclusively in light of Martyr Theology. Moreover, he is certainly correct about the importance of the OT and the New Exodus motif in Paul (cf. 1 Cor 5:7). His specific critiques, however, against a martyrological background behind Paul's conception of Jesus's death would be more appropriate (1) if everyone who affirms that Martyr Theology shaped Paul's conception of Jesus's death also denies that the OT shaped Paul's conception of Jesus's death[33] and (2) if everyone who affirms that Martyr Theology shaped Paul's conception of Jesus's death also denies that the martyrs died as atoning sacrifices and as a saving event for Israel.[34] Since I argue neither of the preceding, Holland's critiques (even

27. So Holland, *Contours*, 157–82, esp. 179–81.

28. Ibid.

29. Ibid.

30. Ibid.

31. Ibid.

32. Ibid.

33. For example, Williams, *Jesus's Death*.

34. For example, Seeley, *The Noble Death*, 100–01. Seeley argues that Jesus's death was not a vicarious, atoning sacrifice. Agreeing with Sanders (*Paul*, 467–68) that Jesus's death was an example to be followed rather than an atoning sacrifice for sin, Seeley states that "E.P. Sanders makes this significance even clearer when he places Rom 6:3–11 alongside Rom 7:4; Gal 2:19–20; 5:24; 6:14; and Phil 3:10–11. Like these other passages, but more fully, Romans 6 shows that dying with Christ is the real means by which the vicarious effect of Jesus's death is conveyed." Seeley, then, quotes Sanders to support his assertion: "We see in all these passages that the prime significance which the death of Christ has

if generally correct) do not disprove my thesis. Moreover, Holland seems to force Paul's atonement imagery into one model.[35] In addition, his statements could also be charged with overreacting against scholars who argue that Martyr Theology shaped Paul's conception of Jesus's death,[36] while they simultaneously maintain that Martyr Theology does not teach that the martyrs died as atoning sacrifices and as a saving event for Israel.[37]

Holland's concerns are understandable since several scholars have argued that Paul does not conceive of Jesus's death as an atoning sacrifice or as a saving event precisely because Martyr Theology shaped his conception of Jesus's death. Stanley K. Stowers, for example, argues that Martyr Theology shaped Paul's conception of Jesus's death, but rejects that Paul conceives of Jesus's death as an atoning sacrifice and as a saving event in Rom 3:25.[38] Stowers denies that the martyrs died sacrificial deaths to achieve atonement and salvation for Israel.[39] He insists that Judaism nowhere teaches that a person could atone for the sins of others.[40] He contends that 4 Maccabees (esp. 6:28–29 and 17:21–22) does not teach that the martyrs' blood accomplished atonement, but that the martyrs' faithful endurance merited God's favor.[41] Fourth Maccabees demonstrates that

---

for Paul is not that it provides atonement for past transgressions. . . but that, by sharing in Christ's death, one dies to the power of sin or to the old aeon, with the result that one belongs to God. The transfer is not only from the uncleanness of idolatry and sexual immorality to cleanness and holiness, but from one lordship to another. The transfer takes place by participation in Christ's death." Against Lohse, *Römer*, 134–35. Lohse argues that Martyr Theology (esp. 4 Macc 17:21–22) was the primary background behind Paul's conception of Jesus's death. Paul conflated Martyr Theology with OT cultic language.

35. Finlan (*Atonement Metaphors*, 123) offers a similar critique of the theses of Stowers (*A Rereading of Romans*, 206–30) and McLean (*The Cursed Christ*). Finlan states that "my efforts amount to a refutation of McLean's and Stowers' assertions that there is no sacrificial imagery in Rom 3:25 or anywhere else in Paul's teachings. . . But both scholars mistakenly try to compel Paul's metaphors to fit one pattern, to deny Paul's imagery its full range of inventive flair, with all its shocking (even bloody) vividness and its blunt condemnation of common behaviors, Gentile and Jewish."

36. If Holland overstates his case, Dunn (*Theology*, 207, esp. 215) understates his case. In his Pauline theology, Dunn acknowledges that Martyr Theology could have been the background behind Paul's conception of Jesus's death, but he states that it makes little difference.

37. For example, Seeley's thesis (*The Noble Death*).

38. Stowers, *A Rereading of Romans*, 206–30.

39. Ibid., 206–30, esp. 206–07.

40. Ibid., 212–13.

41. Ibid.

the "language of Rom 3:25 could be used without sacrificial connotations."[42] According to Stowers, "if the key to Paul's thought about Christ rests in the idea of his death as a sacrifice of vicarious atonement for sin, then why does the only plausibly arguable evidence for that conception depend on the meaning of one word in Paul's extant letter?"[43] Stowers concludes that "the sacrificial interpretation simply proves insufficient to do the interpretive work that exegetes want it to do and therefore is not able to provide the most historically plausible reading of [Rom] 3:21–26" (brackets mine).[44]

Stowers' thesis, as well as his exegesis of Rom 3:21–26, is provocative. However, his analysis of the text cannot withstand exegetical scrutiny. His efforts to rebut that Paul presents Jesus's death as an atoning sacrifice and as a saving event and Holland's attempts to prove that Martyr Theology did not shape Paul's conception of Jesus's death in Rom 3:24–26 fall short. Stowers does not satisfactorily evaluate the evidence in 2 and 4 Maccabees or the key texts in Paul. Stowers neither adequately explains how Paul could apply cultic and sacrificial concepts to Jesus's death in Rom 3:21–26 (and in other places in his letters [e.g., 2 Cor 5:18–21]) in ways that reflect Martyr Theology, but not intend for these concepts to convey sacrificial meanings.

On the other hand, Holland's New Exodus model provides a helpful background by which to understand the soteriological value of Jesus's death, but his New Exodus model does not correlate in every way (as Holland assumes) with Paul's conception of Jesus's death. Nor does his model perfectly correlate with every metaphor that Paul applies to Jesus's death. Martyr Theology, however, more likely was Paul's fundamental background behind his conception of Jesus's death because the martyrs died as atoning sacrifices and as a saving event for Israel instead of animals, just as Jesus (a human) died as an atoning sacrifice and a saving event for Jews and Gentiles.

Therefore, contrary to Holland and Stowers, my argument is that the martyrs died for Israel as atoning sacrifices for the nation's sin to save the nation from God's wrath (2 Macc 7:32–38; 4 Macc 6:28–29; 17:21–22). The author of 4 Maccabees applies ἱλαστήριον to the martyrs' deaths in 4 Macc 17:22 in a sacrificial and soteriological context. The context

42. Ibid., 213.
43. Ibid.
44. Ibid.

suggests that the martyrs' blood secured purification for sin, was shed for sin, and delivered the nation from God's wrath.[45] Paul borrows from the concepts and ideas in Martyr Theology to present Jesus's death as an atoning sacrifice and a saving event for Jews and Gentiles.[46] Fourth Maccabees 17:21–22 specifically states that the martyrs' deaths were a ransom that purified the homeland and saved the nation from God's judgment. Paul states in Rom 3:24–25 that Jesus's death dealt with sin and delivered Jews and Gentiles from God's righteous judgment.

Any allusions to a New Exodus or Yom Kippur in Rom 3:25 can be ascribed to Martyr Theology's appropriation of the cultic language and (especially) the Yom Kippur ritual to the sacrificial deaths of the martyrs.[47] The OT cult alone cannot fully explain Paul's presentation of a human's death as a sacrifice of atonement for sin in order to achieve soteriological benefits for the nations, whereas Martyr Theology can.[48] Furthermore, a New Exodus model or the Yom Kippur ritual as the exclusive background behind Paul's conception of Jesus's death does not make sense of Paul's conception of Jesus's death since (1) animals were offered as atonement in the OT cult in which ἱλαστήριον occurs in the LXX, but the martyrs and Jesus were human sacrifices (Macc 5:1–8:5; 4 Macc 6:28–29; 4 Macc 17:20–22; Rom 3:24–26). (2) The animals that the priests offered as atonement in the OT did not actually atone for sin nor provide salvation (hence, the Day of Atonement), whereas the martyrs and Jesus accomplished both for those whom they died (2 Macc 5:1–8:5; esp. 7:32–38; 4 Macc 17:21–22; Rom 3:21–5:11).

---

45. See Finlan, *Atonement Metaphors*, 201–02.

46. Commenting on whether the sacrificial language that Paul attaches to Jesus's death was literal or metaphorical, Williams (*Paul's Metaphors*, 247) insightfully asserts that "Paul has used the images and language of sacrifice merely to aid us in understanding what Christ has achieved on our behalf." Williams (*Paul's Metaphors*), however, does not discuss Martyr Theology's influence on Paul.

47. Against Stuhlmacher, *Romans*, 58–68. In contrast to Stuhlmacher, see Becker, *Paul the Apostle*, 182–212, esp. 203–5. Becker states that Paul received a creedal statement in Rom 3:25 that had been influenced by 2 and 4 Maccabees.

48. Cf. de Jonge, "Jesus's Death for Others," 142–51; reprinted in *Jewish Eschatology*, 125–34; idem, *Christology*, 12–33. Schnelle (*Apostle Paul*, 442–54, esp. 446–51) asserts that Paul's "Christ died for us statements" came from Greco-Roman ideas. He cites 2 Macc 7:37–38; 4 Macc 6:27–29, and 4 Macc 17:21–22 as evidence of this. Still, he acknowledges that the Eucharistic traditions and LXX Isa 53:11–12 likewise influenced the early church's idea of the vicarious death of the righteous.

Martyr Theology's influence on Paul's conception of Jesus's death in Rom 3:25 is furthermore supported by the sacrificial language with which Paul surrounds ἱλαστήριον in Rom 3:21–26. Paul mentions sin (1:18–3:20, 23, 25–26), salvation (3:21–22, 3:24), redemption (3:24), offering of blood (3:25), and God's justice (3:25–26) in a context where he asserts that a human dies for others. Once more, Paul states that God offered Jesus as a ἱλαστήριον "by means of his blood" (3:25).[49] Προέθετο conveys sacrificial connotations in the context of Rom 3:23–26 (Exod 29:23; 40:23; 2 Macc 1:8),[50] because of its combination with blood in Rom 3:25. That ἱλαστήριον only refers to a human in 4 Macc 17:22 and in Rom 3:25 in any extant literature is striking. Hebrews 9:5 is the only other place in the NT where this term appears,[51] but there it clearly refers to the mercy seat. That 4 Macc 17:22 and Rom 3:25 are the only two texts in which ἱλαστήριον refers to a human's death as an atoning sacrifice and a saving event for others suggests the strong possibility that Martyr Theology shaped Paul's conception of Jesus's death.[52]

Since the articular use of ἱλαστήριον occurs in 4 Macc 17:22 in which ἱλαστήριον functions adjectivally and modifies an articular noun (cf. Rom 3:25), some scholars have argued that ἱλαστήριον does not refer

49. Contra Cranfield, *Romans*, 1:208–09. Cranfield disagrees that προέθετο means "to set forth." Instead, he argues for the meaning "to purpose/plan." He bases his argument on other occurrences of προέθετο in the NT that conveys the latter meaning (cf. Rom 1:13; 8:28; 9:11; Eph 1:9). In light of the verb πεφανέρωται ("to manifest") in Rom 3:21 and the verb ἀποκαλύπτεται ("to reveal") in Rom 1:17, both of which have δικαιοσύνη θεοῦ as their subject, προέθετο likely means "to set forth" in Rom 3:25. Additionally, ἔνδειξιν ("demonstration") in Rom 3:25–26 also supports the translation "set forth" for προέθετο. The latter verb likely, then, refers to Jesus's public death. Rightly Sanday and Headlam, *Romans*, 87; Dunn, *Romans*, 1:170; Moo, *Romans*, 170, 231–32; Schreiner, *Romans*, 178.

50. So Hultgren, *Paul's Gospel*, 56–57; recently Finlan, *Atonement Metaphors*, 140. Thielman (*Paul & the Law*, 56) argues that Martyr Theology did not shape Paul's conception of Jesus's death in Rom 3:25, but the Yom Kippur ritual did. Following Dunn (*Romans*, 1:170), Thielman argues that προέθετο "in connection with the shedding of Christ's blood is also reminiscent of the public display of sacrificial blood at the institution of the Mosaic Covenant in Exod 24:5–8."

51. Its cognate (ἱλασμός) occurs in the LXX and in the NT (Lev 25:9; Num 5:8; Ps 129:4; Ezek 44:27; 2 Macc 3:33; 1 John 2:2; 4:10).

52. Van Henten ("Tradition-Historical Background," 107) states that Rom 3:25 and 4 Macc 17:22 are the only texts in which ἱλαστήριον refers to "an expiation by the death of human beings." Van Henten also notes that 4 Macc 6:28–29 is closely connected to 4 Macc 17:21–22.

to the mercy seat and to the Yom Kippur ritual in Rom 3:25.[53] Others have maintained that ἱλαστήριον does not refer to sacrificial atonement at all in Rom 3:25.[54] Nevertheless, that Paul applies ἱλαστήριον to Jesus's death for others in Rom 3:25 is clear, although this use of the term is unprecedented in the NT. Yet, ἱλαστήριον occurs in both cultic (Lev 16:14–15) and in non-cultic (Ezek 43:14; 17, 20; Amos 9:1) contexts in the LXX. In cultic contexts, it refers to the mercy seat. The translators of the LXX often render ἱλαστηριον as mercy seat from the root כפר.[55] The former refers to the mercy seat in contexts in the LXX where priests atoned for sin through the sacrifice of blood (Leviticus 16–17; 25), where God commands Israel to put the ἱλαστήριον above the ark of the covenant in the holy of holies, the place where only the high priest could enter (Exod 25:17–20; 37:6), where God commands the priest to sprinkle blood over the ἱλαστήριον (Exod 25:18–22; 31:7; 35:12; 37:6–8; Lev 16:14–15), and in contexts where God appears above the ἱλαστήριον to show his acceptance of blood (Exod 25:22; Lev 16:2; Num 7:89).

At some level, God's public setting forth of Jesus as a ἱλαστήριον in Rom 3:25 alludes to Leviticus 16 and the Yom Kippur ritual (LXX Lev 16:14–16), because the concepts of sacrificial offering for sin, God's glory, and blood also occur in Leviticus 16.[56] However, the Yom Kippur ritual cannot exclusively provide the background behind Rom 3:25, because Paul argues that Jesus (a human) was sacrificed to save Jews and Gentiles, just as the martyrs (humans) were sacrificed to save Israel. Neither Jesus nor the martyrs were animals offered as atonement, and they were neither objects sprinkled with blood (e.g., the mercy seat).[57] Paul's purpose in calling Jesus a ἱλαστήριον was not to equate him with an object or to

---

53. Lyonnet and Sabourin (*Sin*, 159) do not espouse this view, but note that some have suggested that the absence of the article speaks against the mercy seat reading of ἱλαστήριον. For the above grammatical argument against the mercy seat, see Campbell, *Rhetoric*, 109.

54. So Talbert, *Romans*, 110–15.

55. For a discussion of כפר, see Finlan, *Atonement Metaphors*, 36–44.

56. So Thielman, *Paul & the Law*, 181.

57. Stowers (*A Rereading of Romans*, 210) unconvincingly argues against the mercy seat interpretation of ἱλαστριον, stating that "there had never been a כפרת in the Second Temple." Even if this assertion is correct, it does not disprove the mercy seat imagery, for Second Temple Jews would still have the mercy seat imagery in mind as they practiced the cult since they offered their sacrifices in compliance with the Torah (cf. 1 Maccabees 1).

elevate one cultic metaphor above another, but to present Jesus as an atoning sacrifice and a saving event for Jews and Gentiles (cf. Rom 3:20–26). Likewise, 4 Macc 17:22 refers to the martyrs' deaths as a ἱλαστήριον to affirm that they died as atoning sacrifices and as a saving event for Israel.[58] Therefore, just as ἱλαστήριον reveals that the martyrs were atoning sacrifices and a saving event for Israel in 4 Macc 17:22 (cf. 4 Macc 6:28–29), Paul employs ἱλαστήριον in Rom 3:25 to affirm that Jesus's death was an atoning sacrifice and a saving event for Jews and Gentiles.[59]

More to the point, ἱλαστήριον *only* refers to the mercy seat and *only* alludes to the Yom Kippur ritual in Heb 9:5 since the author is contrasting Jesus's high priestly ministry with the priests of the old covenant (Hebrews 9–10; cf. Leviticus 16). In Rom 3:25, it is not clear that the term exclusively alludes to the mercy seat or the Yom Kippur ritual,[60] although some of the same cultic vocabulary from Leviticus 16 occurs in Rom 3:23–26 (e.g., sin, blood, and death). It is plausible, however, from the context of Rom 3:21–26 that Martyr Theology shaped Paul's use of ἱλαστήριον and that he refers to Jesus's death as an atoning sacrifice and a saving event for Jews and Gentiles because of the parallels between Martyr Theology and Rom 3:21–26.[61]

---

58. See Deissmann, "ἱλαστήριον," 193–211; Campbell, *Rhetoric*, 102–230, esp. 107–13, 130–37, 219–28; Knöppler, *Sühne*, 112–17.

59. See Campbell, *Rhetoric*, 102–230, esp. 219–28. He argues for a late date of 4 Maccabees (ca. AD 135).

60. Against Fryer, "Hilastērion," 99–116, esp. 103–04; Hengel, *The Atonement*, 45; Bailey, "Mercy Seat;" recently Ben Ezra, *Yom Kippur*, 198–202. Interestingly enough, even Williams (*Jesus's Death*, 41) and Seeley (*The Noble Death*, 20–28, esp. 25–28) both assert that ἱλαστήριον in 4 Macc 17:22 and in Rom 3:25 refers to a propitiatory expiation. Cf. Seeley (*The Noble Death*, 27–28, esp. 28) where he states, "Paul does not speak of sins being forgiven or atoned for, but of reconciliation between hostile forces." Seeley makes this statement while explaining the meaning of Rom 5:9 and while arguing that Rom 5:9, like Rom 3:25, does not allude to the temple cult. Seeley's denial that Paul suggests that Jesus's death provided atonement for sin and accomplished reconciliation between warring sides in Rom 5:9–10 contradict his assertion that ἱλαστήριον in Rom 3:25 refers to a propitiatory expiation. Before his statement that Paul does not speak of sins being forgiven or atoned, Seeley states that "this suggestion of two warring sides is more akin to sin as a power opposed to God than to sin as a collection of individual transgressions." Finally, Seeley's thesis that Jesus's vicarious death should be understood in terms of a mimetic death suggests that he ultimately does not affirm that there was any notion of propitiatory expiation in Jesus's death in Paul's view (cf. Seeley, *The Noble Death*, 100–01).

61. Against Fryer, "Hilastērion," 103–04; Stowers, *A Rereading of Romans*, 206–30; Travis, "Christ," 21–38, esp. 27–30; Talbert, *Romans*, 110–15.

Stowers is correct to assert that there is nothing inherently sacrificial about the term ἱλαστήριον,[62] since it occurs in non-cultic (Ezek 43:14; 17, 20; Amos 9:1) and in cultic contexts (Leveticus 16). Stowers is wrong, however, to conclude from this that ἱλαστήριον does not carry sacrificial and soteriological overtones in Rom 3:25.[63] The context of and the cultic language in Rom 3:21–26 support that ἱλαστήριον should be interpreted as a reference to Jesus's death, that his death was an atoning sacrifice for the soteriological benefit of others, and that his atoning sacrifice dealt with sin,[64] for Paul employs ἱλαστήριον in a context in which he speaks of salvation (Rom 3:20–22, 26), sin (Rom 3:20, 23, 25), redemption (Rom 3:24), a human's death for others (Rom 3:25), and blood (Rom 3:25).[65]

Just as the martyrs offered their blood to God as a ransom as a ἱλαστήριον to deal with Israel's sin-problem and to save the nation from God's judgment (4 Macc 6:28–29; 17:21–22), Paul asserts that God set forth Jesus to be a ἱλαστήριον to deal with the sin-problem of Jews and Gentiles and to save them from God's judgment (Rom 3:24–26; 5:9).[66] As God's ἱλαστήριον, Paul suggests that Jesus's blood dealt with sin, and it publicly revealed God's righteous judgment against it (Rom 3:25–26),[67] just as the martyrs' blood dealt with sin and publicly revealed God's righteous judgment against it (cf. 4 Macc 6:28–29; 17:21–22). For example, Paul states in Rom 3:25b-26 that God offered Jesus as a ἱλαστήριον "by means of his blood for the demonstration of his righteousness because of

---

62. So Stowers, *A Rereading of Romans*, 210.

63. Ibid., 211. Cf. Versnel, "Making Sense of Jesus's Death," 221–94.

64. Rightly Nicole, "C.H. Dodd and the Doctrine of Propitiation," 117–57; Morris, *Apostolic Preaching*, 144–213; Tidball, *The Message*, 196; Hofius, "Erwägungen," 186–99.

65. Friedrich (*Verkündigung*, 78–79) remarks that αἷμα does not refer to Jesus's sacrificial death, but to his violent death.

66. Dunn ("Paul's Understanding of the Death of Jesus," 35–56) argues that Paul presents Jesus's death as an atoning sacrifice, but he opposes that Paul presents Jesus's death as a propitiatory substitute in Rom 3:25, for "substitution shares the defects of propitiation as a description of Jesus's death. It still tends to conjure up pagan ideas of Jesus's standing in man's place and pleading with an angry God. Substitution does not give sufficient prominence to the point of primary significance—that God was the subject: God provided Jesus as the hilastērion; God sent his Son as a sin-offering; God passed judgment on sin in the flesh; God was in Christ reconciling the world to himself." Cf. Hooker, "Interchange in Christ," 349–61.

67. Against Dodd, *The Bible and the Greeks*, 94. See, however, Josephus' use of ἱλαστήριον (*Ant.* 6.124; 8.112; 10.59).

the passing over of previously committed sins."[68] Regardless of how one understands the statement "previously committed sins" in 3:25b, the text clearly states that Jesus's blood was offered to deal with these sins since Paul asserts in 3:25 that God offered Jesus as a ἱλαστήριον "by means of his blood" and since he states twice (once in 3:25 and once in 3:26) that God offered Jesus "for the demonstration of his righteousness" (cf. 4 Macc 6:28–29; 4 Macc 17:21–22).

Δικαιοσύνη in 3:25b–26 is the same term as in 3:21–22. However, the term emphasizes salvation in 3:21–22, but in 3:25b–26 it emphasizes God's judgment since 3:21–22 states that God's righteousness is revealed to others by faith and since 3:25–26 asserts that God demonstrated his righteousness against sin in Jesus's death. Romans 3:25b–26 suggests, then, that one reason that God offered Jesus as a ἱλαστήριον was to judge sin. Romans 8:3 supports that God judged sin in Jesus's death, because Paul states in 8:3 that God sent Jesus concerning sin (περὶ ἁμαρτίας) to condemn sin in his flesh.[69] Therefore, just as the martyrs died as a ἱλαστήριον to remove God's wrath away from the nation (4 Macc 6:28–29; 4 Macc 17:21–22; esp. 17:22), Paul suggests that Jesus died as a ἱλαστήριον to remove God's wrath away from those for whom he died in order to deliver them from God's judgment of their sin.[70] Paul's discussion of God's wrath

---

68. Romans 3:25–26 introduces multiple exegetical difficulties with (1) διὰ, (2) πά ρεσις, and (3) ἀνοχη. For a discussion of these issues, see Kümmel's influential article ("*Paresis*," 1–13).

69. The phrase περὶ ἁμαρτίας (lit., "concerning sin") in Rom 8:3 is cultic and alludes to the OT's "sin-offering" since the LXX uses this phrase on numerous occasions to refer to the "sin-offering" in cultic contexts (cf. LXX Lev 5:6–11; 7:37; 9:2–3; 12:6, 8; 14:13, 22, 31; 15:15, 30; 16:3, 5, 9; 23:19; Num 6:11, 16; 7:16, 22, 28, 34; Ps 39:7) and since Paul uses the phrase in Rom 8:3 to refer to Jesus's death for sin. Cranfield (*Romans*, 1:382) rejects the reading of "sin-offering" for περὶ ἁμαρτίας in 8:3 in spite of the fact that the LXX often uses this phrase in cultic contexts to refer to a "sin-offering." Cranfield argues that a sacrificial reading is forced in 8:3 since the context of Paul's argument does not support a sacrificial interpretation. Contra Dunn, *Romans*, 1:422; Wright, *People of God*, 1:220–25; Bell, "Sacrifice and Christology in Paul," 1–27, esp. 5–8.

70. Williams (*Jesus's Death*, 40–41) affirms that ἱλαστήριον in Rom 3:25 speaks to both expiation and propitiation, but he argues that ἱλαστήριον primarily highlights the expiatory aspect of Jesus's death, because Paul states that God previously passed over sins in his patience in Rom 3:25–26a. Williams also states that propitiation should not be excluded from 4 Macc 17:22, but the expiatory aspect of the martyrs' deaths in 4 Macc 17:22 is primary.

in Romans 1–5 supports that God's offering of Jesus as a ἱλαστήριον ends his wrath against Jews and Gentiles.[71]

First, Paul states in 1:18 that the "wrath of God" currently abides upon all who suppress the truth. As he develops his argument in 1:19–32, Paul demonstrates that the abiding presence of God's wrath in the present age is seen in that God has given the immoral over to commit various sins. As a result, the unrighteous stand condemned before God's righteous judgment, and God will rightly judge them (2:1–3:5). Second, Paul states in 2:5 that Jews and Gentiles store up wrath for themselves because of their disobedience to God. The wrath to which Paul refers in 2:5 is God's eschatological wrath that he will dispense on the last day to all who re-ject the truth, for Paul refers to God's "kindness" in 2:4, and he contrasts God's "kindness" with God's "righteous revelation" and "judgment" in 2:5. The latter is a future event. Third, Paul subsequently refers to God's future judgment of Jews and Gentiles. They will receive their judgment in ac-cordance with their works in (2:6–11). He states that those who obey the truth will receive "eternal life" (2:7), but those who disobey the truth will receive "wrath," "anger," "affliction," and "distress" (2:7–8). The context sug-gests that God will personally impart this distress.

Fourth, Paul states in 3:5 that the "unrighteousness" of men demon-strates the "righteousness" of God in that God unleashes wrath upon those who reject him by suppressing his truth (cf. 1:18–32). This interpretation is certain, because Paul asks in 3:5 "God, who brings wrath, is not unrigh-teous—is he?" Paul responds in 3:6a with an emphatic "*no!*" (μὴ γένοιτο). The wrath to which Paul refers here is not the present, abiding wrath that currently resides upon all who suppress the truth (1:18–32), but to God's eschatological wrath that he will unleash on the last day upon all who suppress the truth about Jesus. Paul, thus, follows his statements in 3:5 about God's wrath with a question pertaining to God's future judgment of the world in 3:6b: "otherwise, how will God judge the world?" Paul's question is a corollary of his answer in 3:6 pertaining to whether God is unrighteous. Paul's line of reasoning is "if God is unrighteous because he condemns the unrighteous for unrighteousness, how will he judge the

---

71. Regarding God's wrath in Paul, compare Hanson, *Wrath*; Macgregor, "The Concept of the Wrath of God," 101–09; Dodd, *Romans*, 20–24, 77; Whitley, *St. Paul*, 61–72; Gorringe, *God's Just Vengeance*, 72; Lincoln, "From Wrath to Justification," 156; Gathercole, "Justified by Faith," 2:168.

world?" His answer in 3:9–18 is that God will condemn and judge both Jews and Gentiles for their unrighteousness, because he is righteous.

Fifth, Paul refers in 5:9–10 again to God's eschatological wrath that he will bestow upon those who suppress the truth and reject the gospel. Here he explicitly states that Jesus's blood/death is the means through which God will save Jews and Gentiles from his wrath and reconcile them to himself. That Jesus's death will deliver Jews and Gentiles from God's wrath suggests that they would be the objects of his eschatological fury apart from Jesus's blood/death, for Paul states that they will be saved from God's wrath through Jesus's blood/death in 5:9–10. According to 1:18–3:20 and 5:9–10, Jews and Gentiles need salvation from God's wrath (to which they are subject) because of their sin. Thus, according to Rom 3:25–26, God patiently and mercifully delayed his judgment against previously committed sins (cf. Rom 1:18–2:5) until God offered Jesus as a ἱλαστήριον for sin to be received by faith by means of his blood.[72]

Therefore, in Rom 3:23–26, Martyr Theology appears to have shaped Paul's conception of Jesus's death in the following ways: (1) Jesus died because of sin (Rom 3:23–26; cf. 2 Macc 7:32; 4 Macc 6:28–29; 17:21–22). (2) He was a payment of ransom for sin (Rom 3:24–25; cf. 4 Macc 6:28–29; 17:21–22). (3) He was a human sacrifice for sin (Rom 3:24–25; cf. 2 Macc 7:32–38; 4 Macc 6:28–29; 4 Macc 17:21–22). (4) He was a ἱλαστήριον (Rom 3:25; 4 Macc 17:22). (5) He was an offering for sin (Rom 3:25; 4 Macc 6:28–29; 17:21–22), and (6) he saved others from God's wrath because of sin (Rom 3:26; 2 Macc 5:1–8:5; 4 Macc 6:28–29; 4 Macc 17:21–22).

---

72. So Dunn, *Romans*, 1:173; Moo, *Romans*, 241; Fitzmyer, *Romans*, 352. I understand διὰ πίστεως to modify ἱλαστήριον. Against Johnson, "Romans 3:21–26," 89; idem, *Reading Romans*, 60. Cf. also Keck, "Jesus in Romans," 456. For examples where διὰ πίστεως modifies a noun, see Phil 3:9; 2 Tim 3:15. Both Bailey ("Mercy Seat," 204–07) and Finlan (*Atonement Metaphors*, 146–47) offer compelling arguments for taking ἐν τῷ αὐτου αἵματι with προέθετο instead of taking both ἐν τῷ αὐτου αἵματι and προέθετο with ἱλαστήριον. I understand the construction in the latter way. However, if opposing arguments better explain the syntax of Rom 3:25, my understanding of Rom 3:25 is still possible: God offered Jesus as a sacrifice of atonement for sin to provide a solution to the sin-problem and the problem of his wrath since Paul states that God set forth Christ to deal with the sin-problem. Although van Henten ("Tradition-Historical Background," 104–28) unconvincingly suggests that πίστις in Rom 3:25 refers to the faith of Jesus, he convincingly demonstrates that διὰ πίστεως ἐν τῷ αὐτου αἵματι was a common pattern that occurred in martyrological texts. Since Paul employs this construction in Rom 3:25, he likely was familiar with and was influenced by martyrological ideas when composing Rom 3:25.

Romans 5:6–11
Jesus's Death and Sin

The first connection between Martyr Theology and Paul's conception of Jesus's death in Rom 5:6–11 occurs in Rom 5:6.[73] In Rom 5:6, Paul states that "Christ died for the ungodly."[74] The latter statement suggests that Jesus died voluntarily and vicariously for Jews and Gentiles because of the active verb (ἀπέθανεν, "he died") and the prepositional phrase ὑπὲρ ἀσεβῶν ("for the ungodly").[75] The vicarious element of Jesus's death in Rom 5:6 is supported by Paul's later statements in 5:8–10 that Jesus's death for the ungodly accomplishes reconciliation and guarantees future salvation from God's wrath.

The context of Rom 5:6–11 does not support David Seeley's thesis that Paul only presents Jesus as an example to be imitated instead of a substitute for sin.[76] Seeley argues that Jesus's death was mimetic based on various Pauline texts.[77] He asserts that Jesus's death benefits others when they re-enact his death either literally or imaginatively.[78]

Romans 5:6–11 calls Seeley's thesis into question. Paul begins Rom 5:7 with a γάρ. The latter explains the previous statement in 5:6 that "Christ died for the ungodly." Romans 5:7 expresses that those who are righteous and good rarely (if ever) need someone to die for them. The ὑπέρ-formula occurs twice in 5:7 (ὑπὲρ δικαίου ["for a righteous person"]; ὑπὲρ τοῦ ἀγαθοῦ ["for a good person"]), and both occurrences modify the infinitive ἀποθανεῖν ("to die"). Such a construction does not emphasize the exemplary nature of Jesus's death, but the sacrificial and

---

73. Contra Shum (*Paul's Use of Isaiah in Romans*, 196) argues that Isa 53:8 was Paul's background behind his statements in Rom 5:6, 8b.

74. The Χριστὸς ἀπέθανεν ὑπέρ-formula or simply the ἀπέθανεν ὑπέρ-formula occurs more than once in the Pauline corpus. I do not interact with every verse in Paul that contains this formula. Rather, I have limited my investigation of vicarious atonement in Paul to those texts in which there appears to be additional data that demonstrate a martyrological influence on Paul.

75. Hengel (*Atonement*, 51) asserts that "the formula Χριστὸς ἀπέθανεν ὑπέρ . . . expressed the uniqueness of the death of Jesus and its soteriological significance over against the constant atoning sacrifices in the temple; in contrast to the universal atoning effect of the death of Jesus these latter only had a very limited force and therefore had to be repeated constantly."

76. Seeley, *The Noble Death*, 99–102.

77. Ibid.

78. Ibid.

soteriological nature of it, for the ὑπέρ-formula in 5:7 suggests that the righteous did not die for the righteous in their place in the Greco-Roman world, but the righteous died for the unrighteous to achieve their salvation (cf. Eur., *Iph.* 3–10; Pl., *Menexenus* 237–462; 2 Macc 7:32–38; 4 Macc 6:28–29; 17:20–22). Paul suggests here, then, that he was aware of righteous humans who died for the benefit of others, a practice that occurs in 2 and 4 Maccabees.

Paul's knowledge of such a practice is elucidated by the precision with which he speaks about it in Rom 5:7 when he says that it is quite rare for someone to die for a righteous man. Paul would only know this to be true if he were familiar with traditions that teach that righteous humans die for the benefit of others. Since this practice is prominent in Martyr Theology, since Paul's description of Jesus's death in Romans closely parallels Martyr Theology, and since both the martyrs and Jesus were humans and righteous Jews who died for the sins of others, Paul therefore alludes to Martyr Theology in Rom 5:7. For example, Eleazar and the martyrs, died for the sin of unrighteous Jews, and Jesus (a righteous Jew) died for the sin of unrighteous Jews and Gentiles (cf. 2 Macc 7:32–38; 4 Macc 6:28–29; 17:21–22; Rom 3:24–26; 5:6).

Romans 5:8–9 confirms Martyr Theology's influence on Paul's conception of Jesus's death. Paul states in Rom 5:8 that "God demonstrates his own love toward us that while we were sinners, Christ died for us." Here Paul accentuates the sacrificial nature of Jesus's death with an adversative δέ ("but") and another use of the ὑπέρ-formula (ὑπὲρ ἡμῶν, "for us") with the active verb ἀπέθανεν ("he died").[79] The ὑπέρ-formula in 5:8 identifies the "weak" in 5:6 as sinners. Moreover, the ὑπέρ-formula and the active verb ἀπέθανεν in 5:8 support Paul's point in 5:7 that ungodly sinners need a substitute, but that the righteous or good do not need one. That Jesus's death in 5:8 is both sacrificial and soteriological is sustained by the fact that his death deals with the sin-problem, reconciles the ungodly to God, and saves from God's wrath those for whom he dies.

Cilliers Breytenbach argues against interpreting Rom 5:8–10 in a sacrificial sense since neither blood nor death "connotes anything cultic or sacrificial."[80] But both the broad and immediate contexts of these verses suggest otherwise. In Rom 1:16–5:21, Paul speaks of Jesus's death

79. Contra Breytenbach, "Salvation of the Reconciled," 284–85.
80. Ibid.

in the context of sin, wrath, law, redemption, justification, ἱλαστήριον, blood/death, righteousness, salvation, and reconciliation. Furthermore, Paul includes himself in Rom 5:8 as part of those for whom Jesus died when he asserts that Jesus died "for us." The "us" in the phrase "for us" in 5:8 are the "weak" (ἀσθενῶν) and the "ungodly" (ἀσεβῶν) in 5:6. The clause "while we were sinners" and the clause "Christ died for us" in 5:8 affirm that Jesus's death was an atoning sacrifice and a saving event for others, because these statements suggest that Jesus died for the sins of others (cf. 2 Macc 5:1–8:5; 4 Macc 6:28–17:22).

Jesus's Blood, God's Wrath, and Reconciliation

Romans 5:9–11 further supports Martyr Theology's influence on Paul's conception of Jesus's death. In Rom 5:9, Paul states that Jesus's blood accomplishes justification, reconciliation, and future salvation from God's wrath: "Therefore, how much more because we have been justified by his blood, we will be saved through him from wrath." The martyrs' blood was the means through which salvation came to Israel and God's wrath ceased from the nation (2 Macc 5:1–8:5, esp. 7:32–38; 4 Macc 6:28–29; 17:21–22). Likewise, Paul states that Jesus's blood in Rom 5:9 is the means through which Jews and Gentiles are justified and will be saved from God's wrath.[81] The martyrs provided salvation for the nation by their deaths (4 Macc 6:28–29; 17:21–22), and Jesus provided salvation for the nations by his death (Rom 5:9–11). The martyrs removed God's wrath away from the nation by their deaths (2 Macc 5:1–8:5; 4 Macc 6:28–17:22), and Jesus removed God's wrath away from the nations by his death (Rom 5:9).

Regarding God's wrath in Rom 5:8, similar to Martyr Theology, his wrath refers to his personal anger that he displays against all who commit sin (cf. 2 Macc 5:20; 7:38). Paul supports this when he refers to the revelation of God's wrath as a future judgment against disobedience to the truth (Rom 2:5–5:10), and Paul's consistent use of ὀργη ("wrath") throughout Romans supports this (2:5; 3:5; 4:15; 9:22).[82] In Rom 5:9, however, Paul

81. For the sacrificial nature of Jesus's death in Rom 5:9, see Martin (*Reconciliation*, 147). Cf. Fitzmyer, "Reconciliation in Pauline Theology," 162–67. Fitzmyer asserts that there is an absence of allusions to expiation, propitiation, and sacrifice in the texts where Paul speaks of reconciliation.

82. Cf. also Eph 2:3; 5:6; Col 3:6; 1 Thess 1:10; 2:16; 5:9. For ὀργη as a reference to personal anger against someone, see the LXX of Gen 27:45; 39:19; Exod 4:14; Exod 32:10–12; Num 11:1, 10; 12:9; 14:34; 16:22; 17:11; 25:4; 32:14; Deut 11:17; 13:18; 29:19, 23; Jos 7:1.

states that Jesus's blood provides salvation from God's future wrath, because he states in 5:10 that Jesus's death for sin reconciles to God those for whom he died.[83]

Paul's assertions in 5:9–10 closely resemble Martyr Theology when he suggests that a human's sacrificial death for the sins of others saves them from God's wrath and reconciles them to God (cf. 2 Macc 5:1–8:5, esp. 7:32–38). Καταλλάσσω ("to reconcile") occurs in 2 Macc 7:33. Two forms of this verb occur in Rom 5:10 (κατηλλάγημεν and καταλλαγέ ντες).[84] Καταλλάσσω does not convey theological overtones outside of the Pauline corpus anywhere in the NT.[85] Καταλλάσσω neither occurs in a context that refers to the sacrificial and soteriological nature of a human's death anywhere in the NT outside of the Pauline corpus.[86] Similar examples, however, of the meaning that Paul attaches to καταλλάσσω in Rom 5:10 are found in Greco-Roman literature,[87] but Paul's use especially resembles 2 Macc 7:33.

Just as in 2 Macc 7:33, καταλλάσσω in Rom 5:10 refers to the accomplishment of peace between hostile parties (2 Macc 1:5; 7:33; 8:29).[88] These parties were once at enmity with one another. Because of Paul's argument in Rom 3:21–5:11, this peace is the inevitable result of justification by faith in Christ on the basis of Jesus's death (cf. Rom 3:21–5:1, 9).[89] Paul's dependence on Martyr Theology is evident in Rom 5:10 when

---

The authors of 1, 2, 3, and 4 Maccabees use ὀργή to refer to a personal manifestation of wrath: 1 Macc 1:64; 15:36; 2 Macc 5:20; 7:38; 8:5; 3 Macc 6:22; 4 Macc 9:32.

83. Porter (Καταλλάσσω, 158) acknowledges that Paul "equates being a sinner with being an enemy of God" in Rom 5:8–10.

84. The noun καταλλαγή ("reconciliation") occurs in Rom 5:11.

85. Breytenbach, *Versöhnung*, 40–83.

86. Prior to the work of Porter and Breytenbach, Dupont (*La reconciliation*) provides the most detailed investigation of the concept of reconciliation and related terms. He rightly affirmed that it is incorrect to deny that Paul's theology of reconciliation reflects 2 and 4 Maccabees. Cf. Käsemann, "Reconciliation," 49–64.

87. See Porter (Καταλλάσσω, 13–116). Although the meaning that Paul attaches to the word occurs elsewhere in Hellenistic literature, Breytenbach (*Versöhnung*, 40–83) argues that the terminology for reconciliation in relationships largely refer to the peace-treaty process in political or military contexts and that the terminology for reconciliation did not occur in religious contexts as a reference to the relationship between God and human beings in Hellenistic literature. Porter (Καταλλάσσω, 39–76) agrees.

88. Rightly Porter, Καταλλάσσω, 154; Morris, *Apostolic Preaching*, 225–32.

89. So Porter, Καταλλάσσω, 154. Michel, (*Römer*, 13), Barrett (*Romans*, 108), Sanday and Headlam (*Romans*, 129), and Porter (Καταλλάσσω, 155) are right to assert that

he states that "we were reconciled to God through the death of his son." Therefore, just as the martyrs' deaths provided reconciliation for those whom they died (2 Macc 5:1–8:5), Jesus's death provided reconciliation for those whom he died.[90] Thus, in Rom 3:21–26 and 5:6–10, Paul mentions the concept of sin and ransom with 4 terms that appear in Martyr Theology (ἱλαστήριον, Rom 3:25 and 4 Macc 17:22; αἷμα ["blood"], Rom 3:25; 5:9 and 4 Macc 6:29; ὀργη["wrath"], Rom 5:9 and 2 Macc 7:38; καταλλάσσω ["to reconcile"], Rom 5:10 and 4 Macc 7:21–22) and applies them to a human to express that his death was an atoning sacrifice and a saving event (Rom 5:9–10), just as Martyr Theology (4 Macc 17:21–22). This sort of a conflation suggests that Martyr Theology shaped Paul's conception of reconciliation.

Some scholars have strongly rejected that Martyr Theology shaped Paul's use of καταλλάσσω.[91] Their major arguments are as follows: (1) God is the recipient of reconciliation in 2 Macc 7:33, whereas Paul states that the ungodly are the recipients of reconciliation through Jesus's death in Rom 5:10–11.[92] (2) The martyrs prayed that God would receive their deaths as the means through which he would be reconciled again to the nation, but 2 Maccabees nowhere explicitly states that God answered this prayer. On the other hand, Paul clearly states that Jesus's death actually accomplished salvation and reconciled the ungodly to God.[93] (3) Paul's presentation of reconciliation is unique to him.[94] (4) Καταλλάσσω in

---

the themes of justification, peace, and reconciliation in Rom 5:1, 9–10 are overlapping metaphors that suggest different components of God's work of salvation.

90. Breytenbach (*Versöhnung*, 100) correctly states that reconciliation is not semantically related to atonement in the LXX. So also Fitzgerald, "Paul and Paradigm Shifts," 243. However, both Breytenbach and Fitzgerald incorrectly conclude that Jewish tradition provides no evidence that atonement could make reconciliation possible. Second Maccabees 5:1–8:5 and 4 Macc 6:28–17:22 speak against their conclusion.

91. For example, Martin, *Reconciliation*, 105–06; Porter, "Reconciliation," iii-iv, 175–78, 188–89; Grayston, "Atonement and Martyrdom," 250–63; Thrall, *Second Corinthians*, 429–39, esp. 429–30; Breytenbach, "Salvation of the Reconciled," 277.

92. Ibid.

93. Grayston, "Atonement and Martyrdom," 250–63.

94. So Breytenbach, *Versöhnung*, 40–83; Thrall, *Second Corinthians*, 429–39, esp. 429–30; Porter, "Reconciliation," iii-iv, 175–78, 188–89. Commenting on reconciliation in 2 Cor 5:18–20, Porter states that "God is the agent and goal of reconciliation, in the sense that he is the one who initiates reconciliation and the one toward whom it is directed, all through or by means of the work of Christ" (Καταλλάσσω, 143).

Paul is a relational metaphor between God and man, and this metaphor "spans the initial act of justification and the final act of salvation."[95]

(5) Paul speaks of reconciliation with passive verbs "to refer to God removing the cause of his own anger against man, an idea barely glimpsed by the Hebrews and unknown to the Greeks."[96] (6) Paul speaks of reconciliation as a process and condition in which the ungodly are positioned through Jesus's death.[97] (7) Similar to the Hebrew tradition, "Paul intensifies the emotional sense [of the term] to depict reconciliation as a personal and intimate relationship between two parties" (brackets mine).[98] (8) Paul's theology of reconciliation comes from Hellenistic literature in which reconciliation terminology neither refers to the relationship between God and humans nor occurs in religious contexts.[99] Instead, reconciliation only appears in Hellenistic literature in political or military contexts, and it does not refer to the OT cult.[100] (9) Paul's reconciliation theology does not "imply a change on the side of God."[101] Rather, Paul states that reconciliation is an expression of divine love toward the ungodly, whereas 2 Macc 5:1–8:5 suggests that God changed and therefore ended his wrath against Israel as a result of the martyrs' deaths.[102] Therefore, καταλλάσσω in Paul is distinct from its use in 2 Maccabees.[103]

The arguments against a martyrological background behind Paul's conception of reconciliation illustrate that some differences occur between the two traditions. The above arguments also demonstrate that Martyr Theology and Paul do not perfectly correlate with one another in their use of καταλλάσσω in reference to the death of a human for the soteriological benefit of others. Moreover, the arguments against a martyrological background behind Paul's use of καταλλάσσω demonstrate that he does not equate the martyrs' deaths and Jesus's death as qualitatively providing the same soteriological significance for others. Martyr

95. Porter, "Reconciliation," iii-iv, 175–78, 188–89.

96. Ibid.

97. Ibid.

98. Ibid.

99. So Breytenbach, *Versöhnung*, 40–83; idem, "Christus starb für uns," 447–75; idem, "Salvation of the Reconciled," 271–86. Cf. also Porter, Καταλλάσσω, 39–77.

100. Breytenbach, *Versöhnung*, 40–83.

101. Breytenbach, "Salvation of the Reconciled," 278.

102. Ibid.

103. Ibid.

Theology clearly states that the martyrs died for Israel (2 Macc 7:32–38; 4 Macc 17:21–22), but Paul states that Jesus died for Jews and Gentiles (Rom 1:16; 3:4–26; 5:6–10).

Still, strong contextual evidence supports that Martyr Theology provided the background behind Paul's use of καταλλάσσω in Rom 5:10 and that Martyr Theology possibly "provided the catalyst to the development of Paul's use of the category of reconciliation."[104] First, like ἱλαστήριον in 4 Macc 17:22 and in Rom 3:25, καταλλάσσω occurs in both 2 Macc 7:33 and in Rom 5:10 to refer to the soteriological benefit that a human's sacrificial death for sin achieves for those whom he dies (cf. 2 Cor 5:18–20). Second, the martyrs suffered and died for others because of sin in order to satisfy God's wrath against the nation (2 Macc 7:32–38).[105] Paul likewise asserts that Jesus suffered and died for the sins of others to satisfy God's wrath against Jews and Gentiles (Rom 5:8–9).[106] Third, the martyrs offered themselves to God in death to reconcile God to the nation. Second Maccabees 5:1–8:5, 4 Macc 6:28–29, and 17:21–22 suggest that their deaths achieved reconciliation for the nation, because 2 Macc 8:5 and 4 Macc 17:21–22 suggest that peace came to Israel both after and by means of the martyrs' deaths. Paul likewise states that Jesus's death provided reconciliation for others (cf. Rom 5:9–11).

Fourth, 2 Macc 7:33 states that God would be reconciled to individuals through the martyrs' deaths, and Paul states in Rom 5:10 that individuals would be reconciled to God through Jesus's death. However, the difference in the grammatical subject and the voice of the verbs in 2 Macc 7:33 and in Rom 5:10 is irrelevant, because both grammatical constructions affirm the same theological point: God reconciled two parties who were at enmity with him by means of a human's sacrificial death for those who needed reconciliation. Fifth, that Paul refers to humans as being reconciled to God in Rom 5:10 instead of saying that God was reconciled to humans is contextually necessary, because Paul emphasizes throughout Rom 5:1–11 that humans are the beneficiaries of justification by faith because of Jesus's death for them. Like 2 Macc 7:33, Paul uses καταλλάσσω to demonstrate that a human's death was an atoning sacrifice and a saving

---

104. So Marshall, "The Meaning of Reconciliation," 117–32, esp. 120–21, 129–30.

105. Ibid.

106. Ibid.

event for others, and he is the only NT writer to apply καταλλάσσω to Jesus's death for sin (cf. 2 Cor 5:15–20; Col 1:15–24).

Therefore, Martyr Theology's influence on Paul in Rom 5:6–11 is evident in at least three ways. (1) Paul states that Jesus (a human) died for the unrighteous (Rom 5:6–8; cf. 4 Macc 6:28–29; 4 Macc 17:20–22). (2) Paul states that Jesus's blood saves from God's wrath those for whom he died (Rom 5:9; cf. 4 Macc 6:28–29; 17:21–22). (3) Paul states that Jesus's death for others provides reconciliation between God and the ungodly (Rom 5:10–11; cf. 2 Macc 7:32–38).

2 Corinthians 5:14–21
Jesus's Death and Sin

Martyr Theology's influence on Paul is evident in 2 Cor 5:14–21 in at least two ways.[107] First, Paul states that Jesus died for sin. Second, he states that Jesus's death for sin reconciled Jews and Gentiles to God.

Second Corinthians 5:14–21 states that the reason that Paul endured sufferings for the sake of the gospel was because Christ's love compelled him to do so.[108] The phrase ἡ ἀγάπη τοῦ Χριστοῦ ("the love of Christ") echoes Paul's statement in Rom 5:8 regarding God's love. Furthermore, in both Rom 5:8 and in 2 Cor 5:14, Paul's focus is the love that God has shown to Jews and Gentiles through the death of his son.[109] In both Rom 5:8 and 2 Cor 5:14, Paul connects God's love to Jesus's death for sin and he asserts that his death achieved salvation for others.

In Rom 5:8, with the ὑπέρ-formula, Paul states that God has shown his love for the ungodly by sending Jesus to die for them. Likewise, with the ὑπέρ-formula in 2 Cor 5:14–15, Paul refers to Jesus's death for the ungodly and the soteriological benefits that it achieved for those for whom he died. Furthermore, just as in Rom 5:8, Paul highlights the voluntary nature of Jesus's death in 2 Cor 5:14–15 with the active verb (ἀπέθανεν) and the active participle (ἀποθανόντι).[110]

107. For discussion on various literary issues in 2 Corinthians, see Furnish, *II Corinthians*, 29–48; Betz, *2 Corinthians 8–9*, 3–36; Martin, *2 Corinthians*, xl–lii; Bultmann, *Second Corinthians*, 16–18; Georgi, *Opponents*, 9–14, 335–38; Harris, *Second Corinthians*, 127.

108. Similarly Harris, *Second Corinthians*, 418.

109. In Rom 5:8, however, Paul speaks of the love of God, whereas in 2 Cor 5:14 he speaks of the love of Christ.

110. Against Breytenbach, "Salvation of the Reconciled," 280–81. Breytenbach rightly

More to the point, Paul reveals a connection with Martyr Theology
in 2 Cor 5:19 and in 5:21, because he suggests that Jesus died as a sacrifice of atonement for sin to achieve salvation for others.[111] He states in
2 Cor 5:19 that God did not count transgressions against the transgressors, because Jesus died for them. In 2 Cor 5:21, Paul uses the concept
of sin-offering to refer to Jesus's death: "he appointed the one who did
not know sin to be sin for us."[112] Paul does not employ the normal grammatical construction in the LXX (περὶ ἁμαρτίας, lit. "concerning sin")
to convey the idea of sin-offering (cf. LXX Lev 5:6–7; 5:11; 7:37; 9:2–3;
12:6, 8; 14:13, 22, 31; 15:15, 30; 16:3, 5, 9; 23:19, Num 6:11; et al.; NT
Rom 8:3). Nevertheless, the concept of sin-offering is present in 2 Cor
5:21 for at least four reasons. (1) Second Corinthians 5:14–15 suggests
that Jesus's death was on behalf of others. (2) Second Corinthians 5:17–18
suggests that Jesus brought about a new creation and reconciliation for
those whom he died. (3) Second Corinthians 5:19 suggests that God does
not judge the transgressors for their transgressions, because Jesus died for
them. (4) God made Jesus sin for others so that they would become God's
righteousness in him (2 Cor 5:21).

The concept of sin-offering is sacrificial language and certainly alludes to the OT cult (cf. Leviticus 1–4) and Isa 53:10.[113] However, such
allusions do not prove that Martyr Theology was not Paul's background,

acknowledges that the "dying formula" so prominent in the Greek tradition influenced
Paul here. However, he goes too far when he states that this tradition did not suggest "the
categories of atonement or expiation." He suggests that the Greek tradition taught that
humans died as representatives for the city-state or for an individual to relieve that person or group from death. The Greek tradition did not teach that humans voluntary died
as substitutionary sacrifices. Breytenbach also wrongly implies that other traditions (e.g.,
the OT cult and 2 and 4 Maccabees) did not inform Paul's language in 2 Cor 5:14–21.
According to him, Paul only employs the Greek tradition. He adds a twist to it by using
this formula "to express how humanity benefits from Christ dying for all."

111. Thrall (*Second Corinthians*, 445–49) rejects Käsemann's thesis ("Reconciliation,"
52–57) that 2 Cor 5:18–21 is a fragment from a pre-Pauline hymn. She also rejects
Martin's thesis (*Reconciliation*, 94–95) that 2 Cor 5:18–21 contained a pre-Pauline tradition regarding reconciliation and that Paul adds an interpretive gloss to this tradition in
2 Cor 5:19b and 2 Cor 5:20c.

112. Hooker ("Interchange in Christ," 349–61; idem, "Interchange and Atonement,"
462–81) broadens Paul's statement in 2 Cor 5:21 (that God appointed Jesus to be sin)
to include the incarnation and the cross. Cf. Bell, "Sacrifice and Christology in Paul,"
14–15.

113. Against Thrall, "Salvation Proclaimed," 230; Breytenbach, "Salvation of the
Reconciled," 276."

because the concept of sin-offering also appears in 2 and 4 Maccabees. The martyrs died for the nation's sin (2 Macc 7:32–33). They prayed that their blood would provide cleansing for the nation's sin (4 Macc 6:28–29), and the author states that their blood purified Israel from its sin and saved the nation from God's wrath (4 Macc 17:21–22). In addition, Martyr Theology's influence on Paul in 2 Cor 5:19 and 5:21 is also evident by the appearance of καταλλάσσω. As in 2 Macc 7:33 and Rom 5:10, this verb occurs in a context that highlights the sacrificial death of a human that achieves salvation for those whom he dies.[114]

Paul elaborates in 2 Cor 5:15–17 the salvation that Jesus achieved for those for whom he died. He states that Jesus's death for others provides reconciliation for the nations. Having argued that God creates new life for Jews and Gentiles on the basis of Jesus's death (2 Cor 5:15–17), Paul states that God reconciles Jews and Gentiles to himself through Jesus in 2 Cor 5:18 (τὰ δὲ πάντα ἐκ τοῦ θεοῦ τοῦ καταλλάξαντος ἡμᾶς ἑαυτῷ διὰ Χριστοῦ).[115] The "all things" (τὰ πάντα) in 2 Cor 5:18 should be interpreted in light of the "on behalf of us all" (ὑπὲρ) for whom Jesus died in 2 Cor 5:14–15 and in light of the language of "new creation" in 2 Cor 5:17.[116] According to 2 Cor 5:17, new creation takes place within those who are in Christ as a result of Jesus's death for them.

The phrase διὰ Χριστοῦ "through Christ" in 2 Cor 5:18 supports that Jesus's death was vicarious, for Paul previously states that Jesus died for the soteriological benefit of others (2 Cor 5:14–15),[117] and because he subsequently states that God does not count transgressions against the transgressors in 2 Cor 5:19 since he appointed Jesus to be an offering for their sin (2 Cor 5:21; cf. Rom 8:3).[118] Second Corinthians 5:19 further supports a martyrological influence on Paul, because he again states that

114. That the Servant of Isaiah 52–53 provided Paul with the background for his reconciliation terminology, see Hengel, "Der Kreuzestod Jesu Christi," 75; Breytenbach, "Salvation of the Reconciled," 280–81; Beale, "Reconciliation in 2 Corinthians 5–7," 550–81; Hofius, "Erwägungen," 186–99; Kim, "2 Cor 5:11–21," 360–84, esp. 361–66; idem, *Origin*.

115. Breytenbach ("Salvation of the Reconciled," 282) limits ἡμᾶς to Paul. He states that God is the subject (i.e., everything has its source in God's action) of everything mentioned in 2 Cor 5:14–17.

116. Rightly Porter (καταλλάσσω, 130).

117. Porter, καταλλάσσω, 139. Contra Breytenbach, "Salvation of the Reconciled," 280.

118. For Jesus as sin-offering in Paul, see Bell, "Sacrifice," 8–26.

Jesus's death for others provides salvation for them: "namely,[119] God was by means[120] of Christ reconciling the world to himself in that he was not counting their transgressions against them and in that he set forth in us the word of reconciliation." Paul suggests here that God himself was reconciling those for whom Jesus died to himself by means of Jesus's death (cf. διὰ Χριστου in 2 Cor 5:18).[121] Paul and the other apostles were both recipients and instruments of God's reconciliation,[122] but both the efficacy and the means of reconciliation were accomplished by virtue of Jesus's death.[123] Therefore, just as the martyrs died to accomplish reconciliation between God and the nation, Paul states that Jesus died to reconcile Jews and Gentiles to God (cf. 2 Macc 5:1–8:5; 4 Macc 6:28–29; 17:20–22).[124]

Galatians 1:4, 3:10–14

Martyr Theology's influence on Paul is apparent in Galatians in 1:4 and in 3:10–14.[125] Galatians 1:4 states that Jesus "gave himself for our sins, so that he would deliver us from this present evil age."[126] At least four martyrological components occur in Gal 1:4. (1) Jesus voluntarily gave himself in death (cf. 2 Macc 7:32–39; 4 Maccabees 6–7). (2) His death was vicarious. (3) He died for sins (cf. 2 Macc 7:32; 4 Macc 6:28–29). (4) The goal of his death was to achieve salvation for others (cf. 4 Macc 17:21–22).

119. I understand ὡς ὅτι epexegetically. So also Porter, Καταλλάσσω, 132. Against Schlatter, *Paulus*, 566; Bachmann, *die Korinther*, 266.

120. Some have challenged the accuracy of reading ἐν Χριστῷ as "by means of Christ" instead of "in Christ" because of the construction θεὸς ἦν ἐν Χριστω κόσμον καταλλάσσων ἑαυτῷ. Porter (*Verbal Aspect,* 453) responds to this challenge: "except for connectives, εἰμί and the participle may be separated only by adjuncts or complements of the participle as predicate."

121. At least three views exist as to how one should understand the syntax of 2 Cor 5:19, all of which contain an element of theological truth. For a concise discussion of each view, see Porter, Καταλλάσσω, 133–36. Recently Bell, "Sacrifice and Christology in Paul," 9–11; Fee, *Pauline Christology*, 197–98.

122. The phrases "word of reconciliation" in 2 Cor 5:20 and "ministry of reconciliation" in 2 Cor 5:18 refer to the apostolic gospel.

123. Rightly Porter, Καταλλάσσω, 135.

124. See Fitzmyer, *Gospel*, 164–66.

125. Against Longenecker, *Galatians*, 7. He states that Paul's statement in Gal 1:4 likely derives from Isa 53:5–6 and 53:12.

126. Longenecker (*Galatians*, 7) states that Gal 1:4 is an early confessional statement and that the words "who died for our sins" are similar to "Christ died for our sins" in 1 Cor 15:3. Cf. Martyn, *Galatians*, 95.

Galatians 3:10–14
Jesus's Death as a Ransom

Martyr Theology's influence on Paul's conception of Jesus's death is especially evident in Gal in 3:10–14.[127] Paul presents Jesus's death as a ransom for sin that achieves salvation. Galatians 3:10–14 cites multiple OT texts, but a connection between Martyr Theology and Gal 3:13 is nevertheless present. Paul states in Gal 3:13 that Jesus's death redeems those under the law from the law's curse. The verb ἐξηγόρασεν ("he redeemed") in Gal 3:13 is conceptually related to the noun ἀντίψυχον ("ransom") in 4 Macc 6:29 and 4 Macc 17:22,[128] for both terms convey the idea that a price was paid for the benefit of another and that the payment achieved salvation for others (cf. 1 Cor 6:20; 7:23).[129] In 2 and 4 Maccabees, the price for salvation was the martyrs' deaths (4 Macc 17:21–22), and the soteriological benefits achieved by their deaths were reconciliation between God and the nation, purification for the land, and deliverance from God's wrath (2 Macc 7:33; 4 Macc 6:28–29; 17:21–22).[130] In Gal 3:13, Jesus's death was the price that was paid for the redemption, and the soteriological benefits achieved by it for those whom he died were deliverance from the curse of the law and Gentile-reception of the Abrahamic blessing (Gal 3:13–14).

Ephesians 1:7
Jesus's Death and Salvation

Paul shows a connection with Martyr Theology in Eph 1:7 by arguing that Jesus's death provides redemption, purification, ransom, and reconciliation for others.[131] In his doxology in Eph 1:3–14, Paul states that Jesus's

---

127. Contra Davis (*Christ as Devotio*), who argues that the Roman *devotio* was Paul's background behind Gal 3:13. Against McLean, "Christ as a Pharmakos," 187–207.

128. For evidence that ἐξαγοράζω and ἀγοράζω refer to a ransom, see Gen 41:57; 42:5, 7; 43:4, 22; 44:25; 47:14; Deut 2:6; 1 Chr 21:24; 2 Chr 1:16; 34:11; 2 Esd 20:32; Tob 1:13–14; 1 Macc 12:36; 13:49; Sir 20:12; 37:11; Isa 24:2; 55:1; Jer 44:12; Bar 1:10; Ep. Jer. 1:24. For a detailed analysis of the Greek terms for redemption, see Morris, *Apostolic Preaching*, 15–64.

129. Against Martyn, *Galatians*, 317.

130. Although he does not speak of a martyrological influence on Paul in Gal 3:13, Longenecker (*Galatians*, 122) acknowledges that Paul probably employs a pre-Pauline Jewish Christian formula that originally spoke of "Jesus's death as a redeeming and atoning self-sacrifice."

131. For a discussion on the authorship of Ephesians, see Hoehner, *Ephesians*, 1–60.

death provides redemption. He states in 1:7 that "in him,[132] we have re-demption by means of his blood." Paul's term for redemption in 1:7 is the same term that he uses in Rom 3:24 (ἀπολύτρωσις). As I argued above, ἀπολύτρωσις in Eph 1:7 is conceptually related to ἀντίψυχον ("ransom") in 4 Macc 6:29 and 17:21, because both terms in their respective contexts suggest that a human's blood (i.e., his death) is the required price for the specific soteriological benefit. The phrase "by means of his blood" in Eph 1:7 confirms that the price that Jesus paid to achieve re-demption was his life.[133] Like the blood of the martyrs (4 Macc 6:28–29 and 17:21–22), Jesus's blood was the required price for redemption. Paul explains in Eph 1:7 that this redemption for which Jesus's blood paid was "the forgiveness of sins."[134] Therefore, Jesus's blood purchased redemption because it was the payment of ransom offered for sin and the necessary price to achieve salvation,[135] just as the martyrs' blood was a payment of ransom for Israel's sin and the necessary price to achieve the nation's sal-vation (cf. 4 Macc 6:28–29; 17:21–22).[136]

Ephesians 2:11–22
Reconciliation

Martyr Theology's influence on Paul is evident in Eph 2:11–22. In the latter text, he states that Jesus's blood both reconciles Jews and Gentiles to God and to one another (cf. 2 Macc 5:1–8:5; 4 Macc 6:28–17:22), and Paul connects reconciliation with Jesus's blood and salvation (Eph 2:13; cf. 4 Macc 6:28–29; 17:21–22).[137] The verb καταλλάσσω ("to rec-oncile") appears in 2 Macc 7:33, Rom 5:10, and 2 Cor 5:18–20, but it is not the term that Paul uses in Eph 2:16. Instead, he uses a cognate verb

---

132. The preposition ἐν does not denote agency here, but it is spherical. It highlights the close relationship between Jesus and the redeemed. Rightly Hoehner, *Ephesians*, 205.

133. Similarly Hoehner, *Ephesians*, 206.

134. So Hoehner, *Ephesians*, 207.

135. Similarly Marshall, "The Development," 165. Against Hill, *Greek Words*, 73–74; Lincoln, *Ephesians*, 28.

136. Contra Hoehner (*Ephesians*, 206–207) who argues for an OT cultic background behind Eph 1:7.

137. For a history of research of ἀποκαταλλάσσω, see Michl, "Die Versöhnung," 442–62. For a history of interpretation of Eph 2:11–22, see Rader, *The Church and Racial Hostility*.

(ἀποκαταλλάσσω) in Eph 2:16, but it too refers to reconciliation.[138] Moreover, the concept of reconciliation explicitly appears throughout Paul's argument in Ephesians 2. Ephesians 2 argues for unity between Jews and Gentiles in the church. Ephesians 2:1–10 argues that Jews and Gentiles were dead in trespasses and sins prior to God's work in their lives. Then, Paul infers in Eph 2:11–22 that Jews and Gentiles should be united to one another in the church, because God has shattered the wall between Jews and Gentiles, erected by the law (*Ep. Arist.* 142), through Jesus's death (Eph 2:11–22).

Similar to the salvation-historical shift that Paul presents in Rom 3:21 with the words "but now," Paul offers an emphatic antithesis in Eph 2:13. The antithesis accentuates that Jews and Gentiles relate differently to God and to another after Jesus's death for their sin than they did before it. They have been reconciled to God and to one another by faith through the cross of Christ: "but now, by means of Christ Jesus you who were formerly far off were brought near by means of the blood of Christ." The phrase "those who were far off" in Eph 2:13 refers specifically to Gentiles, because during the old covenant Gentiles were separated from the promises that God made with Israel since they were not ethnic Jews (Eph 2:11–12). Because of Jesus's death for Jews and Gentiles, the Mosaic Law has been abolished (Eph 2:13–15). Consequently, Jews and Gentiles are reconciled to God and to one another because of Jesus's death. As a result, both groups inherit in Christ soteriological promises. Thus, as in 2 and 4 Maccabees, a human's death accomplishes reconciliation for those whom he dies.

Colossians 1:13–23; 2:13–14
Jesus's Death, Reconciliation, and Purification

Martyr Theology's influence on Paul is evident in Colossians 1–2 by observing at least two soteriological connections between the latter and Martyr Theology.[139] First, Paul states that Jesus's death provides recon-

---

138. Porter (Καταλλάσσω, 163) states that "there does not appear to be any earlier attested usage of ἀποκαταλλάσσω than in Col 1:20, 22 and Eph 2:16." This confirms, says Porter, that the earliest usage of ἀποκαταλλάσσω appears in Paul if he wrote Colossians and Ephesians. Büchsel ("ἀποκαταλλάσσω," 258) states that ἀποκαταλλάσσω was a Pauline creation.

139. The origin of Col 1:15–20 has been debated in NT studies. The debate has consisted of whether the passage was original or whether it was an interpolation. Most

ciliation with God for those for whom he died (Col 1:20–22; cf. 2 Macc 5:1–8:5). Second, he asserts that Jesus's death cleanses sin and achieved forgiveness for those for whom he died (Col 2:13–14; cf. 2 Macc 5:1–8:5; 4 Macc 6:28–17:22).

Paul speaks of Jesus's death in Col 1:14 with virtually the same grammatical construction as in Eph 1:7 (ἐν ᾧ ἔχομεν τὴν ἀπολύτρωσιν διὰ τοῦ αἵματος αὐτοῦ τὴν ἄφεσιν τῶν παραπτωμάτων κατὰ τὸ πλοῦτος τῆς χάριτος αὐτου; Col 1:14: ἐν ᾧ ἔχομεν τὴν ἀπολύτρωσιν τὴν ἄφεσιν τῶν ἀπολύτρωσιν). "Son" in Col 1:13 is the antecedent to "in whom" in Col 1:14.[140] In Col 1:13, Paul states that God has provided salvation through Jesus's death. Paul asserts in Col 1:13 that God "delivered us from this present evil age and placed us into the kingdom of his beloved son." Paul says in Col 1:14 that this salvation is redemption and that the redemption is "the forgiveness of sins."

Paul's reference to the death of Jesus as a means of reconciliation in Col 1:20 is especially pertinent for my thesis. The syntax of Col 1:20 is difficult because of the infinitive ἀποκαταλλάξαι and because of the participle εἰρηνοποιήσας. The absence of a verb in Col 1:20 adds to the syntactical difficulty, but both the infinitive and the participle should be construed with the main verb εὐδόκησεν ("to bless") in Col 1:19,[141] since the nearest main clause occurs with the preceding verb in Col 1:19. Colossians 1:19–20 composes a ὅτι-clause that grounds Col 1:17–18. Thus, Paul states that Jesus is before all things; God holds all things together in him; he is the beginning and the firstborn from the dead, so that he would be first in all things, "because he [God] became well-pleased to cause all the fullness to dwell in him and [he became well-pleased] to reconcile all things in him, whether things upon the earth or things in heaven, because he made peace through the blood of his cross."[142]

---

scholars accept Col 1:15–20 as an interpolation. For example, see Robinson, "A Formal Analysis of Col 1:15–20," 270–87; Käsemann, "A Primitive Christian Baptismal Liturgy," 149–68; Sanders, *Christological Hymns*, 12–14, 75–87; Vawter, "The Colossians Hymn and the Principle of Redaction," 62–81; Lohse, *Colossians and Philemon*, 41–46; Martin, "Reconciliation and Forgiveness in Colossians," 109–16; idem, *Reconciliation*, 111–26; Burger, *Schöpfung und Versöhnung*, 3–79; Dunn, *Christology*, 187–94.

140. So O'Brien, *Colossians, Philemon*, 28.

141. Against Porter, Καταλλάσσω, 173–74.

142. See the Greek text of Col 3:19–20.

Paul clarifies the scope of God's universal reconciliation of all things through the death of Jesus with an explicative καὶ in Col 1:21–22 and with an adversative clause in Col 1:22: "That is, you were formerly estranged and enemies by means of your evil works with respect to understanding, but now he reconciled [you] by means of the body of his flesh through death so that you would be holy and blameless and above reproach in his presence." God's reconciliation of all things through Jesus's blood in Col 1:19–20 includes the eschatological redemption for which all of creation eagerly awaits (cf. Rom 8:23). However, in Col 1:22 reconciliation specifically refers to the promise of salvation that Jesus has accomplished by dying for sin.

Paul expresses in Col 1:22 that Jesus's death achieves salvation in that it reconciled the Colossians to God, so that they would be holy and blameless. Paul emphasizes the cathartic nature of Jesus's death in Col 2:13–14: "and while you were dead in transgressions and in your body of flesh, God made you alive with [Jesus], because he freely forgave all transgressions against us and he wiped away our record of debts with the decrees, which [i.e., the record of debts] were against us, and he took them away from the midst in that he nailed them to the cross." Thus, similar to the martyrs' deaths (2 Macc 7:32–38; 4 Macc 6:28–29; 4 Macc 17:21–22), Jesus's death purified the sins of others and reconciled to God those for whom he died.

1 Timothy 2:6
Jesus's Death as Ransom

Martyr Theology's influence on Paul is evident in 1 Timothy. Paul states in 1 Tim 2:6 that Jesus voluntarily died as a ransom for sin to save those for whom he died (2 Macc 7:32–38; 4 Macc 6:28–29; 17:21–22). The participial phrase ὁ δοὺς ἑαυτον ("the one who gave himself") reveals the voluntary nature of Jesus's death.[143] The voluntary aspect of Jesus's death is also evident in 2:6 since the participle appears in the active voice and takes as its direct object the reflexive pronoun ἑαυτον.[144] Along with the ὑπέρ-formula, the former construction suggests that Jesus's death was both voluntary and vicarious.[145]

---

143. See Towner, *Timothy and Titus*, 183.
144. Ibid.
145. Ibid., 185.

Furthermore, the noun ἀντίλυτρον in 1 Tim 2:6 has a conceptual relationship with ἀπολύτρωσις in Rom 3:24, Eph 1:7, and Col 1:14 and with ἀντίψυχον in 4 Macc 6:29 and 17:21, because each term in its respective contexts suggests that a human's death for others was the required price to achieve soteriological benefits for those whom the human died. The latter point is not obvious in 1 Tim 2:6 alone, but the context of 2:6 supports the above interpretation of ἀντίλυτρον. For example, Paul calls God a "Savior" in 1 Tim 2:3 with the term σωτῆρος, and he suggests that God desires all men to be saved with the cognate infinitive σωθῆναι in 1 Tim 2:4. In 1 Tim 2:5, Paul states that Jesus is the mediator between God and man. Thus, 2:6 expresses that Jesus's death for others was the necessary price for the salvation that God (the Savior) provides. Therefore, similar to the martyrs' deaths (2 Macc 5:1–8:5; 4 Macc 6:28–29; 17:21–22), Paul suggests that Jesus's death provides salvation for others, because his death was a ransom.

Titus 2:14
Purification and Salvation

Finally, Martyr Theology's influence on Paul is present in Titus. Titus 2:14 states that Jesus "gave himself for us, so that he would redeem us from all lawlessness and purify for himself a special people, who are zealous for good works." Similar to the construction ὁ δοὺς ἑαυτὸν ἀντίλυτρον ὑπὲρ πάντων in 1 Tim 2:6, Paul asserts that Jesus's death was an atoning sacrifice and a saving event in Titus 2:14 in ways that suggest a dependence on Martyr Theology, because he states that (1) Jesus voluntarily gave himself in death (cf. 4 Macc 6:28–29). (2) He states that Jesus vicariously died for others (2 Macc 7:32–38; 4 Macc 6:28–29; 17:21–22).[146] (3) He asserts that Jesus died to redeem/ransom the ungodly (4 Macc 6:28; 17:21–22). (4) Paul states that Jesus died to purify the ungodly (4 Macc 6:28–29). I will elaborate the latter parallel with Martyr Theology.

Eleazar prayed in 4 Macc 6:28–29 that God would use his blood to provide purification (καθάρσιον) for Israel. Paul states in Titus 2:14 that Jesus died so that he would purify (καθαρίσῃ) sin. Eleazar and the other martyrs voluntarily and vicariously died to redeem, save, and purify Israel from their sin (2 Macc 7:32–38; 4 Macc 6:28–29; 17:21–22). Paul states

---

146. Mounce (*Pastoral Epistles*, 431) agrees that Titus 2:16 speaks to the vicarious nature of Jesus's death, but Mounce does not affirm a martyrological influence on Paul.

that Jesus voluntarily and vicariously died to redeem a people and to purify them from their sin.

CONCLUSION

The following similarities and parallels between Martyr Theology and Paul's conception of Jesus's death support that Martyr Theology shaped Paul's conception of Jesus's death. (1) The martyrs and Jesus died to save others (4 Macc 17:21–22; Rom 5:9–10). (2) The martyrs' blood and Jesus's blood was the means by which salvation was accomplished for others (4 Macc 6:28–29; Rom 3:25). (3) Martyr Theology and Paul use καταλλά σσω and ἱλαστήριον along with other sacrificial language to describe the soteriological significance of a human's death for others (2 Macc 7:33; 4 Macc 17:22; Rom 3:25; 5:10; 2 Cor 5:18–19). (4) Martyr Theology and Paul suggest that a human served as a ransom to achieve salvation for others (4 Macc 6:29; 17:21; Rom 3:24–25; 1 Tim 2:6; Titus 2:14). (5) The martyrs and Jesus died both because of and for the sins of others (2 Macc 7:32–38; 4 Macc 6:28–29; 17:21–22; Rom 3:23–26; 5:6–10; 2 Cor 5:19, 21). (6) The martyrs and Jesus died to remove God's wrath away from those for whom they died (2 Macc 7:32–38; 4 Macc 6:28–29; 17:21–22; Rom 3:25–26; 5:9–10). (7) The martyrs and Jesus died to provide reconciliation for those for whom they died (2 Macc 5:1–8:5, esp. 7:33; Rom 5:9–11; 2 Cor 5:15–21). (8) The martyrs and Jesus were offerings for sin (2 Macc 7:32; 4 Macc 6:28–29; 17:21–22; Rom 3:23–26; 5:8–9; 2 Cor 5:14–21).

5

Conclusion

PAUL PRESENTS JESUS'S DEATH as an atoning sacrifice and as a saving event for Jews and Gentiles, because Martyr Theology shaped his conception of Jesus's death. Chapter 1 introduced the thesis and presented a history of research of the relevant scholars and their most important work pertaining to the thesis. Chapter 2 argued that 2 and 4 Maccabees present the deaths of the Jews martyrs as atoning sacrifices and as a saving event for Israel with language that resembles the Greco-Roman world, the OT cult, and Isaiah 53. Chapter 3 argued that with the possible exception of Isaiah 53, the sort of human sacrifice that appears in 2 and 4 Maccabees and in Paul is not present in any one of the OT texts that I investigated.

Chapter 4 argued that Paul conceived of Jesus's death as an atoning sacrifice and as a saving event for Jews and Gentiles, because Martyr Theology shaped his conception of Jesus's death. Chapter 4 also endeavored to highlight the specific parallels with and similarities between Martyr Theology and Paul's conception of Jesus's death that warrant the thesis that Martyr Theology shaped his conception of Jesus's death. This final chapter offers some conclusions and implications in light of the thesis that has been argued. The attempt is made here to tie together the arguments from chapters 2–4.

THE ROLE OF GRECO-ROMAN IDEAS AND THE OT CULT IN PAUL'S CONCEPTION OF JESUS'S DEATH

To affirm that Martyr Theology shaped Paul's conception of Jesus's death does not suggest that Greco-Roman ideas, the OT cult, or Isaiah 53 were not a background for Paul. That the OT served as an important background behind Paul's conception of Jesus's death seems incontrovertible since his writings clearly reveal a connection with the OT scriptures. For example,

Paul states that "Jesus died for our sins according to the Scriptures" (1 Cor 15:3) and that Jesus was "our Passover lamb" (1 Cor 5:7).

My thesis affirms that Martyr Theology shaped Paul's conception of Jesus's death in addition to Greco-Roman ideas, the OT cult, and Isaiah 53. This affirmation suggests that more than one stream of tradition was available for Paul from which he could have borrowed to help formulate an interpretation of Jesus's death for others. It is my view, then, that Paul used each tradition and applied each tradition to Jesus's death in his own way to present his death as an atoning sacrifice and a saving event for Jews and Gentiles, but that he especially relied on Martyr Theology to formulate his conception of Jesus's death. The probability of this thesis is strengthened by the close parallels and similarities between Martyr Theology and Paul's conception of Jesus's death in his letters.

THE SOTERIOLOGICAL VALUE OF JESUS'S DEATH FOR JEWS AND GENTILES

Martyr Theology's influence on Paul's conception of Jesus's death does not undermine the soteriological value of Jesus's death for Jews and Gentiles. As I suggested in chapter 4, Tom Holland has argued that to give credence to a martyrological influence on Paul's conception of Jesus's death is in essence to deny substitutionary atonement. His critique would be an accurate assessment of my thesis if I both argued that (1) the authors of 2 and 4 Maccabees did not present the deaths of the martyrs as atoning sacrifices and as a saving event for Israel or (2) if (while arguing the preceding point) I maintained that Martyr Theology shaped Paul's conception of Jesus's death.

As I suggested in chapters 1, 2 and 4, Sam K. Williams, David Seeley, and Stanley K. Stowers have argued that the martyrs were not atoning sacrifices that saved Israel. The thesis argued in this monograph has been different from the above scholars. I by no means deny that Paul suggests that Jesus died as a sacrifice to achieve salvation for Jews and Gentiles. My exegesis of 2 and 4 Maccabees and of the key texts in Paul in chapters 2 and 4 tested the readings of Williams, Seeley, and Stowers. The exegesis supports that Martyr Theology presents the deaths of the Jewish martyrs as atoning sacrifices and as a saving event for Jews and that Paul applied Martyr Theology's sacrificial theology to Jesus' death to present his death as an atoning sacrifice and as a saving event for Jews and Gentiles.

ANIMAL SACRIFICES IN THE OT VERSUS HUMAN
SACRIFICE IN MARTYR THEOLOGY AND IN PAUL

One of the clearest points of disjunction between the OT cult and Paul's conception of Jesus's death is animal sacrifice. In the OT cult, Yahweh commands Israel to offer animals as atonement (e.g., Leviticus 16). The animals were not efficacious for atonement unless Israel and the priests offered them with an obedient and repentant heart (Psalm 51). This could explain why Yahweh rejects Israel's sacrifices on more than one occasion, for Israel often worshipped Yahweh with their lips and with their offerings, but rejected him with their hearts (cf. Isaiah 1).

The author of Hebrews explicitly adds an additional reason why the OT cultic sacrifices cannot alone sufficiently explain Paul's conception of Jesus's death: OT sacrifices did not atone for sins (Heb 10:1–10; cf. 8:1–10:18). The inability of the OT cultic sacrifices to atone for sin was why Israel celebrated the Yom Kippur ritual every year (cf. Leviticus 16 with Heb 8:1–10:18). Even Paul alludes to the insufficiency of the OT sacrificial system in providing atonement for sin in Rom 3:25–26 when he states that God set forth Jesus as a ἱλαστήριον to deal with those sins that he previously passed over during the Mosaic Covenant.

However, one could argue that the OT was the most probable background behind Paul's conception of Jesus's death in spite of the fact that the cult offered animals as atonement and that Paul states that Jesus died as atonement, because Paul could have typologically interpreted the OT cult in light of Jesus. Nevertheless, to suggest that a typological hermeneutic was the foundation underneath Paul's OT exegesis does not disprove that Martyr Theology shaped Paul's conception of Jesus's death, for one must still explain why his presentation of Jesus's death has so many similarities and parallels with Martyr Theology.

A DEATH FOR ISRAEL VERSUS A DEATH
FOR JEWS AND GENTILES

Just as there is an element of disjunction between OT cultic sacrifices and Jesus's death in Paul, there is also a point of disconnect between the deaths of the martyrs and Jesus's death: viz., the martyrs died as sacrifices for Israel's salvation, whereas Paul states that Jesus died as a sacrifice of atonement for the salvation of Jews and Gentiles. This fundamental difference might initially seem to counter my thesis. But it would only counter my thesis (1) if I would have argued that Paul applied every aspect of Martyr Theology to Jesus's death apart from any other metaphor or model or apart from his reconstruction of the tradition, (2) if I would have argued that Martyr Theology determined Paul's conception of Jesus's death instead of the thesis that Paul borrowed from the concepts and ideas in Martyr Theology to formulate his conception of Jesus's death, or (3) if Martyr Theology does not teach that the martyrs died as atoning sacrifices and as a saving event for Israel. The thesis argued in this monograph affirms that Paul used different metaphors, language, and imagery from multiple traditions to convey the message that he wanted to convey about Jesus's vicarious and sacrificial death for Jews and Gentiles, but Martyr Theology was foundational.

MARTYR OR GOD CRUCIFIED?

Does Martyr Theology's influence on Paul suggest that he thought that Jesus was nothing more than an innocent sufferer? Martyr Theology shaped Paul's conception of Jesus's death. However, Paul's purpose in writing about Jesus's death was not martyrological, but soteriological and theological. That is, his purpose was not to exhort his readers to imitate Jesus's death (contra Seeley's thesis), though Paul would agree that Christians should imitate Christ. His purpose was to articulate the nature and significance of Jesus's death with vocabulary and metaphors that his Hellenistic-Jewish audience would have understood.

Often NT scholars read Paul with the assumption that his readers were well schooled in the OT Scriptures. Although this assumption might be true of the Pauline audiences in general, I would hardly affirm that Paul's readers universally knew equally well the OT Scriptures. It would, then, make sense for Paul to present Jesus's death in known vocabulary and with the help of certain traditions that represent the ideas (i.e., Greco-Roman, OT cultic, and martyrological) that were prominent during the time he wrote his letters. These ideas would have enabled both Jews and Gentiles in a Greco-Roman and Hellenistic world to understand more precisely the magnitude of Jesus's death for the nations.

SUGGESTIONS FOR FURTHER STUDY

This monograph has not offered the final word regarding the background behind Paul's conception of Jesus's death. It has neither offered an impervious thesis as to whether Martyr Theology shaped Paul's conception of Jesus's death. I have provided an up to date study that has endeavored to interact with the major scholars who have discussed this issue and that has endeavored to interact with the key texts by providing an exegesis of those texts. I have also endeavored to argue against those who have denied that Paul presents Jesus's death as an atoning sacrifice and a saving event. After my investigation, I am aware of more questions that need to be answered and that could push the discussion forward.

First, a detailed analysis of Isaiah 53 and a detailed comparison and contrast between Isaiah 53 and Martyr Theology, every Second Temple text that speaks of human sacrifice, and a comparison between every atonement text in Paul's letters would be beneficial to the discussion. Second, further work should be done to answer the question why Paul would borrow the concepts and ideas of Martyr Theology since Isaiah 53 was available to him. Third, a discussion about Paul's Hellenistic-Jewish education would also shed light on whether Martyr Theology and the stories of the martyrs were part of his academic training. Fourth, attention should be given to whether Paul actually borrowed from Martyr Theology or reacted against it. Fifth, further work should be done to see whether the differences between Martyr Theology and Paul's conception of Jesus's death extinguish any possibility that the former shaped the latter. Sixth, one should investigate whether Martyr Theology and Paul were dependent on the same stream of tradition (i.e., the OT), but used that tradition to form two different trajectories (e.g., the sacrificial nature of the martyrs' deaths and the sacrificial nature of Jesus's death).

Bibliography

Aland, Barbara, et al. *The Greek New Testament*. Edited by Barbara Aland, et al. 4th rev. ed. Stuttgart: Deutsche Bibelgesellschaft, 1998.

Alexander, Philip S. "Torah and Salvation in Tannaitic Literature." In *Justification and Variegated Nomism: The Complexities of Second Temple Judaism*, edited by D. A. Carson et al., 1:261–301. Tübingen: Mohr Siebeck. Grand Rapids: Baker, 2001.

Anderson, H. "4 Maccabees (First Century AD): A New Translation and Introduction." In *Old Testament Pseudepigrapha*, Edited by James H. Charlesworth, 531–64. New York: Doubleday, 1985.

Avery-Peck, Alan J., Daniel Harrington, and Jacob Neusner (eds.), *When Judaism and Christianity Began: Essays in Memory of Anthony J. Saldarini*. Leiden: Brill, 2005.

Bailey, Daniel P. "Concepts of Stellvertretung in the Interpretation of Isaiah 53." In *Jesus and the Suffering Servant: Isaiah 53 and Christian Origins*, edited by William H. Bellinger et al., 223–50. Harrisburg, PA: Trinity Press International, 1998.

———. "Greek Heroes Who Happen to be Jewish: The Meaning of Hilastērion in 4 Macc 17:22." Paper Presented at the 2002 Annual Meeting of the Society of Biblical Literature.

———. "Jesus as the Mercy Seat: The Semantics and Theology of Paul's Use of Hilastērion in Romans 3:25." PhD diss., Cambridge University, 1999.

Barclay, John and J. Sweet. *Early Christian Thought in Its Jewish Context*. New York: Cambridge University Press, 1996.

Barnett, Paul. *The Second Epistle to the Corinthians*. The New International Commentary on the New Testament. Grand Rapids: Eerdmans, 1997.

Barrett, C. K. *A Commentary on the Epistle to the Romans*. Harper's New Testament Commentary Series. San Francisco: Harper & Collins Row, 1957.

Barth, Gerhard. *Der Tod Jesus Christi im Verständis des Neuen Testaments*. Nerkirchen-Vluyn: Neukirchener Verlag, 1992.

Barth, Karl. *The Epistle to the Romans*. 6th ed. Translated by Edwyn C. Hoskyns. London: University of Cambridge Press, 1950.

Baumeister, Theofried. *Die Anfänge der Theologie des Martyriums*. Münsterische Beiträge zur Theologie. Münster: Aschendorf, 1980.

Beale, G. K. "Reconciliation in 2 Corinthians 5–7 and Its Bearing on the Literary Problem in 2 Corinthians 6:14–7:1." *NTS* 35 (1989) 550–81.

Beck, Brian. "Imitatio Christi and the Lukan Passion Narrative." In *Suffering and Martyrdom in the New Testament: Studies Presented to G. M. Styler by the Cambridge New Testament Seminar*, edited by William Horbury et al., 28–47. Cambridge: Cambridge University Press, 1981.

Becker, J. C. *Paul, the Apostle: The Triumph of God in Life and Thought*. Philadelphia: Fortress, 1980.

Bell, Richard. "Sacrifice and Christology in Paul." *JTS* 53 (2002) 1–27.

Ben Ezra, Daniel Stökl. *The Impact of Yom Kippur on Early Christianity*. Wissenschaftliche Untersuchungen zum Neuen Testament. Tübingen: Mohr Siebeck, 2003.

Bickerman, E. "The Date of IV Maccabees." In *Studies in Jewish and Christian History*, Part 1, 275–81. Leiden: Brill, 1976.

———. *The God of the Maccabees: Studies on the Meaning and Origin of the Maccabean Revolt*. Translated by Horst R. Moehring. Leiden: Brill, 1979.

Bockmuhel, Markus. *This Jesus: Martyr, Lord, Messiah*. Edinburgh: T. & T. Clark, 1994.

Bossmann, David. "In Christ: A Midrashic Approach to Paul's in Christ." PhD diss., St. Louis University, 1973.

Bowersock, G. W. *Hellenism in Late Antiquity*. Ann Arbor: The University of Michigan Press, 1990.

———. *Martyrdom and Rome: The Wile's Lectures Given at the Queen's University of Belfast*. Cambridge: Cambridge University Press, 1995.

Boyarin, Daniel. *Dying for God: Martyrdom and the Making of Christianity and Judaism*. Stanford: Stanford University Press, 1999.

Brandon, Owen. "Atonement through Suffering: An Interpretation of a New Testament Idea." *CQR* 163 (1963) 282–92.

Brandscheidt, R. "Das Opfer des Abrahams (Genesis 22:1–19)." *TZ* 110 (2001) 1–19.

Breitenstein, U. *Beobachtungen zu Sprache, Stil und Gedankengut des Vierten Makkabäerbuchs*. Basel: Schwabe, 1976.

Breytenbach, Cilliers, *Versöhnung: Eine Studie zur paulinischen Soteriologie*. Wissenschaftliche Monographien zum Alten und Neuen Testament 60. Neukirchener-Vluyn: Neukirchener Verlag, 1989.

———. "Versöhnung, Stellvertretung und Sühne: Semantische und traditionsgeschictliche Berkmungen am Beispel der Paulinischen Briefe." *NTS* 39 (1993) 59–79.

———. "Christus starb für uns: Zur Tradition und paulinischen Rezeption der sogennanten Sterbeformeln." *NTS* 49 (2003) 447–75.

———. "Salvation of the Reconciled (with a Note on the Background of Paul's Metaphor of Reconciliation)." In *Salvation in the New Testament: Perspectives in Soteriology*, edited by J. G. der Watt, 271–86. Leiden: Brill, 2005.

Brown, F., S. et al. *The Brown-Driver-Briggs Hebrew and English Lexicon*. Peabody, MA: Hendrickson, 2000.

Brown, William H. "From Holy War to Holy Martyrdom." In *The Quest for the Kingdom of God: Studies in Honor of George E. Mendenhall*, edited H. B. Huffmon, et al., 281–92. Winona Lake, IN: Eisenbrauns, 1983.

Bruce, F. F. *The Epistle of Paul to the Romans*. The New Testament Commentary. Grand Rapids: Eerdmans, 1963.

———. *New Testament History*. New York: Doubleday, 1980.

Brutti, Maria. *The Development of the High Priesthood during the pre-Hasmonean Period*. Leiden: Brill, 2006.

Buchannan, George Wesley. "The Day of Atonement and Paul's Doctrine of Redemption." *NovT* 32 (1990) 236–49.

Bultmann, Rudolph. *Theology of the New Testament*. 2 vols. Translated by Kendrick Grobel. New York: Charles Scribner's Sons, 1951.

———. *Theology of the New Testament*. Translated by Kendrick Grobel. Waco: Baylor University Press, 2007.

Burger, C. *Schöpfung und Versöhnung: Studien zum liturgischen Gut im Kolosser-und-Epheserbrief.* Neukirchen: Neukirchener Verlag, 1975.

Byrne, Brendon. *Romans.* Sacra Pagina 6. Collegeville, MN: Liturgical Press, 1996.

Calvin, John. *Commentary on the Epistle of Paul to the Romans.* Edited and Translated by John Owen. Grand Rapids: Eerdmans, 1947.

———. *The Epistles of Paul to the Romans and to the Thessalonians.* Translated by R. McKenzie. Grand Rapids: Eerdmans, 1960.

Campbell, Douglas A. "The Atonement in Paul." *Anvil* 11 (1994) 237–50.

———. *The Rhetoric of Righteousness in Romans 3:21–26.* Journal for the Study of the New Testament 65. Sheffield: Sheffield Academic Press, 1992.

Capps, E., et al. *Plato, with an English Translation.* 9th ed. Edited by E. Capps, et al. Translated by Harold North Fowler. Vol. 1. Cambridge, MA: Harvard University Press, 1943.

Carson, D. A. "Atonement in Romans 3:21–26." In *The Glory of the Atonement,* edited by Charles E. Hill et al., 119–39. Downers Grove, IL: InterVarsity Press, 2004.

Cathcart, Kevin, et al. *The Targums: Targums Neofiti 1 and Pseudo—Jonathon: Leviticus,* edited by Kevin Cathcart, et al. Translated by Martin McNamara and Michael Maher. Vol. 3. Collegeville, MN: Liturgical Press, 1994.

Ceresko, A. R. "The Rhetorical Strategy of the Fourth Servant Song (Isa 52:13–53:12): Poetry and the New-Exodus." *CBQ* 56 (1994) 42–55.

Charlesworth, James H. *The Old Testament Pseudepigrapha,* edited by James H. Charlesworth. 2 vols. New York: Doubleday, 1983.

Childs, Brevard. *Isaiah.* The Old Testament Library. Louisville: Westminster/John Knox, 2001.

———. *The Struggle to Understand Isaiah as Christian Scripture.* Grand Rapids: Eerdmans, 2004.

Chilton, B. D. "Isaac and the Second Night: A Consideration." *Bib* 61 (1980) 78–88.

Clines, David J. *I, He, We, and They: A Literary Approach to Isaiah 53.* Journal for the Study of the Old Testament 1. Sheffield: Sheffield Academic Press, 1976.

Cole, Dennis R. *Numbers.* New American Commentary 3b. Nashville: Broadman & Holman, 2000.

Collins, John J. *Daniel, First Maccabees, and Second Maccabees, with an Excursus on the Apocalyptic Genre.* 2nd ed. Old Testament Monograph. Wilmington, DE: Michael Glazier Incorporation, 1989.

———. *Between Athens and Jerusalem: Jewish Identity in the Hellenistic Diaspora.* 2nd ed. Grand Rapids: Eerdmans, 2000.

———. *Jewish Cult and Hellenistic Culture: Essays on the Jewish Encounter with Hellenism and Roman Rule.* Leiden: Brill, 2005.

Cousar, Charles B. *A Theology of the Cross: The Death of Jesus in the Pauline Letters.* Minneapolis: Augsburg Fortress, 1990.

Cranfield, C. E. B. *Romans 1–8.* International Critical Commentary. Edinburgh: T. & T. Clark, 1975.

Cullmann, Oscar. *The Christology of the New Testament.* Translated by Shirley C. Guthrie and Charles A. M. Hall. Philadelphia: Westminster, 1959.

Cummins, Stephen Anthony. *Paul and the Crucified Christ in Antioch.* Cambridge: Cambridge University Press, 2001.

Dahl, Nils. *Studies in Paul: Theology for the Early Christian Mission.* Minneapolis: Augsburg, 1977.

Daly, R. J. "The Soteriological Significance of the Sacrifice of Isaac." *CBQ* 39 (1977) 45–75.

———. *Christian Sacrifice: The Judaeo Christian Background before Origen*. Washington, DC: The Catholic University of America, 1978.

Danker, Frederick William. *A Greek—English Lexicon of the New Testament & Other Early Christian Literature*. 3rd ed. Chicago: University Press, 2000.

Das, Andrew A. *Paul, The Law, and the Covenant*. Peabody, MA: Hendrickson, 2001.

Davies, P. R. "Passover and the Dating of the Akedah." *JJS* 30 (1979) 59–67.

Davies, W. D. *Paul and Rabbinic Judaism: Some Rabbinic Elements in Pauline Theology*. London: SPK, 1948.

Davis, Basil S. *Christ as Devotio: The Argument of Galatians 3:1–14*. Lanham, MD: University Press of America, 2002.

Davis, Christopher A. *The Structure of Paul's Gospel: "The Gospel which is Truth."* Lewisten, NY: Mellen Biblical Press, 1995.

De Jonge, Marinus. "Jesus' Death for Others and the Death of the Maccabean Martyrs." In *Text and Testimony: Essays in Honour of A. F. J. Klijn*, edited by T. Baarda et al., 142–51. Kampen: Kok, 1988.

———. *Christology in Context: The Earliest Response to Jesus*. Philadelphia: Westminster, 1988.

———. *Jesus, The Servant-Messiah*. New Haven: Yale University Press, 1991.

———. *God's Final Envoy: Early Christology and Jesus' Own View of His Mission*. Grand Rapids: Eerdmans, 1998.

Deissmann, Adolf. *Bible Studies*. Translated by A. Grieve. Edinburgh: T. & T. Clark, 1895.

———. "ἱλαστήριος und ἱλαστήριον." *ZW* 4 (1903) 193–212.

———. *Light from the Ancient Near East*. New York: Harper, 1927.

DeSilva, David. *Introducing the Apocrypha: Message, Context, and Significance*. Grand Rapids: Baker, 2002.

———. *4 Maccabees*. Sheffield: Sheffield Academic Press, 1998.

———. *An Introduction to the New Testament: Contexts, Methods, & Ministry Formation*. Downers Grove, IL: InterVarsity Press, 2004.

———. *4 Maccabees*. Septuagint Commentary Series. Leiden: Brill, 2006.

Dibelius, Martin. *From Tradition to Gospel*. 2nd ed. Translated by Bertram Lee Woolf. London: Ivor, Nicholson, and Watson, 1934.

Dobbeler, A. von. *Glaube als Teilhabe*. Wissenschaftliche Monographien zum Alten und Neuen Testament 2. 22. Tübingen: Mohr Siebeck, 1987.

Dodd, C. H. "Hilaskesthai, Its Cognates, Derivatives, and Synonyms in the Septuagint." *JTS* 32 (1931) 352–60.

———. *The Epistle of Paul to the Romans*. Moffat New Testament Commentary. New York: Harper and Brothers, 1932.

———. *The Bible and the Greeks*. 2nd ed. London: Hodder and Stoughton, 1954.

Downing, John. "Jesus and Martyrdom." *JTS* 14 (1963) 279–93.

Droge, Arthur J. and James D. Tabor. *A Noble Death*. San Francisco: Harper, 1992.

Duhm, B. *Das Buch Jesaja*. Göttinger Handkommentar zum Alten Testament 3. Güttingen: Vandenhoeck & Ruprecht, 1892.

Dunn, James D. G. "Paul's Understanding of Jesus' Death." In *Reconciliation and Hope*, edited by Robert J. Banks, 125–41. Grand Rapids: Eerdmans, 1974.

———. *Christology in the Making: A NT Inquiry into the Origins of the Doctrine of the Incarnation*. Philadelphia: Westminster, 1980.

———. *Romans 1–8*. Word Biblical Commentary 38. Dallas: Word Books, 1988.

———. *Jesus, Paul, and the Law: Studies in Galatians and Mark*. London: SPK, 1990.

———. "Paul's Understanding of the Death of Jesus as Sacrifice." In *Sacrifice and Redemption: Durham Essays in Theology*, edited by S. W. Sykes, 35–56. Cambridge: Cambridge University Press, 1997.

———. "Once More ΠΙΣΤΙΣ ΧΡΙΣΤΟΥ." In *Pauline Theology, Looking Back, Pressing Forward*, edited by E. Elizabeth Johnson et al., 4:61–81. Atlanta: Scholars Press, 1997.

———. *The Theology of Paul, the Apostle*. Grand Rapids: Eerdmans, 1998.

Dupont, Jacques. *La reconciliation dans la théologie de Saint Paul*. Paris: Desclée de Brouwer, Universitaies de Louvain, 1953.

Dupont-Sommer, A. *Le Quatrième Livre des Machabées*. Paris: Champion, 1939.

Durham, John I. *Exodus*. Word Biblical Commentary 3. Waco, TX: Word, 1987.

Elliger, Karl. *Leviticus*. Tübingen: Mohr Siebeck, 1966.

Evans, Craig A. *Ancient Texts for New Testament Studies: A Guide to the Background Literature*, edited by Craig A. Evans. Peabody, MA: Hendrickson, 2005.

Farmer, William R. *Maccabees, Zealots, and Josephus: An Inquiry into Jewish Nationalism in the Greco-Roman Period*. New York: Columbia University Press, 1956.

Fee, Gordon D. *Pauline Christology: An Exegetical-Theological Study*. Peabody, MA: Hendrickson, 2007.

Feldman, Louis H. *Judaism and Hellenism Reconsidered*. Supplemental Journal for the Study of Judaism 107. Leiden: Brill, 2006.

Finlan, Stephen. *The Background and Content of Paul's Cultic Atonement Metaphors*. Atlanta: SBL, 2004.

Fischer, Georg, and Knut Backhaus. *Sühne und Versöhnung: Perspectiven des Alten und Neuen Testaments*. Die Neue Echter Bibel 7. Würzburg: Echter, 2000.

Fitzgerald, John T. "Paul and Paradigm Shifts: Reconciliation and Its Linkage Group." In *Paul Beyond the Judaism/Hellenism Divide*, edited by Troels Engberg-Pedersen, 241–62. Louisville: Westminster/John Knox, 2001.

Fitzmyer, Joseph A. "The Sacrifice of Isaac in Qumran Literature." *Biblica* 83 (2002) 211–29.

———. *Romans*. Anchor Bible Commentary. New York: Doubleday, 1993.

———. "Reconciliation in Pauline Theology." In *No Famine in the Land*, edited by J. L. Flanagan et al., 155–77. Missoula: Scholars Press, 1975.

———. *To Advance the Gospel*. 2nd ed. Grand Rapids: Eerdmans, 1998.

Fohrer, G. "Stellvertretung und Schuldopfer in Jes 52, 13–53." In *Studien zu alttestamentlichen Texten und Themen, 24–43*. Berlin: de Gruyter, 1988.

France, R. T. *Jesus and the Old Testament*. Grand Rapids: Baker, 1982.

Frazier, Charles D. "A Comparison of the Function of Cultic AIMA in the Pauline Corpus with that of Non-Rabbinic Judaism and the Mystery Cults." PhD diss., New Orleans Theological Seminary, 1996.

Frend, W. H. C. *Martyrdom and Persecution in the Early Church: A Study of a Conflict from the Maccabees to Donatus*. Oxford: Alden Press, 1965.

Freudenthal, J. *Die Flavius Josephus beigelegte Schrift über die Herrschaft der Vernunft (IV Makkabäerbuch), eine Predigt aus dem ersten nachchristlichen Jahrhundert*. Breslau: Schletter, 1969.

Friedrich, Gerhard. *Die Verkündigung des Todes Jesu im Neuen Testament*. Biblische-theologische Studien. Neukirchener-Vluyn: Neukirchener Verlag, 1982.

Fryer, Nico S. L. "The Meaning and Translation of Hilastērion in Romans 3:25." *EvQ* 59 (1987) 99–116.

Furnish, V. P. *II Corinthians*. New York: Doubleday, 1984.

Gaffin, Richard. "Atonement in the Pauline Corpus." In *The Glory of the Atonement: Biblical, Theological, and Practical Perspectives*, edited by Charles E. Hill et al., 140–62. Downers Grove, IL: InterVarsity Press, 2004.

Garlington, D. B. "'The Obedience of Faith in the Letter to the Romans: Part 3, The Obedience of Christ and the Obedience of the Christian." *WTJ* 55 (1993) 87–112.

Garnet, P. "Atonement Constructions in the Old Testament and the Qumran Scrolls." *EvQ* 46 (1974) 131–63.

———. *Salvation and Atonement in the Qumran Scrolls*. Tübingen: Mohr Siebeck, 1977.

Garrison, Roman. "Innocent Suffering in the Greek, Roman, and Biblical Traditions." *EGLMBS* 19 (1999) 37–51.

Gathercole, Simon J. "Romans 3:25–26: An Exegetical Study." Lecture Presented at the Annual Atonement Conference of the London School of Theology. London, July 2005.

———. "The Cross and Substitutionary Atonement." *SBET* 21 (2003) 152–65.

———. *Where is Boasting? Early Jewish Soteriology and Paul's Response in Romans 1–5*. Grand Rapids: Eerdmans, 2002.

Gayston, Kenneth. *Dying, We Live: A New Inquiry into the Death of Christ in the New Testament*. New York: Oxford University Press, 1990.

Georgi, D. *The Opponents of Paul in Second Corinthians*. Philadelphia: Fortress, 1986.

Gibbs, J. G. *Creation and Redemption: A Study in Pauline Theology*. Leiden: Brill, 1971.

Ginzberg, L. *The Legends of the Jews*. Philadelphia: Jewish Publication Society, 1909.

Gnilka, J. "Martyriumsparänese und Sühnetod in synoptischen und jüdischen Traditionen." In *Die Kirche des Anfangs: Festschrift für Heinz Schürman*, 223–46. Leipzig: St. Benno-Verlag, 1977.

Goldingay, John. *God's Prophet, God's Servant: A Study in Jeremiah and Isaiah 40–55*. Carlisle, UK: Paternoster, 1995.

Goldstein, Jonathan A. *2 Maccabees*. Anchor Bible Commentary. New York: Doubleday, 1983.

Goodenough, R. R. *Jewish Symbols in the Greco-Roman Period*. 13 vols. New York: Pantheon Books, 1954.

Gorringe, Timothy. *God's Just Vengeance*. Cambridge: Cambridge University Press, 1996.

Gray, George Buchanan. *Sacrifices in the Old Testament: Its Theory and Practice*. New York: KTAV Publishing House, 1971.

———. *Numbers*. International Critical Commentary. Edinburgh: T. & T. Clark, 1912.

Grayston, Kenneth. "Atonement and Martyrdom." In *Early Christian Thought in Its Jewish Context*, edited by John Barclay et al., 250–63. Cambridge: Cambridge University Press, 1996.

Green, Joel B. and Mark D. Baker. *Recovering the Scandal of the Cross: Atonement in New Testament & Contemporary Contexts*. Downers Grove, IL: InterVarsity Press, 2000.

Greenberg, L. Arik. "My Share of God's Reward: Exploring the Roles and Formulations of the Afterlife in Early Christian Martyrdoms." PhD diss., Claremont University, 2005.

Groves, J. Alan. "Atonement in Isaiah 53." In *The Glory of the Atonement*, edited by Charles E. Hill, 61–89. Downers Grove, IL: InterVarsity Press, 2004.

Gummere, Richard M. *Seneca, Ad Lucilium Epistulae Morales*. Translated by Richard M. Gummere. Cambridge, MA: Harvard University Press, 1967.

Grundmann, Walter. "Die Übermacht der Gnade: Eine Studie zur Theologie des Paulus." *NovT* 2 (1957) 50–72.

Gundry, Robert H. "The Nonimputation of Christ's Righteousness." In *Justification: What's at Stake in the Current Debates*, edited by Mark Husbands, 17–45. Downers Grove, IL: InterVarsity, 2004.

Haacker, Klaus. *Der Brief des Paulus an die Römer.* Leipzig: Evangelische Verlagsanstalt, 1999.

Hadas, M. *The Third and Fourth Books of Maccabees.* New York: Harper and Brothers, 1953.

Hafemann, Scott J. *Paul, Moses, and the History of Israel: The Letter/Spirit Contrast and the Argument from Scripture in 2 Corinthians 3.* London: Paternoster, 2005.

Hannah, Darrell D. "Isaiah within Judaism of the Second Temple Period." In *Isaiah in the New Testament*, edited by Steve Moyise et al. London: T. & T. Clark International, 2005.

Hanson, A. T. *The Wrath of the Lamb.* London: SPK, 1957.

Haran, Menahem. *Temples and Temple-Service in Ancient Israel: An Inquiry into Biblical Cult Phenomena and the Historical Setting of the Priestly School.* Winona Lake, IN: Eisenbrauns, 1985.

Hardie, R. P., et al. *The Pocket, Aristotle.* Translated by R. P. Hardie, et al. New York: Pocket Books, 1958.

Harris, Murray J. *The Second Epistle to the Corinthians.* New International Greek Text Commentary. Grand Rapids: Eerdmans, 2005.

Hartley, John E. *Leviticus.* Word Biblical Commentary 4. Dallas: Word, 1992.

Hayward, Ray. "The Present State of Research into the Targumic Account of the Sacrifice of Isaac." *JJS* 32 (1981) 127–50.

Heard, Warren Joel. "Maccabean Martyr Theology: Its Genesis, Antecedents, and Significance for the Earliest Soteriological Interpretation of the Death of Jesus." PhD diss., University of Aberdeen, 1989.

Hedderic, Ronald L. "An Investigation of the Implications of the Akedah Hypothesis for the Pauline Concept of Atonement." PhD diss., Southwestern Theological Seminary, 1993.

Hengel, Martin and Anna Maria Schwemer. *Paul between Damascus and Antioch: The Unknown Years.* Louisville: Westminster/John Knox, 1997.

———. "Der Kreuzestod Jesu Christi als Gottes souveräne Erlösungstat: Exegese über 2 Korinther 5, 11–21." In *Theologie und Kirche: Reichenau-Gesprächder Evangelischen Landessynode Württemberg*, edited by Peter Stuhlmacher et al., 60–89. Stuttgart: Calwer, 1967.

———. "The Effective History of Isaiah 53 in the Pre-Christian Period." In *The Suffering Servant: Isaiah 53 in Jewish and Christian Sources*, edited by Bernd Janowski et al. Translated by Daniel P. Bailey, 75–146. Grand Rapids: Eerdmans, 2004.

———. *Judaism and Hellenism: Studies in their Encounter in Palestine in the Early Hellenistic Period.* Translated by John Bowden. Minneapolis: Fortress, 1990.

———. *The Atonement: A Study of the Origins of the Doctrine in the New Testament.* London: SCM, 1981.

———. *The Zealots: Investigations into the Jewish Freedom Movement in the Period between Herod I and 70 A. D.* Translated by David Smith. Edinburgh: T. & T. Clark, 1989.

Hill, David. *Greek Words and Hebrew Meanings: Studies in the Semantics of Soteriological Terms.* Society for the New Testament Monograph Series 5. Cambridge: Cambridge University Press, 1967.

Hoehner, Harold W. *Ephesians.* Grand Rapids: Baker, 2002.

Hofius, Otfried. "Erwägungen zur Gestalt und Herkunft des paulinischen Versöhnungsgedankens." In *Paulusstudien I*, Wissenschaftliche Untersuchungen zum Neuen Testament 51, 186–99. Tübingen: J. C. B. Mohr, 1981.

———. "Isaiah 53 in the New Testament Letters." In *The Suffering Servant: Isaiah 53 in Jewish and Christian Sources*, edited by Bernd Janowski et al. Translated by Daniel P. Bailey, 163–88. Grand Rapids: Eerdmans, 2004.

Holland, Tom. *Contours of Pauline Theology: A Radical New Survey of the Influences on Paul's Biblical Writings*. Scotland, UK: Mentor, 2004.

Hooker, M. D. "Interchange and Atonement." *BJRL* 60 (1978) 462–81.

———. *From Adam to Christ: Essays on Paul*. Cambridge: Cambridge University Press, 1990.

———. *Jesus and the Servant*. London: SPCK, 1959.

———. *Not Ashamed of the Gospel: New Testament Interpretations of the Death of Christ*. Grand Rapids: Eerdmans, 1994.

———. "Interchange in Christ." *JTS* 22 (1974) 349–61.

House, Paul. *Old Testament Theology*. Downers Grove, IL: InterVarsity Press, 1998.

Hüllstrung, Wolfgang, et al. "A Classified Bibliography on Isaiah 53." In *The Suffering Servant: Isaiah 53 in Jewish and Christian Sources*, edited by Bernd Janowski, et al. Translated by Daniel P. Bailey, 462–92. Grand Rapids: Eerdmans, 2004.

Hultgren, Arnold J. *Christ and His Benefits: Christology and Redemption in the New Testament*. Philadelphia: Fortress, 1987.

———. *Paul's Gospel and Mission: The Outlook from His Letter to the Romans*. Philadelphia: Fortress, 1985.

Janowski, Bernd. "He Bore Our Sins: Isaiah 53 and the Drama of Taking Another's Place." In *The Suffering Servant: Isaiah 53 in Jewish and Christian Sources*, edited by Bernd Janowski et al. Translated by Daniel P. Bailey, 67–70. Grand Rapids: Eerdmans, 2004.

———. *Sühne als Heilsgeschehen*. 2nd ed. Wissenschaftliche Monographien zum Alten und Neuen Testament. Neukirchener-Vluyn: Neukirchener Verlag, 2000.

Jerrow, Janet. "Arguing with God in the Wake of the Golden Calf Episode: The Rabbis Read Exodus 32." PhD diss., Southern Methodist University, 2006.

Joüon, Paul and T. Muraoka. *A Grammar of Biblical Hebrew:* Pt. 3, Syntax. Rome: Editrice Pontificio Instituto Biblico, 2003.

Johnson, Luke Timothy. "Romans 3:21–26 and the Faith of Jesus." *CBQ* 44 (1982) 77–90.

———. *Reading Romans: A Literary and Theological Commentary*. New York: Crossroad, 1997.

Jowett, Benjamin, et al. *The Dialogues of Plato*. Translated by Benjamin Jowett, et al. New York: Bantam Books, 1986.

Kümmel, Werner Georg. *Introduction to the New Testament*. 17th ed. Translated by Howard Clark Lee. Nashville: Abingdon, 1973.

Käsemann, Ernst. "Erwägungen zum Stichwort: Versöhnungslehre im Neuen Testament." In *Zeit und Geschichte: Danksgabe an Rudolph Bultmann zum 80*, edited by Erich Dinkler, 47–59. Tübingen: Mohr, 1964.

———. "Zum Verständis von Römer 3:24–26." *ZW* 43 (1950–1951) 150–54.

———. *Commentary on Romans*. Translated by Geoffrey W. Bromiley. Grand Rapids: Eerdmans, 1980.

———. "Some Thoughts on the Theme of the Doctrine of Reconciliation in the New Testament." In *The Future of Our Religious Past: Essays in Honour of Rudolph*

Bultmann, edited by James M. Robinson. Translated by Charles E. Carlston et al., 49–64. London: SCM, 1971.

———. "The Saving Significance of Jesus' Death." In *Perspectives on Paul.* Translated by Margaret Kohl, 32–59. Philadelphia: Fortress, 1971.

Kautzsch, E. and A. E. Cowley. *Gesenius' Hebrew Grammar.* 2nd ed. Oxford: Clarendon Press, 1909.

Kellermann, U. "Zum traditionsgeschichtlichen Problem des stellvertretenden Sühnetodes in 2 Makk 7:37." *BN* 13 (1980) 63–83.

———. *Auferstanden in den Himmel: 2 Makkabäer 7 und die Auferstehung der Märtyrer.* Stuttgart: Neukirchener Verlag, 1979.

Kertelge, K. "Das Verständis des Todes Jesu bei Paulus." In *Der Tod Jesu: Deutungen im Neuen Testament.* 2nd ed. Edited by K. Kertelge, 114–36. Freiburg: Herder, 1976.

Kim, Jintae. "The Concept of Atonement in 1 John: A Redevelopment of the Second Temple Concept of Atonement." PhD diss., Westminster Theological Seminary, 2003.

Kim, Seyoon. "2 Cor. 5:11–21 and Reconciliation." *NovT* 38–39 (1996–1997) 360–84.

———. *The Origins of Paul's Gospel.* Wissenschaftliche Untersuchungen zum Neuen Testament 2. Tübingen: Mohr Siebeck, 1981.

———. *Paul and The New Perspective: Second Thoughts on the Origins of Paul's Gospel.* Grand Rapids: Eerdmans, 2002.

Klauck, H. J. *4 Makkabäerbuch: Jüdische Schriften aus hellenistisch-römischer Zeit.* Gütersloh: Gerd Mohn, 1989.

Klawans, Jonathan. *Purity, Sacrifice, and the Temple: Symbolism and Supersessionism in the Study of Ancient Judaism.* Oxford: Oxford University Press, 2006.

Knöppler, Thomas. *Sühne im Neuen Testament.* Wissenschaftliche Monographien zum Alten und Neuen Testament 88. Neukirchener-Vluyn: Neukirchener Verlag, 2001.

Kraus, Wolfgang. *Der Tod Jesu als Heiligtumsweihe: Eine Untersuchung zum Umfeld der Sühnevorstellung im Römer 3:25–26a.* Wissenschaftliche Monographien zum Alten und Neuen Testament 66. Neukirchener-Vluyn: Neukirchener Verlag, 1991.

Kurtz, J. H. *Offerings, Sacrifices, and Worship in the Old Testament.* Translated by James Martin. Peabody, MA: Hendrickson, 1998.

Lato, A. *The Servant of YHWH and Cyrus.* Stockholm: Almqvist and Wiksell International 1992.

Lebrahm, J. C. H. "Die Literarische form des Vierten Makkabäerbuches." *VC* 28–29 (1974–1975) 81–96.

Lerch, David. *Isaaks Opferung Christlich Gedeutet: Eine Auslegungsgeschichtlich Untersuchung.* Tübingen: Mohr, 1950.

Levenson, Jon D. *The Death and Resurrection of the Beloved Son: The Transformation of Child Sacrifice in Judaism and Christianity.* New Haven: Yale University Press, 1993.

Levi, Israel. "Le Sacrifice d' Isaac et la Mort de Jesus." *RJS* 64 (1912) 161–235.

Liddell, Henry George and Robert Scott. *A Greek-English Lexicon.* Oxford: Clarendon Press, 1940.

Lightfoot, Joseph. *St. Paul's Epistle to the Galatians.* London: Macmillan, 1865.

Lincoln, Andrew T. "From Wrath to Justification." In *Pauline Theology: Romans,* edited by David M. Hay et al., 3:130–59. Atlanta: SBL, 2002.

———. *Ephesians.* Word Biblical Commentary 42. Nashville: Thomas Nelson, 1990.

Lohse, Eduard. *Colossians and Philemon.* Philadelphia: Fortress, 1971.

———. *Märtyrer und Gottesknecht: Untersuchungen zur urchristlichen Verkündigung vom Sühne Jesus Christi.* 2nd ed. Göttingen: Vandenhoeck & Ruprecht, 1963.

———. *Der Brief an die Römer: Kritisch-exegetischer Kommentar über das Neue Testament.* The Meyers Commentary 4. Göttingen: Vandenhoeck & Ruprecht, 2003.

Longenecker, Richard N. *Galatians.* Word Biblical Commentary 41. Nashville: Thomas Nelson, 1990.

———. *St. Paul's Epistles to the Colossians and to Philemon.* London: Macmillan, 1886.

Luther, Martin. *Lectures on Romans.* Edited and Translated by Wilhelm Pauck. Philadelphia: Westminster, 1961.

Lyonnet, Stanislas and Lèopold Sabourin. *Sin, Redemption, and Sacrifice: A Biblical and Patristic Study.* Rome: Biblical Institute Press, 1970.

———. "De notione expiationis." *VT* 37 (1959) 336–52.

Macgregor, G. H. C. "The Concept of the Wrath of God in the NT." *NTS* 7 (1960–1961) 101–9.

Manson, T. W. "ἱλαστήριον." *JTS* 46 (1945) 1–10.

Marshall, I. Howard. "The Death of Jesus in Recent New Testament Study." *WW* 3 (1983) 12–21.

———. "The Development of the Concept of Redemption in the New Testament." In *Reconciliation and Hope,* edited by Robert J. Banks, 153–69. Exeter: Paternoster, 1974.

Martin, Ralph P. "Reconciliation and Forgiveness in Colossians." In *Reconciliation and Hope,* ed. Robert J. Banks, 104–24. Exeter: Paternoster, 1974.

———. *2 Corinthians.* Word Biblical Commentary 40. Waco, TX: 1986.

———. *Reconciliation: A Study of Paul's Theology.* 2nd ed. Atlanta: John Knox, 1981.

Martyn, J. Louis. *Galatians.* Anchor Bible 33 A. New York: Doubleday, 1997.

Mathews, Kenneth A. *Genesis 11:27–50:26.* New American Commentary 1b. Nashville: Broadman & Holman, 2006.

McKnight, Scot. *Jesus and His Death: Historiography, the Historical Jesus, and Atonement Theory.* Waco, TX: Baylor University Press, 2005.

McLean, Bradley H. "The Absence of Atoning Sacrifice in Paul's Soteriology." *NTS* 38 (1992) 531–53.

———. *The Cursed Christ.* Journal for the Study of the New Testament 126. Sheffield: Sheffield Academic Press, 1996.

———. "Christ as a Pharmakos in Pauline Soteriology." *SBLSP* (1991) 187–206.

Meile, Eva. "Isaaks Opferung, eine Note an Nils Alstrup." *ST* 34 (1980) 111–28.

Melanchthon, Philip. *Commentary on Romans.* Edited and Translated by Fred Kramer. St. Louis: Concordia Publishing House, 1992.

Merwe, H. J. et al. *A Biblical Hebrew Reference Grammar.* Sheffield: Sheffield Academic Press, 2002.

Mettinger, Tryggve N. D. *A Farewell to the Servant Song: A Critical Examination of an Exegetical Axiom.* Scriptura Minora 3. Lund: C. W. K. Gleerup, 1983.

Metzger, Bruce M. *The Text of the New Testament: Its Transmission, Corruption, and Restoration.* 3rd ed. Oxford: Oxford University Press, 1992.

———. *A Textual Commentary on the Greek New Testament.* 2nd ed. Edited by Bruce M. Metzger. Stuttgart: Deutsche Bibelgesellschaft, 1994.

Meyer, B. F. "The Pre-Pauline Formula in Rom 3:25–26a." *NTS* 29 (1983) 198–208.

Michel, O. *Der Briefe an die Römer.* Göttingen: Vandenhoeck und Ruprecht, 1955.

Michl, J. "Die Versöhnung (Kol 1:10)." *TQ* 128 (1948) 442–62.

Milgrom, Jacob. *Cult and Conscience: The Asham and the Priestly Doctrine of Repentance.* Leiden: Brill, 1976.

———. *Studies in Cultic Theology and Terminology*. Leiden: Brill, 1983.

———. *Numbers*. The Jewish Publication Society Torah Commentary. Philadelphia: Jewish Publication Society, 1990.

Miller, J. W. "Prophetic Conflict in Second Isaiah: The Servant Songs in the Light of Their Context." In *Wort, Gebot, Glaube*, 77–85. Zürich: Zwingli-Verlag, 1970.

Minear, Paul S. "The Truth about Sin and Death." *Interpretation* 7 (1953) 142–55.

Moberly, R. W. L. *At The Mountain of God: Story and Theology in Exodus 32–34*. Journal for the Study of the Old Testament 22. Sheffield: Sheffield Academic Press, 1983.

Modica, Joseph Benjamin. "The Function and Purpose of Suffering, Persecution, and Martyrdom in Luke-Acts: An Exegetical and Theological Inquiry." PhD diss., Drew University, 1995.

Moo, Douglas J. *The Epistle to the Romans*. New International Commentary on the New Testament. Grand Rapids: Eerdmans, 1996.

Moore, George Foot. *Judaism in the First Centuries of the Christian Era: The Age of the Tannaim*. 3 vols. Cambridge, MA: Harvard University Press, 1950.

Morris, Leon. "The Meaning of ΗΙΛΑΣΤΗΡΙΟΝ in Romans 3:25." *NTS* (1955–1956) 3–43.

———. *The Atonement: Its Meaning and Significance*. Downers Grove, IL: InterVarsity Press, 1983.

———. *The Cross in the New Testament*. Grand Rapids: Eerdmans, 1965.

———. *The Apostolic Preaching of the Cross*. 3rd ed. Grand Rapids: Eerdmans, 1965.

———. "The Use of Hilaskēsthai in Biblical Greek." *JETS* 62 (1950–1951) 227–33.

———. *The Epistle to the Romans*. Pillar New Testament Commentary. Grand Rapids: Eerdmans, 1988.

Motyer, J. Alec. *The Prophecy of Isaiah*. Downers Grove, IL: InterVarsity Press, 1993.

Moule, C. F. D. *The Origins of Christology*. Cambridge: Cambridge University Press, 1977.

Mounce, William D. *Pastoral Epistles*. Word Biblical Commentary 46. Nashville: Nelson, 2000.

———. *An Analytical Lexicon to the Greek New Testament*. Grand Rapids: Zondervan, 1993.

Murphy, Frederick J. *Early Judaism: The Exile to the Time of Jesus*. Peabody, MA: Hendrickson, 2002.

Murray, John. *The Epistle to the Romans*. New International Commentary on the New Testament. 2 vols. Grand Rapids: Eerdmans, 1968.

Neusner, Jacob. *Early Rabbinic Judaism: Historical Studies in Religion, Literature, and Art*. Leiden: Brill, 1975.

Newton, M. *The Concept of Purity at Qumran and in the Letters of Paul*. Society of New Testament Studies Monograph Series 53. Cambridge: Cambridge University Press, 1985.

Nicole, Roger. "C. H. Dodd and the Doctrine of Propitiation." *WTJ* 17 (1954–55) 117–57.

North, C. R. *The Suffering Servant in Deutero-Isaiah*, 2nd ed. London: Oxford University Press, 1956.

———. *The Second Isaiah: Introduction, Translation, and Commentary to Chapters XL–LV*. Oxford: Clarendon Press, 1964.

Noth, Martin. *Leviticus*. Philadelphia: Westminster, 1965.

Nygren, Anders. *Commentary on Romans*. Translated by C. C. Rasmussen. Philadelphia: Muhlenburg Press, 1949.

O'Brien, Peter T. *Colossians, Philemon*. Word Biblical Commentary 44. Waco, TX: Word, 1982.

———. *The Letter to the Ephesians*. Pillar New Testament Commentary. Grand Rapids: Eerdmans, 1999.

O'Connor-Visser, E. A. M. E. *Aspects of Human Sacrifice in the Tragedies of Euripides*. Amsterdam: B. R. Grüner, 1987.

O'Hagan, A. "The Martyr in the Fourth Book of Maccabees." *SBFLA* 24 (1974) 94–120.

Oesterly, W. O. E. *The Psalms: Translated with Text-Critical and Exegetical Notes*. London: SPCK, 1939.

Origen. *Commentary on the Epistle to the Romans: Books 1–5*. Translated by Thomas P. Scheck. Washington, DC: The Catholic University of America, 2001.

Orlinsky, H. M. "The So-Called Servant of the Lord and Suffering Servant in Second Isaiah." In *Studies in the Second Part of the Book of Isaiah*, edited by H. M. Orlinsky et al., 1–133. Leiden: Brill, 1967.

Oswalt, John N. *The Book of Isaiah: Chapters 40–66*. New International Commentary of the Old Testament. Grand Rapids: Eerdmans, 1998.

Page, T. E., et al. *Euripides, with an English Translation*. 6th ed. Edited by T. E. Page, et al. Translated by Arthur S. Way. 4 vols. Cambridge, MA: Harvard University Press, 1950.

Park, Sung Kun. "The Influence of 2 and 4 Maccabees for the Concept of Piety in Luke-Acts." PhD diss., Southwestern Baptist Theological Seminary, 1992.

Passenemeck, Stephen M. "The Jewish Mandate for Martyrdom." *HUCA* 74 (2004) 215–41.

Pate, C. Marvin. *The Reverse of the Curse*. Wissenschaftliche Untersuchungen zum Neuen Testament 114. Tübingen: Mohr Siebeck, 2000.

Piper, John. *Counted Righteous in Christ: Should We Abandon the Imputation of Christ's Righteousness?* Wheaton: Crossway, 2002.

———. *The Justification of God: An Exegetical & Theological Study of Rom 9:1–23*. 2nd ed. Grand Rapids: Baker, 1993.

Pobee, John S. *Persecution and Martyrdom in the Theology of Paul*. Journal for the Study of the New Testament Supplement Series 6. Sheffield: Sheffield Academic Press, 1986.

Porter, Stanley E. "Reconciliation (ΚΑΤΑΛΛΑΣΣΩ) in Romans 5:1–11." M. A. thesis, Trinity Evangelical Divinity School, 1983.

———. *Idioms of the Greek New Testament*. 2nd ed. Sheffield: Sheffield Academic Press, 1999.

———. Καταλλάσσω *in Ancient Greek Literature, with Reference to the Pauline Writings*. Cordoba: Ediciones El Almendro, 1994.

———. *Verbal Aspect in the Greek of the New Testament with Reference to Tense and Mood*. New York: Peter Lang, 1989.

Powers, Daniel G. *Salvation through Participation: An Examination of the Notion of the Believer's Corporate Unity with Christ in Early Christian Soteriology*, Biblical Exegesis and Theology 29. Leuven: Peeters, 2001.

Röhser, Günter. *Stellvertretung im Neuen Testament*. Stuttgart Bibel-Studien 195. Stuttgart: Katholisches Bibelwerk Verlag, 2002.

Rader, William. *The Church and Racial Hostility: A History of Interpretation of Ephesians 2:11–22: Beiträge zur Geschichte der biblischen Exegese*. Tübingen: Mohr, 1978.

Rahlfs, A. *Septuaginta*, edited by A. Rahlfs Stuttgart: Deutsche Bibelgesellschaft, 1979.

Rashdall, Hastings. *The Idea of Atonement in Christian Theology: Being the Bampton Lectures for 1915*. London: Macmillan, 1925.

Reumann, John. "The Gospel of the Righteousness of God: Pauline Reinterpretation in Romans 3:21–26." *Interpretation* 20 (1966) 432–52.

Reventlow, Henning Graf. "Basic Issues in the Interpretation of Isaiah 53." In *Jesus and the Suffering Servant: Isaiah 53 and Christian Origins*, edited by William H. Bellinger et al., 23–38. Harrisburg, PA: Trinity Press International, 1998.

———. *Opfere deinen Sohn, eine Auslegung von Genesis 22*. Neukirchener-Vluyn: Neukirchener Verlag, 1968.

Ridderbos, Herman. *Paul: An Outline of His Theology*. Grand Rapids: Eerdmans, 1966.

Robert, Louis. *Etudes èpigraphiques et philologiques*. Paris: Champion, 1938.

Robertson, A. T. *A Grammar of the Greek New Testament in the Light of Historical Research*. Nashville: Broadman, 1934.

Roberts, W. *Aristotle, Rhetoric*. Translated by W. Roberts. New York: Random House, 1954.

Robinson, J. M. "A Formal Analysis of Col 1:15–20." *JBL* 76 (1957) 270–87.

Rowley, H. H. "The Servant of the Lord in the Light of Three Decades of Criticism." In *The Servant of the Lord and Other Essays on the Old Testament*. 2nd ed., 3–60. Oxford: Blackwell, 1965.

———. "The Unity of the Old Testament." *BJRL* 29 (1936) 5–15.

Rhys, Ernest. *History of Rome: Titus Livy*, edited by Ernest Rhys. Translated by Canon Roberts, under the title The First Samnite War and Settlement of Latium. Vol. 2. New York: E. P. Dutton and Company, 1926.

Sacchi, Paolo. *The History of the Second Temple Period*. Sheffield: Sheffield Academic Press, 2000.

Sanday, W. and A. C. Headlam. *The Epistle to the Romans*. International Critical Commentary. Edinburgh: T. & T. Clark, 1896.

Sanders, E. P. *Paul and Palestinian Judaism*. Philadelphia: Fortress, 1977.

———. *Paul, the Law, and the Jewish People*. Minneapolis: Fortress, 1983.

Sanders, James T. *The NT Christological Hymns: Their Historical Religious Background*. Cambridge: Cambridge University Press, 1971.

Scaer, Peter J. *The Lukan Passion and The Praiseworthy Death*. New Testament Monograph 10. Sheffield: Sheffield Academic Press, 2005.

Schatkin, Margaret. "The Maccabean Martyrs." *VC* 28 (1974) 97–113.

Schenker, A. *Biblia Hebraica Stuttgartensia*. Edited by A. Schenker. Stuttgart: DeutscheBibelgesellschaft, 1967/77.

Schiffman, Lawrence H. "2 Maccabees." In *Harper's Bible Commentary*, 898–915. San Francisco: Harper and Row, 1988.

———. *Texts and Traditions: A Source Reader for the Study of Second Temple and Rabbinic Judaism*. Edited by Lawrence H. Schiffman. Hoboken, NJ: Ktav Publishing House, 1998.

Schlatter, Adolf von. *Romans: The Righteousness of God*. Peabody, MA: Hendrickson, 1995.

Schnelle, Udo. *Apostle Paul: His Life and Theology*. Translated by M. Eugene Boring. Grand Rapids: Baker, 2005.

Schoeps, H. J. "The Sacrifice of Isaac in Paul's Theology." *JBL* 65 (1946) 385–92.

———. *Paul: The Theology of the Apostle in the Light of Jewish Religious History*. London: Lutterworth Press, 1961.

Schreiner, Thomas R. "The Penal Substitution View." In *The Nature of the Atonement: 4 Views*, edited by James Beilby et al., 67–98. Downers Grove, IL: InterVarsity Press, 2006.

———. *Romans*. Baker Exegetical Commentary of the New Testament. Grand Rapids: Baker, 1998.

———. *The Law and Its Fulfillment: A Pauline Theology of Law*. 2nd ed. Grand Rapids: Baker, 2001.

———. *Paul: An Apostle of God's Glory in Christ*. Downers Grove, IL: InterVarsity Press, 2001.

Scullion, James P. "A Tradition-Historical Study of the Day of Atonement." PhD diss., The Catholic University of America, 1991.

Seeley, David. *The Noble-Death: Greco-Roman Martyrology and Paul's Concept of Salvation*. Journal for the Study of the New Testament 28. Sheffield: Sheffield Academic Press, 1990.

Segal, A. F. "He who did not spare his own son . . . : Jesus, Paul, and the Akedah." In *From Jesus to Paul: Studies in Honour of Francis Wright Beare*, edited by Peter Richardson et al., 169–84. Ontario: Wilfrid Laurier University Press, 1984.

———. *The Other Judaisms of Late Antiquity*. Brown Judaic Studies 127. Atlanta: Scholars Press, 1987.

Seifrid, Mark A. *Christ, Our Righteousness: Paul's Theology of Justification*. New Testament Studies in Biblical Theology 36. Downers Grove, IL: InterVarsity Press, 2000.

Sevier, Paul. "The Truth about Sin and Death: The Meaning of Atonement in the Epistle to the Romans." *Interpretation* 7 (1953) 142–55.

Shepkaru, Shamuel. "The Evolution of Jewish Martyrdom in the Greco-Roman World from the Maccabees through the Middle Ages." PhD diss., New York University, 1997.

Shillington, George V. "Atonement Texture in 1 Corinthians 5:5." *JSNT* 71 (1998) 29–50.

Shum, Shiu-Lun. *Paul's Use of Isaiah in Romans: A Comparative Study of Paul's Letter to the Romans and the Sibylline and Qumran Sectarian Texts*. Wissenschaftlich Untersuchungen zum Neuen Testament 156, 2002.

Smyth, Herbert. *Greek Grammar*. 21st ed. Revised by Gordon M. Gessing. Cambridge, MA: Harvard University Press, 2002.

Snaith, N. "Isaiah 40–66: A Study of the Teaching of the Second Isaiah and Its Consequence." In *Studies on the Second Part of the Book of Isaiah*, edited by H. M. Orlinsky et al., 135–264. Supplement to Vetus Testamentum 14. Leiden: Brill, 1967.

Spieckermann, Hermann. "The Idea of Vicarious Suffering in the Old Testament." In *The Suffering Servant: Isaiah 53 in Jewish and Christian Sources*, edited by Bernd Janowski et al. Translated by Daniel P. Bailey, 1–15. Grand Rapids: Eerdmans, 2004.

Spiegel, Shalom. "Meaggadot Ha-Akedah." In *The Alexander Marx Jubilee Volume*, edited by Saul Liebermann, 471–547. New York: Jewish Theological Seminary of America, 1950.

Stauffer, E. *The Theology of the New Testament*. Translated by John Marsh. London: SCM, 1955.

Stone, Michael E. *Jewish Writings of the Second Temple Period: Apocrypha, Pseudepigrapha, Qumran Sectarian Writings, Philo, and Josephus*, edited by Michael E. Stone. Philadelphia: Fortress, 1984.

Stowers, Stanley K. "4 Maccabees." In *Harper's Bible Commentary*, 922–34. San Francisco: Harper & Row, 1988.

———. *A Rereading of Romans: Justice, Jews, and Gentiles*. New Haven: Yale University Press, 1994.

Stuart, Douglas K. *Exodus*. New American Commentary 2. Broadman & Holman, 2006.

Stuhlmacher, Peter. "Zur neueren Exegese von Römer 3:24–26." In *Versöhnung, Gesetz und Gerechtigkeit*, edited by Earle Ellis et al., 117–35. Göttingen: Vandenhoeck & Ruprecht, 1981.

———. *Paul's Letter to the Romans: A Commentary*. Translated by Scott J. Hafemann. Louisville: Westminster/John Knox, 1994.

Suomala, Karla R. *Moses and God in Dialogue: Exodus 32–34 in Postbiblical Literature*. Society of Biblical Literature 61. New York: Peter Lang, 2004.

Surkau, H. W. *Martyrien in jüdischer und frühchristilicher Zeit*. Forschungen zur Religion und Literatur des Alten und Neuen Testaments 36. Göttingen: Vandenhoeck & Ruprecht, 1938.

Swain, William C. "For Our Sins: The Image of Sacrifice in the Thought of the Apostle Paul." *Interpretation* 17 (1963) 131–39.

Swallow, Frederick R. "Redemption in St. Paul." *Sacrament* 10 (1958) 21–27

Talbert, Charles H. "A Non-Pauline Fragment at Romans 3:24–26?" *JBL* 85 (1966) 287–96.

———. *Romans*. Macon: Smyth and Helwys, 2002.

Tambasco, A. J. *A Theology of Atonement and Paul's Vision of Christianity*. Collegeville, MN: Liturgical Press, 1991.

Tcherikover, V. *Hellenistic Civilization and the Jews*. New York: The Magnus Press, 1959.

Thielman, Frank S. *Paul & The Law: A Contextual Approach*. Downers Grove, IL: InterVarsity Press, 1994.

Thoennes, Erik A. "A Biblical Theology of Godly Human Jealousy." PhD diss., Trinity Evangelical Divinity School, 2001.

Thompson, R. J. *Penitence and Sacrifice in Early Israel outside the Levitical Law*. Leiden: Brill, 1963.

Thornton, T. C. G., "Propitiation or Expiation? ἱλαστήριον and ἱλασμος in Romans and 1 John." *ExpT* 80 (1968–1969) 53–55.

Thrall, Margaret E. *The Second Epistle to the Corinthians*. International Critical Commentary. Edinburgh: T. & T. Clark, 1994.

Tidball, Derek. *The Message of the Cross*. Bible Themes Series. Downers Grove, IL: InterVarsity Press, 2001.

Tigchelar, J. C. *The Dead Sea Scrolls: Study Edition*. Translated by Florentino Garcia Martinez and Eibert J. C. Tigchelar. Vol. 1. Leiden: Brill, 1997.

Towner, Philip. *The Letters to Timothy and Titus*. New International Commentary on the New Testament. Grand Rapids: Eerdmans, 2005.

Townshend, R. B. "The Fourth Book of Maccabees." In *The Apocrypha and Pseudepigrapha of the Old Testament*, edited by R. H. Charles, 656–57. Oxford: Clarendon Press, 1913.

Travis, Stephen H. "Christ as Bearer of Divine Judgment in Paul's Thought about the Atonement." In *Atonement Today*, edited by John Goldingay, 21–38. London: SPK, 1995.

Van Henten, J. W. "Das jüdische Selbsverstädis in den altesten Martyrien." In *Die Entstehung der Jüdischen Martyrologie*, edited by B. A. G. M. Dehandschutter et al., 127–61. Leiden: Brill, 1989.

————. "Einige Prolegomena zum Studium der jüdischen Martyrologie." *Bijdragen* 46 (1985) 381–90.

————. *The Maccabean Martyrs as Saviours of the Jewish People: A Study of 2 & 4 Maccabees.* Leiden: Brill, 1997.

————. "The Martyrs as Heroes of the Christian People." In *Martyrium in Multidisciplinary Perspective*, edited by M. Lamberigts and P. van Deun, 303–22. Leuven: University of Leuven, 1995.

————. "2 Makkabeeën." In *The International Commentaar op de Bijbel*, edited by T. Baarda, 853–67. Kampen: Kok, 2001.

————. "Datierung und Herkunft des Vierten Makkabäerbuches." In *Tradition and Re-Interpretation*, edited by J. W. van Henten, 136–49. Leiden: Brill, 1986.

————. "Die Martyrer als Helden des Volkes." In *Jüdische Schriften in ihrem antic-jüdischen und urchristlichen Kontext: Studien zu den Jüdischen Schriften aus hellenistisch—romischer Zeit*, edited by H. Lichtenberger, 303–22. Guetersloh: Guetersloher Verlagshaus, 2002.

————. "Jewish Martyrdom and Jesus' Death." In *Deutungen des Todes Jesus im Neuen Testament*. Wissenschaftliche Untersuchungen zum Neuen Testament 181, edited by J. Frey et al., 139–68. Tübingen: Mohr Siebeck, 2005.

————. "Martyrdom and Persecution Revisited: The Case of 4 Maccabees." In *Märtyrerakten, Altertumswissenschaftliches Kolloquium* 6, edited by W. Ameling, 59–75. Tübingen: Mohr Siebeck, 2005.

————. "The Tradition-Historical Background of Romans 3:25: A Search for Pagan and Jewish Parallels." In *From Jesus to John: Essays on Jesus and New Testament Christology in Honour of Marinus De Jonge*. Journal for the Study of the New Testament 84, edited by Martinus C. de Boer, 101–128. Sheffield: Sheffield Academic Press, 1993.

————. *Martyrdom and Noble Death: Selected Texts from Graeco-Roman, Jewish, and Christian Antiquity*. London: Routledge, 2003.

————. *Studies in Early Jewish Epigraphy*, edited by J. W. van Henten and P. W. van der Horst. Leiden: Brill, 1994.

Vanderkam, James C. *From Joshua to Caiphas*. Minneapolis: Fortress, 1986.

————. *An Introduction to Early Judaism*. Grand Rapids: Eerdmans, 2001.

Vawter, B. "The Colossians Hymn and the Principle of Redaction." *CBQ* 33 (1971) 62–81.

Vermes, G. "Redemption and Genesis xxii—the Binding of Isaac and the Sacrifice of Jesus." In *Scripture and Tradition in Judaism: Haggadic Studies*. 2nd ed. 193–227. Leiden: Brill, 1974.

Versnel, Henk S. "Making Sense of Jesus' Death: The Pagan Contribution." In *Deutungen Todes im Neuen Testament*. Wissenschaftliche Untersuchungen zum Neuen Testament 181, edited by Jörg Frey et al., 221–94. Tübingen: Mohr Siebeck, 2005.

Versnel, Henk S. "Two Types of Roman Devotio." *Mnemosyne* 29 (1976) 365–410.

Vickers, Brian J. *Jesus' Blood and Righteousness*. Wheaton: Crossway, 2006.

Wallace, Daniel B. *Greek Grammar Beyond the Basics*. Grand Rapids: Zondervan, 1996.

Waltke, Bruce K. "Atonement in Psalm 51." In *The Glory of the Atonement*, edited by Charles E. Hill et al., 51–60. Downers Grove, IL: InterVarsity Press, 2004.

————, and M. O'Connor. *An Introduction to Biblical Hebrew Syntax*. Winona Lake, IN: Eisenbrauns, 1990.

Warfield, B. B. "Redeemer," and "Redemption." *PTR* 14 (1916) 177–201.

Watson, Wilfred G.E. *The Dead Sea Scrolls Translated: The Qumran Texts in English*, edited by Florentino Garcia Martinez. Translated by Wilfred G. E. Watson. 2nd ed. Leiden: Brill, 1994.

Weiner, Eugene and Anita Weiner. *The Martyr's Conviction: Sociological Analysis*. Brown Judaic Studies 203. Atlanta: Scholars Press, 1990.

Wengst, K. *Christologische Formeln und Lieder des Urchristentums*. Gütersloh: Gerd Mohn, 1972.

Westerholm, Stephen. *Perspectives Old and New on Paul: The Lutheran Paul and His Critics*. Grand Rapids: Eerdmans, 2004.

Westermann, Claus. *Isaiah 40–66*. Old Testament Library. London: SCM, 1969.

Whitley, D. E. H. *The Theology of St. Paul*. 2nd ed. Oxford: Blackwell, 1974.

Whybray, R. N. *Isaiah 40–66*. New Century Bible Commentary. Grand Rapids: Eerdmans, 1981.

———. *Thanksgiving for a Liberated Prophet: An Interpretation of Isaiah 53*. Journal for the Study of Old Testament Theology 4. Sheffield: Sheffield Academic Press, 1978.

Wilken, Robert L. "Melito, The Jewish Community at Sardis, and the Sacrifice of Isaac." *TS* (1976) 53–69.

Wilkens, U. *Der Brief an die Römer*. Evangelisch-Katholischer Kommentar zum Neuen Testament 6/1. Zürich: Benziger/Neukirchen-Vlyun: Neukirchener Verlag, 1980.

Williams, David J. *Paul's Metaphors: Their Context and Character*. Peabody, MA: Hendrickson, 1999.

Williams, Jarvis J. *Penal Substitution in Romans 3:25-26*? PTR 13 (2007): 73–81

Williams, Sam K. *Jesus' Death as Saving Event: The Background and Origin of a Concept*. Harvard Dissertation Review. Missoula: Scholars Press, 1975.

Wright, N. T. *Climax of the Covenant: Christ and the Law in Pauline Theology*. Minneapolis: Fortress, 1991.

———. *The Letter to the Romans: Introduction, Commentary, and Reflections*. The New International Interpreter's Bible Commentary 10. Nashville: Abingdon Press, 2002.

———. *What Saint Paul Really Said: Was Saul of Tarsus the Real Founder of Christianity?* Grand Rapids: Eerdmans, 1997.

———. *The New Testament and the People of God*. Minneapolis: Fortress, 1992.

———. *Justification: God's Plan & Paul's Vision*. Downers Grove, IL: InterVarsity, 2009.

Yerkes, Keith Royden. *Sacrifice in Greek and Roman Religions and Early Judaism*. London: Adam and Charles Black, 1953.

Yong, Kukwah Philemon. "'The Faith of Jesus Christ': An Analysis of Paul's Use of Pistis Christou." PhD diss., The Southern Baptist Theological Seminary, 2003.

Young, Eduard J. "The Interpretation of נזה in Isaiah 52:15." *WTJ* 3 (1941) 125–32.

———. *The Book of Isaiah: Chapters 40–66*. Grand Rapids: Eerdmans, 1972.

Young, Francis M. *The Use of Sacrificial Ideas in the Greek Christian Writers from the New Testament to John Chrysostom*. Philadelphia: The Philadelphia Patristic Foundation, 1979.

Young, N. "Hilaskēsthai and Related Words in the New Testament." *EvQ* 55 (1983) 169–76.

Ziesler, John. *Commentary on Romans*. New Testament Commentaries. London: SCM, 1989.